APPLY GLUE TO
FACE

HERBERT HOOVER AS SECRETARY OF COMMERCE:

STUDIES IN NEW ERA THOUGHT

AND PRACTICE

Papers Presented At The

HERBERT HOOVER CENTENNIAL SEMINARS

HERBERT HOOVER PRESIDENTIAL LIBRARY ASSOCIATION

WEST BRANCH, IOWA

APRIL 1974

Edited with introduction by
ELLIS W. HAWLEY

HERBERT HOOVER

AS SECRETARY OF COMMERCE:

Studies in New Era
Thought and Practice

UNIVERSITY OF IOWA PRESS  IOWA CITY

Library of Congress Cataloging in Publication Data

Main entry under title:

Herbert Hoover as Secretary of Commerce.

(Herbert Hoover centennial seminars; 2)
"Papers presented at the Herbert Hoover
centennial seminars, Herbert Hoover Presidential
Library Association, West Branch, Iowa, April 1974."
Includes bibliographical references and index.
1. Hoover, Herbert Clark, Pres. U.S., 1874-1964
—Political career before 1929—Congresses.
2. United States—Economic policy—To 1933—
Congresses. 3. United States—Economic con-
ditions—1918-1945—Congresses. I. Hawley,
Ellis, Wayne, 1929-   II. Hoover Presidential
Library Association. III. Series.
E802.H4   973.91'6'0924   80-26771
ISBN 0-87745-109-5

University of Iowa Press, Iowa City 52242

©1981 by The University of Iowa. All rights reserved

Printed in the United States of America

CONTENTS

Preface
xi

Introduction
Secretary Hoover and the Changing Framework
of New Era Historiography
1

Herbert Hoover and the Harding Cabinet
ROBERT K. MURRAY
17

Herbert Hoover and Economic Stabilization, 1921–22
ELLIS W. HAWLEY
43

Herbert Hoover, the Wage-Earner,
and the "New Economic System," 1919–29
ROBERT H. ZIEGER
80

Herbert Hoover's Agricultural Policies, 1921–28
JOAN HOFF WILSON
115

Herbert Hoover, the "New Era,"
and American Foreign Policy
MELVYN P. LEFFLER
148

Product Diplomacy: Herbert Hoover's
Anti-Monopoly Campaign at Home and Abroad
JOSEPH BRANDES
185

Herbert Hoover's Concept of Individualism Revisited
GEORGE W. CAREY
217

Index
255

Discussants
Second Hoover Seminar-Conference

PERI ARNOLD
University of Notre Dame

BARBARA CHAPMAN
Rockford, Illinois Register

WILLIAM JULIAN
Central College, Iowa

GARY KOERSELMAN
Morningside College, Iowa

JOSEPH MCCABE
Coe College, Iowa

ALAN SELTZER
University of Maryland, Baltimore

GLENN TINDER
University of Massachusetts, Boston

GEORGE TSELOS
Monmouth College, Illinois

Preface

In 1974, as part of a centennial commemoration of Herbert Hoover's birth, the Hoover Presidential Library Association sponsored four seminar-conferences participated in by some seventy-eight scholars from sixty-eight institutions of higher learning in the United States and Canada. The first of these conferences, held in February, focused on those aspects of Hoover's public career that related to the First World War and the postwar peace settlement. The second, convening in April, examined his activities as secretary of commerce, 1921–28. The third, in June, dealt with selected aspects of the Hoover Presidency, 1929–33. And the fourth, meeting in October, considered Hoover's post-1933 role as an "elder statesman." In each case the conference was built around a series of scholarly papers prepared by historians and political scientists interested in particular aspects of Hoover's career and subjected to critical scrutiny by discussants and other participants. In each case, also, there were approximately thirty persons in attendance, a group small enough to allow for an informal exchange of ideas. Most of the sessions met at the Hoover Presidential Library in West Branch, Iowa. Those that did not were held in Iowa City, some on the University of Iowa campus and some at the Highlander Supper Club.

Dr. Francis O'Brien, who then served as director of academic programs for the Hoover Presidential Library Association, arranged, managed, and moderated the four conferences. He drew up the plan for the conference series, invited speakers and discussants, and in some instances suggested topics for the papers. In no other sense, however, did he or the Hoover Presidential Library Association impose constraints on the participants. Diversity and scholarly debate were welcomed, and the papers and commentaries did reflect a broad spectrum of intellectual perspectives and interpretive orientations.

The seven papers published in this volume are slightly revised versions of those given at the seminar-conference held in April 1974. Each deals with an aspect of Hoover's activities as secretary of commerce. And taken together, they constitute the second unit in a series designed to make the scholarship generated by the conferences available in published form. In this sense the present volume stands as a companion and sequel to Lawrence E. Gelfand, ed., *Herbert Hoover, 1914–23: The Great War and Its Aftermath* (Iowa City: University of Iowa Press, 1979).

In 1978 the authors were given an opportunity to revise their original papers, make stylistic improvements, and incorporate any relevant scholarship that had appeared since 1974. The revisions in all
cases were minor. In addition, I made a number of editorial suggestions, most of which were accepted and have been incorporated in the
versions published here. I have also attempted, in my introduction to
the volume, to provide historiographical context and perspective. And
for each paper I have provided a brief editorial introduction and a
short summary of the most significant comments and criticisms that
followed the paper's presentation. The summaries are based on tape
recordings of the sessions that were made by the staff of the Hoover
Presidential Library and are held in its archives.

    To the realization of this volume a number of individuals have
made important contributions. Especially noteworthy have been those
of Dr. Francis O'Brien, professor of politics and constitutional law at
Southwestern University, Georgetown, Texas; Thomas T. Thalken
and Robert S. Wood, respectively director and assistant director of
the Hoover Presidential Library, and their library and archival staff;
John Henry, former executive secretary of the Hoover Presidential
Library Association; and R. Lawrence Angove, the present executive
director of the Association. All of these persons acted on the conviction that the Hoover Centennial papers deserved to be published and
thus made available to the scholarly community and the public-at-
large. I also want to express appreciation for the encouragement provided by the Board of Trustees of the Hoover Presidential Library
Association. Its members are anxious to stimulate active and continuous research, as well as greater public interest, in the life and
career of Herbert Hoover and in his contributions to the world of the
twentieth century.

Ellis W. Hawley
Iowa City, Iowa

Introduction

In American historiography the fortunes of Herbert Hoover and those of the New Economic Era have been closely linked. During the Great Depression both fell under an historiographical cloud, manifested not only in negative images but in convictions that neither warranted serious historical study. For years this cloud persisted. But then, as perceptions of the 1930s changed and new materials became available, it began to dissipate. For many scholars the 1920s became a new historiographical frontier,[1] and the result in recent years has been several streams of revisionist scholarship challenging and altering the historiographical framework erected during the depression era. To these developments the essays in this volume are not unrelated; and for this reason, it seems appropriate to introduce the volume with a brief review of this changing framework of New Era historiography and of its relationship to the ways in which historians have perceived Herbert Hoover and his activities as secretary of commerce.

During the New Era itself, as the historian Henry May has shown,[2] Americans could not fully agree on the kind of historical epoch through which they were living. Some saw it as a time of reaction, irresponsibility, and betrayal of democratic ideals, much as it would be seen by historians in the 1930s and 1940s. But more saw it as the threshold of a new age, a time when democratic goals were being realized through technical and scientific advances, when institutional leaders were becoming increasingly responsive to modern needs, and when responsible self-government was emerging in an economic sector long characterized by destructive conflict. New Era America, so a number of business, academic, and political leaders argued, was not only realizing national dreams but leading the world toward a new and more enlightened international order. And while some historians embraced the perceptions of alienated intellectuals,[3] most seemed inclined to tell a story of democratic and progressive impulses breaking into new channels and creating institutions attuned to modern needs and demands.

Writing in 1927, for example, the progressive historian Charles A. Beard depicted an America being transformed by technology and scientism yet retaining its faith in democratic processes and mass progress. If it was a country that elected seekers of normalcy and wor-shipped captains of commerce, it was also one, as Beard saw it, that had found ways to bridge class divisions, mount an attack on the roots of poverty and distress, and confound the predictions of both classical and Marxian economists. There were flaws to be corrected and chal-lenges to be met. But it was possible, so Beard concluded in his closing sentence, that the American civilization of the new machine age stood at "the dawn, not the dusk, of the gods."[4]

Similarly, in a work published in 1930, the historian Preston W. Slosson depicted New Era America as constituting one of two great experiments in economic revolution, one that unlike its Russian counterpart "had little to do with politics," yet one that had created new patterns of mass life and was perhaps as historically significant as England's industrial revolution at the close of the eighteenth century.[5] In another survey appearing in the same year, one stressing organiza-tional and policy developments, the historian James C. Malin saw not only major economic changes but another forward thrust of the dem-ocratic idea and of the American experiment in balancing individual rights with modern social needs. Those championing government reg-ulation, Malin noted, had gone into eclipse. They had been unable to adjust their theories to a changing political climate. But conservative political victories had not brought forth a personality powerful enough to impose laissez-faire doctrines on public policy. On the con-trary, they had opened the way to a new kind of cooperative ferment, and from this, with some assistance from political agencies, had come a new structure of economic self-government capable of realizing social ideals unattainable through public regulation. The concept of democracy, Malin insisted, had actually been enlarged; the problem of balancing individual liberty with social obligations had been tackled in new and possibly more fruitful ways; and while practicality was their most common justification, these developments were also beginning to produce a new body of political theory.[6]

At the center of these historical developments, moreover, particu-larly for Malin and Slosson, stood the man who had become secretary of commerce in 1921 and had served in that capacity for the next seven years. While advocating a retreat from political forms of regulation, Herbert Hoover had helped the nation's democratic and associative impulses to break into new paths, had hailed science and technology as the new frontiers, and had used political government to nurture and assist the beginnings of responsible self-government in the economic sphere. Under his leadership and prodding, the government had moved to stimulate and guide the cooperative ferment out of which had emerged new controls, standards, and ideals. In addition he had, in his speeches and writings, moved toward a new political theory, one that recognized what was happening and envisioned a liberal order that was neither statist nor devoid of agencies through which needed social actions could be taken.

Also inclined to see Hoover in much the same light was the historian Frederick Jackson Turner. In Hoover's *American Individualism,* in particular, Turner found evidence of a mind seeking to adapt pioneering traditions to the problems of an industrial and urban age.[7] And among journalists who tried to bring some sort of historical perspective to their work, the view that Hoover was engaged in pioneering work of major historical significance was even more pronounced. William Hard saw him as the shaper of a new kind of governmental agency, one that sought not to regulate or subsidize but to make private groups more statesmanlike and hence better able to cope with modern conditions and problems.[8] The *New York Times* saw Hoover's writings as bearing "much the same relation to the problems of the present and the future that the essays of Hamilton, Madison, Jay, and Noah Webster bore to the problems that occupied men's minds when the Constitution was framed."[9] *Time* magazine, which featured the secretary of commerce on its November 16, 1925, cover, saw him not only as the "brains" of the Coolidge administration, with his fingers in an amazing "number of pies," but also as the prime representative of a new breed of public official capable of getting results without much political fuss and with very little legislation.[10] Only a few critics were inclined to see Hoover as the builder of oppressive, undemocratic, and unstable institutions, and even they were unlikely to deny that his administrative domain was a whirlwind of activity or that, as *Time* put it, there was "more Hoover in the Administration than any other one person."[11]

In these contemporary perceptions there was, of course, much that was shortsighted, fallacious, and misleading. They largely ignored the darker aspects of popular experience, accepted establishment rationalizations much too uncritically, and credited theories of economic expansion and social behavior that could not account for what followed. Yet students of the period are now inclined to credit contemporaries with seeing much that was subsequently obscured by the political rhetoric of the 1930s and 1940s. Their age, for all its conservative reaction and aimless frivolity, was one that foreshadowed and helped to lay the institutional and ideological foundations for a new kind of organizational order. It was an age, so it now seems, during which a variety of developments, including those of Hoover's commerce secretariat, were of major historical significance and current relevance. Had the post-1929 search for historical scapegoats been less intense, it seems possible that the historiographical frontier of recent years might have come a generation earlier.

This, however, was not to be. The New Economic Era, after all, did end in the Great Depression. The Hoover programs of the early 1930s failed to bring recovery, either at home or abroad; and while the post-1933 era brought continued depression followed by another world war, these developments were widely viewed not as failings of current policy but as the consequences of what had been done or not done in the 1920s.[12] In the popular mind and in New Deal political rhetoric, the decade became thoroughly disreputable, a period dominated not by democratic or progressive impulses but by economic avarice, political chicanery, and irresponsible pleasure seeking. Among historians there was a growing reluctance to defend earlier perceptions. These faded from the scene, and as they did so the perspectives once associated with alienated intellectuals, journalistic color, or outmoded politicians came into their own. It was the Beardian progressive framework, with the New Deal now cast in the role of progressive democracy and the New Era as reactionary folly, that came to dominate the writing of American history in the 1930s and 1940s. For the 1920s, this meant histories that were a compound of political morality tales and the kind of titillating social froth that Frederick Lewis Allen had offered in his *Only Yesterday* (1931). The period, so it seemed to most writers and teachers of American history, was of interest only because of its amusing eccentricities or because it served as an illustration of what could happen when a democratic people relaxed its vigilance or allowed itself to be deluded and manipulated.[13]

As these views became established, Hoover and his associates did try to break the linkages between his activities and those that were now perceived to be at the core of the New Economic Era.[14] But among historians these efforts were all but completely rejected. In most historical accounts, Hoover as secretary of commerce became a backward extension of the highly negative images now associated with his presidency. He was the very embodiment of the illusions and complacencies that had led to economic and social disaster, a man, in other

words, who had never really understood what the American democratic experiment was about, who had turned himself into a tool of entrenched greed and special privilege, and who had masked his ig-
norance and real political connections behind a continual stream of
optimistic boosterism and misleading propaganda. In short, he was
the nation's "Super-Babbitt"; and in a popular jingle that historians
loved to quote, it was Mellon who had "pulled the whistle," Hoover
who had rung "the bell," Wall Street that had given "the signal," and
the country that had gone "to hell."[15]

Ironically, moreover, even those historical accounts in which Hoover
appeared as the champion and defender of American traditions tended
to ignore or play down his organizational and planning activities as
secretary of commerce. Written chiefly by anti-Roosevelt journalists
and academics, these accounts tended to identify the American way
not with government-fostered cooperative action but with adherence
to the teachings of laissez-faire fundamentalism. Their praise was for
a Hoover who had allegedly believed in these teachings and had done
everything in his power to keep the American nation from abandoning
them, a Hoover, in other words, who was not only a foe of the New
Deal but anti-collectivist, anti-planning, and anti-managerial as well.[16]
Since this was the same kind of Hoover that was now being depicted in
mainstream history, few were left to deny that it was historically accurate. Occasionally, to be sure, Hoover himself did so. But given his
increasing penchant toward working with the laissez-faire right and
accepting its praise and support, these denials had little chance of being taken seriously.

Until well into the 1950s, then, neither the developments of the
1920s nor Herbert Hoover as secretary of commerce seemed worthy of
serious historical study. For those committed to the progressive
framework, they were part of an aberration having little to do with the
main currents of twentieth-century development,[17] and for the tiny
group of historians who saw the New Deal as un-American error, they
stood outside the central story of a nation poisoned by foreign ideologies and bureaucratic proliferation. Both groups concentrated their
study on what they had identified as central to an understanding of recent America, and both saw their central stories as unfolding during
the Wilson and Roosevelt eras rather than during the years that lay
between.

It would take changes in these basic perceptions to alter the situation, and these were slow in coming. They waited on the cooling of

political passions, on a growing awareness of the consensual factors and basic continuities in American history, and on the application by historians of insights borrowed from sociology, political science, and institutional economics. Yet if the wait was a long one, the conditions under which established perceptions could change finally did arrive. They did so in the mid and late 1950s, facilitated perhaps by social pressures for national unity and increased prestige for the social sciences. The result, by the end of the decade, was the appearance of three major challenges to the established framework, each helping to stimulate a new interest in the 1920s and eventually in Herbert Hoover as secretary of commerce.

One of these challenges came from the much debated consensus history, with its emphasis on a persisting consensual core rather than democratic revolutions or un-American poisons. The central story of the American past, so historians of this persuasion argued,[18] was neither the coming of a virtuous collectivism nor the sapping and decay of virtuous traditions. It was rather the story of a nation dedicated from its beginnings to the principles of Lockean liberalism, rejecting throughout its history those who would depart from them, and constantly finding ways to adapt these principles to changing economic and social conditions. It was these adaptations that had made up most of what Americans had called reform; and while a number of them had come during the Wilson and Roosevelt eras, these should be seen as part of a continuing process, at work not only during but before, between, and after these periods. Indeed, it was possible that the more important adaptations had taken place during periods like the 1920s and that what had made the Wilsonian and New Deal periods so politically strident was not basic change but temporary narrowings in the ongoing consensus.

The second new framework was that emerging from an enhanced awareness of the work being done in sociology, political science, institutional economics, and management studies. Influenced by these disciplines, a number of historians began seeing an America shaped less by democratic impulses or un-American imports than by status drives, interest-group interaction, managerial impulses, and urban living.[19] They saw, in particular, a society in which traditional ordering mechanisms had been unable to withstand the impact of industrialization and mass mobility; in which a period of disorganization, cultural conflict, and social strain had ensued; and in which a new, more modern, and more rational set of ordering mechanisms had gradually emerged and gained social legitimacy. The central struggle in twenti-eth-century America, as they saw it, had been neither a struggle be-tween the people and the interests nor one between American and alien influences. It had been rather a struggle between modernizers, rationalizers, and urbanizers on the one hand and the forces of rural traditionalism, anti-modernity, and irrational reaction on the other.

Among such interpreters, accounts of this central struggle differed. They differed especially as to when the modernizers achieved domi-nance and how they combined bargaining with technocratic struc-tures. But the new writing did bring a general rethinking and reexam-ination, not only of the Wilsonian and Roosevelt eras but of the New Economic Era that lay between them. Indeed, in this new story of twentieth-century America, the 1920s appeared to be a pivotal rather than an aberrational period, a period, in other words, characterized less by reactionary folly and irresponsible hoopla than by vigorous in-tergroup competition, the emergence of modern institutions and values, and major forward thrusts on the part of technocratic ration-alizers and other seekers of a modern order.

The third departure from established perceptions, appearing to some extent as a response to the first two, was an altered progressive framework broadening the definition of "progressive" and allowing for greater degrees of continuity, ethno-cultural tension, and ideolog-ical consensus. As told within this framework, the central story of modern America was still a story of reformist impulses moving the na-tion onward and upward toward the realization of greater democracy. But the range of those contributing to this process was now broad-ened, obstacles other than entrenched business greed were now recog-nized, and periods like the 1920s were now seen as being less aberra-tional than once thought. They, too, had had their reformers and reformist impulses, or at least linkages between and seedbeds for such impulses; and of even greater importance, they had served as healing or consolidating periods during which reforms could establish them-selves and reform energies be regenerated.[20] Seen from this perspec-tive, the 1920s did merit serious historical study, and like the other new historiographical frameworks this one did stimulate new lines of inquiry. By 1960 historians had become much interested in the per-sistence of "progressivism" during the 1920s, in how the politicians of the period had healed political divisions and contained political re-action, and in a variety of movements that had allegedly laid the foun-dation for the reform politics and measures of the 1930s.

As America entered the 1960s, historical writing and teaching was also influenced by the rise of a new political and intellectual left and by the development within it of new Marxian perspectives on the American past. Rejecting both the progressive framework and its new competitors, the neo-leftists found wisdom in a series of works that mainstream historians had ignored or refused to accept as valid scholarship. They were impressed particularly with the later Charles A. Beard's critiques of Rooseveltian diplomacy, with the kind of radical perspective on the New Deal provided by Broadus Mitchell's *Depression Decade* (1947), and with the reinterpretations of modern America found in William Appleman William's *Tragedy of American Diplomacy* (1959), and *Contours of American History* (1961). They were impressed as well with the discoveries of such radical scholars as C. Wright Mills, Paul Goodman, and Herbert Marcuse. With the aid of such "eye-openers," they began reconstructing a national past having a different set of constancies and continuities. The central story, as they told it, was not one of advancing democracy, ideological consensus, or rational adaptation to modern demands and needs. It was a story rather of an exploitive ruling class, caught in the contradictions of corporate capitalism and unable to mask its true nature from certain elements of the population, yet managing to sustain itself through statist supports, bureaucratic manipulation, and an informal but very real imperialism. It was these threads of class action and of imperialism disguised as trade liberalization that ran through the history of modern America and made it largely of one piece.[21]

For some of the neo-radicals, moreover, the 1920s were important not only because these threads had run through them but because the leading policy makers of the period had understood the social dangers inherent in using the state to save the corporate order. Such men, so it was argued had not been provincial isolationists. Nor had they been foolish reactionaries or mere interest-group brokers. Along with the radicals, they had understood the contradictions of corporate capitalism and their potential for begetting statist repression and international conflict. While they were ultimately doomed to failure, they had acted on these perceptions and had thus sought to work out a capitalist communitarianism capable of preventing the future that they feared. In many ways they had been wiser, more perceptive, and more sophisticated than the policy makers that replaced them in the 1930s and 1940s; and they were worth studying both as men wrestling with the central problems of an advanced capitalist order and as prescient prophets of where liberal statism and efforts to export domestic diffi-culties could eventually lead.[22]

Finally, two developments in conservative intellectual circles also produced new ways of looking at the American past and particularly at what had gone on during the New Economic Era. One was the emergence of a neo-libertarianism skeptical of established conserva-tive heroes and inclined to see those of the 1920s as having been, in ac-tuality, the subverters of true conservative principles. They had worked, so it was argued, not to defend economic liberty but to develop a corporate state that had eventually given birth to the free-dom-destroying measures of the New Deal.[23] The other development was the appearance of a neo-traditionalism seeking to show that tradi-tional America had opposed both the modern bureaucratic state and the errors of Lockean liberalism. The great tradition, from which both rampant individualism and bureaucratic centralism were pernicious departures, had been one emphasizing organic social duties and con-fining government action to the protection of the traditional institu-tions through which such duties had been customarily discharged.[24] It was this that true conservatives should seek to restore and preserve, and in the 1920s it was possible to discern historical figures who had had some understanding of what was needed and had made some ef-forts to secure it.

By the late 1960s, then, growing numbers of historians had broken away from the conceptual frameworks that had once inhibited serious study of the New Economic Era. If they could not agree upon what constituted the central story of modern America, they were no longer inclined to see the 1920s as a barren, frivolous, and irrelevant inter-lude. And as interest grew, materials long closed to researchers were being opened, processed, and made available. The Harding papers, once believed to have been burned, became available in 1964 and proved to be exceptionally rich. Other collections, both organizational and personal, yielded rich finds; and at the new Hoover Presidential Library, opened in 1963, historians finally gained access to collections documenting the main streams of New Era policy and especially the crucial areas of intersection between the governmental and private sec-tors. One result was the growing stream of revisionist scholarship that the historian Burl Noggle described in 1966 and revisited in 1973.[25] Another, or more accurately a part of the first, was the rediscovery of much that had been apparent to contemporaries but had been ob-scured subsequently by the developments of the 1930s and 1940s.

As in the past, moreover, the historiographical fortunes of the New Era remained closely linked to those of Herbert Hoover. Paralleling their revival was a new interest in Hoover's life and public career—one that began with a reconsideration of his presidency, seeking particularly to place it within the progressive framework and to understand how it had paved the way for the New Deal,[26] but which then quickly expanded to include his pre-presidential activities. New studies of the war system disclosed a man who had been one of the most creative, energetic, and fascinating of Wilson's war managers. New biographical studies sought to relate his career to the organizational and technical revolutions and to understand how a Quaker orphan from a rural midwestern village had emerged as a heroic figure in the new world of big administration. New studies of the post-armistice period revealed a man wrestling with a whole range of major problems and eventually serving as a bridge from Wilsonian perspectives to those of the New Era. And stimulated by the new ways of looking at the 1920s, especially those associated with William Appleman Williams, Louis Galambos, Murray Rothbard, and the reexaminers of progressivism and isolationism, scholars began digging into the collections at the Hoover Library and reconstructing Hoover's activities as secretary of commerce. In studies of what they were now labeling as a corporate gentry, an associational system, an embryonic corporate state, a corporative progressivism, a functionalist diplomacy, or an independent internationalism, the figure of America's seventh secretary of commerce assumed a large and often central role.[27]

About this rediscovered Hoover there was still much scholarly disagreement. But to almost all involved, it was clear that Hoover as secretary of commerce had not been the laissez-faire ideologue vilified in progressive history or canonized in its conservative rival. For most, he appeared instead as a modernizing manager and reformer, an official, as Melvyn Leffler notes in this volume, who was "engrossed in the problems of stabilizing modern industrial society, involved in the effort to promote harmony between capital and labor, devoted to the task of fostering cooperative competition among businessmen, committed to the use of scientific techniques to solve national problems, and inclined to accept limited governmental responsibility in the struggle to manage the business cycle and eradicate poverty."[28] Judgments differed as to how he had performed in these roles, why he had assumed them, and what the consequences of his actions had been. But as with the 1920s as a whole, the accepted historical reality around which these interpretive debates revolved bore a much closer resemblance to the perceptions of New Era contemporaries than to what had been accepted as reality in the historical writing and teaching of the 1930s, 1940s, and 1950s.

It was in the midst of these recent historiographical developments, then, that the papers published in this volume were written and presented. In planning the seminar on Hoover as secretary of commerce, efforts were made to secure participants who were or had been involved in developing and testing revisionist perspectives. These efforts were reasonably successful, so that, in some sense, all of the papers published here might be categorized as revisionist. All reject the view that Hoover as secretary of commerce was an outmoded laissez-faire ideologue defending a nineteenth-century liberalism rendered obsolete by the organizational and technical revolutions of the twentieth century. All except one see him as a modernizer and rationalizer, seeking in particular to forge a new synthesis between managerial and libertarian values, to build modern institutions retaining traditional virtues, and to nurture more system-conscious forms of individualism and nationalism. Most of them also view his designs and activities as part of some larger reformist, managerial, stabilizing, or corporative impulse; and while reflecting major interpretive differences, all regard this particular phase of Hoover's public career as being a subject of major historical significance.

This is not to say, however, that the papers represent either the entire range of revisionist scholarship or some calculated balance of revisionist views. The planners of the seminar had no such objectives in mind and would make no claims about the representational character of the scholarship that it produced. Nor is it to say that the sessions at which the papers were presented, criticized, and discussed were so structured as to leave the central claims of revisionist scholarship unchallenged and undebated. In the formal commentaries and the discussion from the floor, as the published summaries of these should make clear, such challenges were made and the cases for the older progressive and conservative views continued to find expression.

The essays, it should also be noted, were never intended to provide a comprehensive history of Hoover's activities as secretary of commerce. Nor do they provide such a history. Their focus instead is on important but selected aspects of this story, chiefly on what was taking place in the spheres of farm, labor, foreign, and business stabilization policy. In addition, they provide insights into Hoover's political philosophy and his relationships with other figures in the executive branch of the government. But none of them deals with business policy after 1922, and left largely unexplored are Hoover's actions in such areas as social welfare policy, urban development, transportation and communication, resource development and management, pollution and environmental controls, the provision of public health facilities, and the improvement of the monetary and banking system. Hoover, after all, was involved during this period in virtually the entire spectrum of governmental activity. He was, as contemporaries noted, "Secretary of Commerce and undersecretary of every other department." To detail this whole range of activity would require several additional essays.

Still, when taken as a whole, the essays do bring out a general pattern of policy permeating almost all of Hoover's programs and activities. Almost invariably, it seems, this pattern combined the outlook and optimism of modern management with deep-seated reservations about the competency of statist institutions, the result being a search for managerial or problem-solving institutions that would be responsive to social needs yet remain ouside the state or at least outside the grasp of its more irrational and corrupting components. The essays, moreover, do complement each other. Their inquiries into differing aspects of a common subject mesh well, and as arranged here they come together to form a larger unity.

The broadest of the essays, and hence the one providing a suitable introduction for the others, is Robert K. Murray's discussion of Hoover and the Harding cabinet. In it the focus is on the political and administrative setting in which Hoover emerged as a major policy maker and proceeded to transform his department from a miscellaneous collection of technical bureaus into a dynamic and growing organization concerned with promoting, guiding, and protecting American economic development. The next three essays, those by Ellis Hawley, Robert Zieger, and Joan Hoff Wilson, then form a unit on how the Commerce secretariat became involved in and helped to shape the nation's economic policies. They focus, in turn, on the responses made to the recession of 1921, the efforts to secure labor participation in building the new economic system, and the search for appropriate ways to restore prosperity in the depressed agricultural sector. The focus then shifts from domestic concerns to the involvement of Hoover and his organization in economic diplomacy. This is the subject of the essays by Melvyn Leffler and Joseph Brandes, the former seeking to understand the general patterns of Hooverian diplomacy and the latter looking in more detail at his campaigns against foreign monopolies and especially against the British rubber cartel. Finally, in the concluding essay by George Carey, Hoover's political thought is analyzed and some conclusions drawn about how it should be categorized, the ways in which it was incomplete, and the kind of system that might have emerged had Hoover's teachings been more closely followed. Like the other essayists in this volume, Carey concludes that Hoover was not a nineteenth-century laissez-faire liberal. But unlike them, he sees Hoover's ideas as fitting into an anti-modern or traditional framework rather than a modernizing one.

Historiographically, the essays can be seen both as reflections of major scholarly developments and as contributions to a continuing search for historical understanding of the New Economic Era and the man who functioned as one of the period's most influential makers of public policy. As to how well the authors deal with their subjects and how much new light they have shed on these two controversial subjects, the reader must judge.

Ellis W. Hawley
University of Iowa

NOTES

1 For an excellent discussion of this development, see Burl Noggle, "The Twenties: A New Historiographical Frontier," *Journal of American History,* 53 (September 1966), 299-314.

2 See Henry F. May, "Shifting Perspectives on the 1920's," *Mississippi Valley Historical Review,* 43 (December 1956), 405-27.

3 See, for example, James Truslow Adams, *Our Business Civilization* (New York, 1929).

4 Charles A. and Mary R. Beard, *The Rise of American Civilization,* vol. 2 (New York, 1927), esp. chapter 30. The quoted phrase is on page 800.

5 Preston W. Slosson, *The Great Crusade and After, 1914-1928* (New York, 1930), esp. chapter 6.

6 James C. Malin, *The United States After the World War* (New York, 1930), esp. chapter 34.

7 Frederick Jackson Turner to E. S. Emmett, January 18, 1923, Herbert Hoover Papers (Hoover Presidential Library, West Branch, Iowa), Commerce Section, Misc.—Tu.

8 William Hard, "The New Hoover," *Review of Reviews,* 76 (November 1927), 478-84.

9 "Hoover's New Federalism," *New York Times,* December 17, 1922, sect. 3, p. 1.

10 *Time,* 6 (November 16, 1925), 6.

11 *Ibid.*

12 For perceptive comments on this phenomenon, see Paul K. Conkin, *The New Deal* (New York, 1967), pp. 26-27.

13 Typical of what was written and taught were Karl Schriftgiesser, *This Was Normalcy* (Boston, 1948); Henry M. Robinson, *Fantastic Interim* (New York, 1943); Samuel Hopkins Adams, *Incredible Era* (New York, 1939); Laurence Greene, *The Era of Wonderful Nonsense* (Indianapolis, 1939); and Mark Sullivan, *Our Times,* vol. 6 (New York, 1935).

14 This was one theme, for example, in books like Ray Lyman Wilbur and Arthur M. Hyde, *The Hoover Policies* (New York, 1937) and William Myers and Walter Newton, *The Hoover Administration* (New York, 1936).

15 Gene Smith, *The Shattered Dream* (New York, 1970), p. 73.

16 See, for example, John T. Flynn, *The Roosevelt Myth* (New York, 1948) and Edgar E. Robinson, *The Roosevelt Leadership, 1933-1945* (Philadelphia, 1955).

17 Reflecting this point of view, for example, were such accounts as Harold U. Faulkner, *From Versailles to the New Deal* (New Haven, 1955), Arthur M. Schlesinger, Jr., *The Crisis of the Old Order, 1919-1933* (Boston, 1957), and John D. Hicks, *Republican Ascendancy, 1921-1933* (New York, 1960).

18 The most influential work was Louis Hartz, *The Liberal Tradition in America* (New York, 1955). Also influential were the historians Daniel Boorstin and Clinton Rossiter.

19 Among the major works reflecting and helping to shape this new perspective were Richard Hofstadter, *The Age of Reform* (New York, 1955); Samuel P. Hays, *The Response to Industrialism* (Chicago, 1957); Robert H. Wiebe, *Businessmen and Reform* (Cambridge, 1962); Robert H. Wiebe, *The Search for Order* (New York, 1967); J. Joseph Huthmacher, *Massachusetts People and Politics, 1919-1933* (Cambridge, 1959); George Mowry, *The Urban Nation* (New York, 1965); Alfred D. Chandler, *Strategy and Structure* (Cambridge, 1962); and Louis Galambos, *Competition and Cooperation* (Baltimore, 1966). See also Louis Galambos, "The Emerging Organizational Synthesis in Modern American History," *Business History Review,* 44 (Autumn 1970), 279-90, and Edward N. Saveth, "American History and Social Science," *International Social Science Journal,* 20 (1968), 319-30.

20 Illustrative of the works emerging from the application of this perspective were Arthur S. Link, "What Happened to the Progressive Movement in the 1920's?" *American Historical Review,* 64 (July 1959), 833-51; Clarke A. Chambers, *Seedtime of Reform* (Minneapolis, 1963); Robert K. Murray, *The Harding Era* (Minneapolis, 1969); Donald B. McCoy, *Calvin Coolidge* (New York, 1967); Preston Hubbard, *Origins of the TVA* (Nashville, 1961); and George B. Tindall, "Business Progressivism," *South Atlantic Quarterly,* 62 (Winter 1963), 92-106.

21 See Barton J. Bernstein, ed., *Towards a New Past* (New York, 1967). See also Ir-

win Unger, "The New Left and American History," *American Historical Review,* 72 (July 1967), 1237-63.

22   See especially William A. Williams, *The Contours of American History* (Cleveland, 1961), pp. 425-38, and Carl P. Parrini, *Heir to Empire* (Pittsburgh, 1969). See also Williams, "The Legend of Isolationism in the 1920s," *Science and Society,* 18 (Winter 1954), 1-20.

23   See especially Murray Rothbard's *America's Great Depression* (Princeton, 1963) and his "Herbert Clark Hoover," *New Individualist Review,* 4 (Winter 1966), 3-12.

24   See especially Willmoore Kendall, *The Conservative Affirmation* (Chicago, 1963) and Willmoore Kendall and George W. Carey, *The Basic Symbols of the American Political Tradition* (Baton Rouge, 1970). Also sharing a part of this orientation was Rowland Berthoff, *An Unsettled People* (New York, 1971).

25   See Burl Noggle, "The Twenties" (cited in footnote 1) and Noggle, "Configurations of the Twenties," in W. H. Cartwright and R. L. Watson, eds., *The Reinterpretation of American History and Culture* (Washington, 1973), 465-90.

26   See especially Harris G. Warren, *Herbert Hoover and the Great Depression* (New York, 1959); Carl N. Degler, "The Ordeal of Herbert Hoover," *Yale Review,* 52 (June 1963), 563-83; and Albert U. Romasco, *The Poverty of Abundance* (New York, 1965).

27   Leading titles in this reexamination of Hoover's career include Joseph Brandes, *Herbert Hoover and Economic Diplomacy* (Pittsburgh, 1962); Ellis Hawley, "Secretary Hoover and the Bituminous Coal Problem," *Business History Review,* 42 (Autumn 1968), 253-70; Barry Karl, "Presidential Planning and Social Science Research," *Perspectives in American History,* 3 (1969), 347-409; Carl Parrini, *Heir to Empire* (Pittsburgh, 1969); Herbert Stein, *The Fiscal Revolution in America* (Chicago, 1969); Robert Zieger, *Republicans and Labor* (Lexington, 1969); Bruce Lohoff, "Herbert Hoover, Spokesman of Humane Efficiency," *American Quarterly,* 22 (Fall 1970), 690-700; Jordan Schwarz, *Interregnum of Despair* (Urbana, 1970); Edwin Layton, *Revolt of the Engineers* (Cleveland, 1971); Joan Hoff Wilson, *American Business and Foreign Policy, 1920-1933* (Lexington, 1971); Peri Arnold, "Herbert Hoover and the Continuity of American Policy," *Public Policy,* 20 (Fall 1972), 525-44; Craig Lloyd, *Aggressive Introvert* (Columbus, 1972); Carolyn Grin, "The Unemployment Conference of 1921," *Mid-America,* 55 (April 1973), 83-107; Ellis Hawley and others, *Herbert Hoover and the Crisis of American Capitalism* (Cambridge, 1973); Martin Fausold and George Mazuzan, eds., *The Hoover Presidency* (Albany, 1974); Donald Lisio, *The President and Protest* (Columbia, 1974); Benjamin Weissman, *Herbert Hoover and Famine Relief to Soviet Russia* (Stanford, 1974); Melvyn Leffler, "Political Isolationism, Economic Expansion, or Diplomatic Realism?" *Perspectives in American History,* 8 (1974), 413-61; Ellis Hawley, "Herbert Hoover, the Commerce Secretariat, and the Vision of an Associative State," *Journal of American History,* 61 (June 1974), 116-40; Joan Hoff Wilson, *Herbert Hoover: Forgotten Progressive* (Boston, 1975); Gary Dean Best, *The Politics of American Individualism* (Westport, 1975); Robert Zieger, "Labor, Progressivism, and Herbert Hoover," *Wisconsin Magazine of History,* 58 (Spring 1975), 196-208; Evan Metcalf, "Secretary Hoover and the Emergence of Macroeconomic Management," *Business History Review,* 49 (Spring 1975), 60-80; Edgar Robinson and Vaughn Bornet, *Herbert Hoover: President of the United States* (Stanford, 1975); Robert Himmelberg, *The Origins of the National Recovery Administration* (New York, 1976); Michael Hogan, *Informal Entente* (Columbia, 1977); James Olson, *Herbert Hoover and the Reconstruction Finance Corporation* (Ames, 1977); Robert Cuff, "Herbert Hoover, the Ideology of Voluntarism, and War Organization during

the Great War," *Journal of American History,* 64 (September 1977), 358–72; Gary Koerselman, "Secretary Hoover and National Farm Policy," *Agricultural History,* 51 (April 1977), 378–95; and David Burner, *Herbert Hoover: A Public Life* (New York, 1978).

28   See below, pages 149–50.

Robert K. Murray

Herbert Hoover and the Harding Cabinet

Editor's Introductory Note

Robert K. Murray, professor of history at Pennsylvania State University, is a recognized authority on the Harding administration. He was one of the first to make use of the Harding papers, opened in 1964 after a long period during which scholars believed that they had been lost or destroyed. And from his researches in these have come works substantially altering the older view of the early 1920s. In *The Harding Era* (1969) and *The Politics of Normalcy* (1973), Murray concluded that Warren G. Harding was in many ways an astute and skillful politician, that his administration had a number of constructive and progressive aspects, and that the history of the Harding years is of major significance for those who would understand modern American development. If there were scandals and defects, there were also actions that helped to build a new national consensus and usher in a remarkable era of economic and social modernization.

In the paper published here, Murray focuses on the political and administrative context in which Herbert Hoover took over the Commerce Department and transformed it into a beehive of promotional and educational activities. Hoover's appointment, as the paper makes clear, was not welcomed by the more conservative elements in the Republican party. It also came with unusual presidential pledges concerning the future status and jurisdictional claims of the Commerce Department. And the cabinet that Hoover joined, so the paper makes equally clear, contained not only some of the worst appointments ever made but also some of the ablest, most energetic, and most aggressive administrators ever to hold cabinet positions. Harding did attempt to create a government of the "best minds," as he perceived them; and in operation this meant a government in which policy making was en-

trusted to master administrators linked to the organizational leadership of the private sector. Although traditionally viewed as a period of
retrenchment, deregulation, and spoilsmanship, the early 1920s can
also be seen as an era of expanding administrative domains seeking to
legitimize and extend a managerial culture and constantly encroaching
on each other's preserves.

Indeed, it is within this context that Hoover's activities as secretary
of commerce now seem to make the most sense. He was not a spoils-
man. Nor was he, in this period, a champion of austerity budgets.
And if he was a deregulator, it was in the special sense of trying to
replace governmental command systems with a government engaged
in developing new systems of self-regulation. His activities seem best
viewed as one facet of a larger quest for new managerial tools, for
techniques, in other words, that could replace unreflective and un-
coordinated endeavors with behavior that was deliberate and rationalized. And the form that these activities took seems best understood by
looking first at these managerial impulses and demands and then examining how they were constrained and modified by Hoover's personal capabilities and values, by the competing thrusts of other
rationalizers, and by an opposition drawing upon anti-managerial
ideologies and resistance to organizational innovation.

On all of these matters, moreover, Professor Murray sheds additional light. He describes and analyzes Hoover's energetic expansionism, relating this both to the new managerial impulses and to the secretary's personal qualities and values. He examines the impact of this
on other departments and jurisdictions, noting how the responses
shaped and constrained Hooverian initiatives. And asserting a view of
Harding developed in earlier works, he stresses the importance of the
president's political skills. The exercise of these, he concludes, not only gave Hoover the opportunity to implement his ideas but also helped
to rescue him from political blunders and carry such initiatives as the
Unemployment Conference and the drive for an eight-hour day in the
steel industry to fruition.

Like most of the other authors in this volume, Murray focuses on
Hoover the modernizer and rationalizer as opposed to Hoover the defender of traditional or established institutions. Some may wonder if
this much needed corrective does not go too far; and among those who
do not, there may be some skepticism about Murray's assessment of
Harding's contributions. But the central points of the essay rest on
solid evidence, and it is difficult to quarrel with its general depiction
of the Harding administration and Hoover's role in it.

Herbert Hoover and the Harding Cabinet

In a precedent-shattering move, one that immediately followed his in-
augural ceremony on March 4, 1921, President Warren G. Harding
appeared before the Senate of the United States and personally presented to that body his slate of cabinet nominees. Among the names
was that of Herbert Clark Hoover as secretary of commerce. Already
well known for his humanitarian activities and for his work as director
of the wartime Food Administration, Hoover thus began the longest
and most productive period in his public life.

Hoover's name was not on Harding's list by accident or because of
expediency. As soon as the Ohioan had been elected in November
1920, he thought of Hoover as a possible cabinet choice. Hoover was
one of the first post-election visitors that Harding invited to Marion,
and the new president-elect "sized him up" at that time for a position
either in Commerce or Interior. The press shrewdly discounted the
cover story that the two men talked only about "our place in international relations" and correctly speculated that Hoover was being considered for a cabinet slot.[1]

The possibility of Hoover's selection unnerved a large segment of
the Republican party which opposed him not only for Commerce or
Interior but for any high governmental appointment. Indeed, no
sooner had Hoover left Marion than these opponents launched a bitter
campaign against him. Senator Hiram Johnson, for example, opposed
Hoover on personal grounds growing out of their differences involving California politics. But most of Hoover's foes were Old Guard
members, some of whom were friends of Harding. Harry M. Daugherty, Harding's campaign manager and closest confidant, told Harding shortly before Christmas that the Hearst newspapers were all
against Hoover, that even such "progressives" as Raymond Robbins,
Gifford Pinchot, Senator William Borah, and Senator George Norris
did not support him, and that almost all "regular" senators wanted
his name omitted. Senators Boies Penrose and Philander C. Knox
complained that Hoover was "too internationally-minded" and not
malleable enough to "get along well" with other cabinet members.[2]
Senator Frank B. Brandegee, one of Harding's closest senatorial
friends, put it bluntly: "Hoover gives most of us gooseflesh."[3]

Hoover early knew of this opposition and sought to minimize the
president-elect's dilemma. On December 22, he wrote Harding that he
had given a "great deal of thought" to the possibility of serving in the

cabinet but that he had no real desire to re-enter public life. Moreover, he added, "I cannot but be aware that there is opposition in certain politically-minded quarters to such an appointment." For these reasons, Hoover concluded, Harding should "dismiss from your mind all thought of my appointment."[4] Harding, on the other hand, refused to consider the matter closed and persisted in his desire to appoint Hoover somewhere in his official family.

Fortuitous circumstances intervened. Harding had wanted Charles G. Dawes, the Chicago banker, as his secretary of the treasury and had offered him the post in mid-December. But in early January Dawes refused the offer, forcing Harding to turn elsewhere. The eastern banking establishment, which had mildly opposed the Dawes selection, quickly came forward with several replacement candidates such as Boston banker John Weeks, ex-Senator Charles Hilles of New York, and Frank Vanderlip, a New York financier. Anxious to effect a compromise between eastern and midwestern banking elements, Senators Knox and Penrose, both of Pennsylvania, suggested the name of Pittsburgh capitalist Andrew W. Mellon. Harding toyed with this idea throughout late January and finally ordered Daugherty to indicate to Knox and Penrose that he would accept Mellon as secretary of the treasury on the condition that they drop their opposition to a cabinet position for Hoover. With Daugherty acting as intermediary, the two senators reluctantly promised Harding that they would cease their anti-Hoover activities and help secure his acceptance by the Senate in exchange for the Mellon appointment.[5]

This was cabinet-making at its best and Harding performed flawlessly. Adamant on a Hoover appointment, he now ignored the remaining pockets of resistance, writing Daugherty on February 9, "The more I consider him [Hoover] the more do I come to think well of him. Of course, I have no quarrel with those who do not think as I do, but inasmuch as I have the responsibility to assume, I think my judgment must be trusted in the matter."[6]

Ironically, it was Hoover, himself, who supplied the last barrier to his selection. Receiving a formal offer from Harding on February 12 to join the cabinet as secretary of commerce (a position Harding understood Hoover preferred), Hoover balked. At the moment he was considering a partnership with Daniel Guggenheim, owner of one of the largest mining and metallurgical complexes in the world. Moreover, Hoover did not relish assuming the traditional role of the secretary of commerce, a position not accorded much respect or possessing much influence. To overcome his reluctance, Harding asked

Charles Evans Hughes, who had already agreed to become secretary of state, and Will Hays, chairman of the Republican National Committee and soon to be postmaster general, to talk with Hoover. Both did so, Hays urging Hoover to take the post and Hughes agreeing to help Hoover expand the powers of the Commerce secretary. Then, on February 22, Harding talked at length with Hoover by phone from his pre-inaugural vacation headquarters in St. Augustine, Florida, promising Hoover virtually a free hand, if he would accept the job, to make Commerce as important and influential as he desired. The next day, February 23, Hoover wired Harding, ". . . I should prefer infinitely not to undertake the burden of public office [but] I have no right to refuse your wish and I will accept the Secretaryship of Commerce."[7]

When Hoover was sworn into office in 1921 he was enthusiastically endorsed by the press and the general public who regarded him as one of the stronger cabinet appointees. In particular, most of the business community was delighted, enthralled by Hoover's desire to reorganize the Commerce Department and make it a significant factor in the governmental process. Hoover's basic pro business bias and his reputation for "getting things done" buoyed the spirits of many business leaders who were currently anxious about the postwar economic slump.

Hoover did not disappoint them. Having extracted from Harding a large measure of autonomy, he proceeded to drive himself and his department unmercifully. Briskly hurrying to his office each day from his house at 2300 S Street, Hoover quickly transformed Commerce from a dusty pigeon hole into a beehive of activity. Hoover's predecessor, Oscar S. Straus, had told him that as secretary of commerce he would need to work only two hours a day "putting the fish to bed at night and turning on the lights around the coast."[8] Instead, by the end of five days Hoover had an information service in operation which was issuing a stream of propaganda about the many functions of the Commerce Department and their importance. By the end of fifteen days he was busily raiding the business world for top administrative talent. Within the first month he enticed twenty-five distinguished business, labor, and agricultural leaders to serve as an advisory board on the policies and programs of his department. Hoover hoped through such whirlwind activities to make Commerce "more nearly meet the needs of the American business public than it does at present."[9]

Helping Hoover in effecting this transformation were some out-

standing men. Claudius H. Huston of Tennessee became Hoover's
assistant secretary. William E. Lamb was appointed solicitor. Dr.
John M. Gries was made head of the Division of Building and Housing. Dr. Julius Klein, professor of Latin American history and economics at Harvard, became director of the Bureau of Foreign and
Domestic Commerce. Christian A. Herter, later secretary of state
under Eisenhower, was made special assistant in charge of publicity.
Under their collective guidance the Commerce Department expanded
markedly both in the number of employees and in the dollars ex-
pended. The department simultaneously became determinedly acquis-
itive. In 1923 it took over the Bureau of Custom Statistics from Treasury and somewhat later acquired the Bureau of Mines and the Patent
Office from Interior. Hoover justified such expansion on the grounds
that it was essential in order for the department to keep pace with the
burgeoning requirements of American industry. Naturally, all this activity delighted the bulk of the business community, which before the
year was out was hailing Hoover as a genius.

Such progress and expansion did not occur without opposition.
Farming interests, especially, were not pleased with many of Hoover's
programs and activities, claiming that he was anti-farmer and possessed the biases of a big business autocrat. Helping to feed this antagonism during the Harding years were frequent difficulties between the
Agriculture and Commerce Departments involving not only basic
philosophy but jurisdictional control. The major dispute centered on
the collection and analysis of accurate marketing and production
data. Hoover contended that all such information should be gathered
by Commerce through its Bureau of Census rather than by Agriculture's Bureau of Markets. Hoover even claimed that all of the data-
gathering functions of the Labor Department's Bureau of Labor
Statistics ought also to be placed under Commerce. Secretary of Agriculture Henry C. Wallace and Secretary of Labor James J. Davis
joined forces to resist successfully such Hooverian attempts at piracy,
but not without prolonged and acrimonious wrangling.

Meanwhile, Hoover and Commerce went their own way, picking up
whatever stray functions appeared and widely publicizing the department's expanding activities for aiding the businessman. In this regard,
Hoover, more than any other cabinet officer, was aware of the importance of a favorable public opinion and avidly cultivated it. To
gain the public ear he worked through journalists, press agents, pub-
licists, and even public relations firms which he sometimes employed.

Hoover saw publicity as a vital link between the centralized ideas of his Washington office and the decentralized execution of those ideas by the public and various business concerns. Publicity to him meant "education"—educating the public to the need for cooperation and the businessman to his public responsibilities.[10]

Acting on the belief that the Commerce Department's usefulness was "dependent solely upon its ability to get information to the country," and despite continuing protests from Agriculture and Labor, Hoover developed a statistical program in Commerce which was distributing its own marketing and production data by the summer of 1922. Disclaiming any intention of usurping the functions of either the Bureau of Markets or the Bureau of Labor Statistics, Hoover bypassed both in providing information which was more meaningful and adaptable to the needs of the business community. Such Commerce data regularly made its way into 160 dailies each Saturday morning, reaching an estimated five million readers. Specific trade information was issued monthly, covering foreign and domestic businesses and involving approximately 19,000 firms. Commerce figures were also made available to trade associations and to American exporters and importers. Undeniably beneficial to the American businessman, such information was regarded by them as an important factor in reviving business prosperity.

During the Harding years, however, the most significant work of the Commerce Department was concentrated in the Bureau of Foreign and Domestic Commerce. Headed by Dr. Klein, a masterful administrator, this agency undertook the task of rejuvenating American foreign trade. By reorganizing the bureau along commodity lines and by creating trade offices in major American cities as well as abroad, Hoover and Klein quickly geared this bureau for more intensive trade activity, publicizing this fact to the nation as a whole. Unfortunately, farmers were suspicious of the bureau's intent and resisted its attempts to make them "overseas conscious." Business, on the other hand, reacted eagerly. Such business enthusiasm permitted Hoover and Klein not only to weather agricultural opposition but to secure an agreement from Secretary Hughes that Commerce would be consulted on all trade-related matters such as foreign loans, war debts, and trade treaties. Moreover, Hoover successfully rebuffed any attempt by the State Department to lessen the importance of commercial attaches overseas or to place them under the sole control of Secretary Hughes's office.

Hoover pushed business interests as secretary of commerce on still other fronts in the years 1921–24. He was always a strong advocate of better housing and a booster of expansion in the home building industry. Consequently, he encouraged the department's Division of Building and Housing to study major housing problems, develop interest in home ownership, encourage the development of honest credit facilities, and standardize building materials. Hoover also supported trade associations. Despite the danger of price malpractices, he believed that trade associations were beneficial because of their ability to undertake industrial research and effect standardization and efficiency within the industrial and commercial field. This latter—industrial standardization and efficiency—particularly appealed to a man with Hoover's engineering background, and he championed all moves in that direction. As a result, the Commerce Department sponsored over 900 group conferences between 1921 and 1924 and had 229 committees at work on various phases of the problem. Hoover simultaneously promoted industrial and scientific economic research as a primary weapon against waste and inefficiency. The National Bureau of Standards, established originally to maintain standards of measurement, was transformed under Hoover into an agency that also handled much scientific and industrial research.[11]

Because he was one of the truly creative minds in the Harding cabinet, Hoover's value to the Harding administration extended far beyond the confines of the Commerce Department. For example, in the summer of 1921 he master-minded and then headed up the American relief effort in the Russian famine crisis. Under his direction some $60 million in relief supplies were distributed with the result that over 10 million Russian children and adults were kept from starving. The next year, 1922, Harding appointed him chairman of the Colorado River Commission, which established a complicated formula for a fair division of water rights in the surrounding seven state area, thus clearing the path for the long-discussed Boulder Dam project. In the summer of 1922 Harding designated him as his chief negotiator in dealing with recalcitrant coal operators during the bitter coal strike. After many frustrations, Hoover was successful in wringing some concessions from the operators on behalf of the striking miners.

Two events, in particular, demonstrated Hoover's importance to the Harding administration. They also revealed his basic economic philosophy as well as his administrative aggressiveness. The first was the Unemployment Conference of 1921 and the second was the twelve-hour day struggle in the steel industry.

Among the most critical problems confronting the Harding administration when it took office was that of unemployment. Inheriting a depressed and unstable labor market from the Wilson years, the new administration faced a gloomy economic future. The first to show concern about this situation was not Secretary of Labor Davis, whose problem it chiefly was, but Herbert Hoover. As unemployment figures climbed above the four million mark, Hoover called for remedial action, predicting that real hardship would occur during the approaching winter unless something was done. Hoover first suggested that local communities begin public works and other building projects immediately, rather than wait for spring. He also suggested that private business keep its workers employed throughout the fall and winter months, eliminating the usual seasonal layoffs. Finally, in late August, when it became apparent that too little was being done, Hoover recommended the convening of a national unemployment conference. President Harding agreed to this idea and ordered Hoover to arrange for the conference at once.[12]

Hoover took this assignment seriously, meticulously planning all phases of the conference and screening all proposed delegates carefully. Harding generally went along with Hoover's various recommendations but persistently complained that Hoover was not including enough women in the conference. Harding finally ordered him to hold up publication of the final delegate list "until there is suitable representation."[13] When the conference convened on September 26, 1921, with the requisite number of women present, Hoover was clearly in charge, although it was the president who welcomed the delegates. Following Harding's brief address which cautioned the conference not to seek relief "from the Public Treasury," Hoover mounted the platform and bluntly told his listeners that voluntary and local action, not federal intervention, could properly solve the unemployment crisis. What was needed, he said, was "the mobilization of cooperative action of our manufacturers and employers, of our public bodies, and local authorities. . . ."[14] In taking this stand Hoover was not only following Harding's wishes but was repeating what he had already told the National Association of Real Estate Boards in Chicago in July: "Unless we would destroy individual initiative and drive ourselves straight into nationalization or paternalism, the Government can not undertake to reduce or raise wages, or fix prices, no matter how it is camouflaged."[15]

Following these opening remarks, the unemployment conference divided into ten committees whose separate reports were ultimately distilled into a series of recommendations which were submitted to the president and then made public. These recommendations closely adhered to the Harding-Hoover theme and called upon local businesses, employers, government officials, and others to move ahead building and construction plans in order to increase employment at once. The conference also recommended that the work be spread and that as many new local public works projects be initiated as local communities could afford. It further recommended that all deferred repairs be undertaken immediately and that a feeling of caution make way for an attitude of "do it now!"

To implement these recommendations, Hoover quickly created a Bureau of Unemployment in the Commerce Department and appealed to the nation to support the work of the conference. The resultant propaganda effort was immense. The new Bureau of Unemployment poured out a stream of information and encouragement. Almost daily during the remainder of the fall and winter, this bureau issued glowing reports of what was being accomplished. By October 10, mayors' emergency committees had been created in thirty-one cities and were being planned in at least twenty more, while an office had been set up for Colonel Arthur Woods in Washington to coordinate all this various state and local activity. Woods, a former police commissioner of New York, enthusiastically assumed the lead in stimulating local action by sending out insistent letters from himself and from Secretary Hoover. Under such prodding, state and local committees matched men with jobs, promoted work projects, and persuaded employers to hire additional help. Simultaneously, various agencies of the federal government, especially Navy, War, Agriculture, and Interior, reexamined their construction and repair plans and let contracts immediately for work that had been scheduled for spring. As a result, by midwinter, Hoover could truthfully report that the federal government, states, and cities, as well as private individuals and companies, "have taken more comprehensive and effective measures than probably have ever been taken before in such a situation."[16]

The winter of 1921–22 passed safely. From a peak of nearly 5.5 million, unemployment figures leveled off and then began to decline.

Consequently both Harding and Hoover regarded the Unemployment Conference as a success. So did organized labor, especially Samuel Gompers, who, although no admirer of either Harding or Hoover, later testified to its accomplishments. In May 1922, after the crisis had passed, Hoover drafted a letter which Harding sent over his own signature to all cabinet officers and conference participants thanking them for their efforts and claiming that through voluntary cooperative action "we have come through [the winter] with much less suffering than in previous years, when unemployment was very much less."[17]

And where was the Department of Labor and Secretary Davis in all this? Such matters, after all, should have fallen under their jurisdiction. Hoover knew this, but he did not let it bother him. He made several half-hearted attempts to consult Davis on unemployment conference matters, but he regarded Davis as only a junior partner in the enterprise, if that. For his part, the secretary of labor followed in Hoover's wake without too much grumbling, although he was stung by Hoover's peremptory placement of the unemployment coordinating agency in Commerce. To one of Davis's few complaining letters, Hoover curtly replied: "My dear Davis: Don't get the notion that we are setting up any employment bureau in this Department. [It is only] a little machinery to . . . bring actual results from the Unemployment Conference by getting team work."[18] Such a disclaimer, however, never really fooled anyone. As one observer humorously but truthfully remarked: "At the conference on unemployment, which was Mr. Hoover's, the best and only example of the unemployed present was the Secretary of Labor."[19]

If the Unemployment Conference showed Hoover's administrative aggressiveness and his preference for voluntary cooperation and educating the businessman to his public responsibilities, so did his actions in the twelve-hour day struggle. From the beginning of the Harding regime, Hoover had been concerned about conditions in the steel industry. Investigations growing out of the steel strike of 1919 had uncovered primeval working conditions in the steel mills, especially the practice of the twelve-hour day, and all observers had recommended reforms. But steel management had consistently ignored such pleas, including any change in the twelve-hour day system. By March 1922, however, some operators were beginning to show a willingness to modify their position, and Hoover, acting for the administration, seized the opportunity to exert pressure for change.

On April 8, 1922, Hoover notified Harding that Judge Elbert Gary, head of United States Steel, might use the occasion of a company meeting on April 17 to make a statement about the twelve-hour day. Hoover suggested that Harding send Gary a letter to "stir his imagination" and even wrote out a proposed draft. Hoover told the president that even if Gary took no action on the twelve-hour day, such a presidential letter "would put the Administration's feeling in the matter right with the public." Harding thought Hoover's idea an excellent one, but altered Hoover's draft completely, eliminating his rather strident language and blunt phraseology. The president merely told Gary that he would be personally delighted if the steelmen would abolish the twelve-hour day.[20]

When no action was forthcoming at the April 17 steel meeting, Hoover urged Harding to apply additional pressure. At Hoover's suggestion, the president invited a group of forty-one top steel executives, including Judge Gary, to dinner at the White House on May 18. Also present, besides Hoover, were Secretaries Mellon and Davis. After dinner, Harding stated that he was "in dead earnest" about wanting the "twelve-hour day blight" eradicated from the steel industry. He then turned to Hoover to present the administration's case. Like the engineer that he was, Hoover offered an array of charts, graphs, and figures to show that any cost involved in the abolition of the twelve-hour-day practice would be offset by a gain in overall worker efficiency. Hoover's statistics produced an immediate sharp rejoinder from the steelmen who threatened to walk out of the meeting. Only Harding's skill at compromise managed to salvage the situation and secure a promise that a committee under Judge Gary would study the matter further and make a recommendation at a later date. Hoover, in turn, was surprised and shocked by the steelmen's angry opposition and later said, "I left the dinner much disheartened."[21]

It is difficult to say which disturbed Hoover more—the steelmen's contrariness on the twelve-hour day or their rejection of his statistics. In any case, he had no intention of allowing the steelmen to seize the initiative and, after the White House dinner, contrary to administration policy, leaked to the press the purpose of the meeting and the trend of the discussion.[22] As he expected, the nation's newspapers almost unanimously took the administration's side. Further, Hoover immediately requested the Federated Engineering Societies (of which he was president) to study the twelve-hour day and issue a report. This report was finally published in November 1922 under the title *The Twelve-Hour Shift in Industry*. Not only did the study support

Hoover's facts and figures concerning relative costs but contained a hard-hitting foreword by President Harding which Hoover actually wrote. This Foreword concluded ominously: "The old order of the twelve-hour day must give way."[23]

For more than a year the Gary committee remained silent. Then, on May 25, 1923, it announced its rejection of the White House appeal for the elimination of the twelve-hour day. Both Harding and Hoover were bitterly disappointed, and on June 13 Hoover drafted a reply to Gary which he submitted to the president for his approval. This letter took sharp issue with the Gary committee and reiterated the president's desire that the steel industry abolish the twelve-hour day forthwith. This time Harding changed Hoover's draft hardly at all.[24]

Harding was passing through the Pacific Northwest on his way to Alaska when he was given the steelmen's reaction to this latest demand. In a telegram dated June 27, Gary and fourteen other steel leaders told Harding: "On account of [public] sentiment, and especially because it is in accordance with your own expressed views, we are determined to [bring about] a total abolition of the twelve-hour day at the earliest time practicable."[25] Delighted by this news, Harding decided to use a scheduled Independence Day address at Tacoma as the occasion for a public announcement. To Hoover fell the responsibility of inserting the proper paragraph in the already-prepared speech. But it was Harding's voice which read: "I wish to congratulate the steel industry on this important step. . . . I should be proud indeed if my Administration were marked by the final passing of the twelve-hour day in American life." Harding stumbled awkwardly over the Hooverian passage, but the audience immediately grasped its significance and burst into wild applause. As he sat down, smiling and nodding, Harding mumbled jovially to Hoover, "Damn it, Hoover, why don't you write the same English as I do?"[26]

Often obscured by the success and the publicity surrounding his numerous activities during the Harding years were Hoover's personal relationships with the important members of the Harding administration. These relationships sometimes aided but also sometimes hindered his overall effectiveness. In several critical instances they markedly affected his future career.

In many respects Hoover was the best known, yet the least known, of all the Harding cabinet officers. Since 1914, when he had first entered public service, newspaper publicity had made Hoover's name a household word. But it was his name, not his person, that had received the attention. Hoover's methods, Hoover's proposals, and Hoover's ideas garnered the publicity and not Hoover himself.

As a person, Hoover was shy and socially awkward. He had a halting, unsure manner toward people and gave the impression of being pompous. Very thin-skinned and sensitive to criticism, Hoover tended to harbor grudges and aggressively struck back at any detractors. In policy discussions he lost his temper too easily, was too prone to argue, and assumed too quickly that he was right. His inclination was to reach decisions rapidly and *tell* people what to do rather than discuss the situation with them.

Such traits proved abrasive and, as a result, Hoover's contacts with other members of the Harding cabinet were never very close. Yet Hoover craved the acceptance of his peers as well as an ever-larger public audience. His decision to move from private life into public service was motivated, at least in part, by this need for acceptance and recognition. Seemingly cold and aloof, Hoover nevertheless derived much excitement from taking part in large-scale governmental ventures and frankly enjoyed the "behind-the-scenes" influence he wielded in the Harding years. As one recent author has said, Hoover was a peculiar blend of opposites—he was an aggressive introvert.

All of this made Hoover controversial, even interesting, but it did not make him politically skilled or particularly likeable. Although Hoover spent the remainder of the decade at the center of American politics, he never developed into a charismatic political leader but remained mainly an "engineer in politics." He enjoyed dealing primarily with matters relating to "productivity" and "efficiency." Although associated with humanitarian activities almost all his life, he could appear to be peculiarly non-sensitive or unfeeling, and even his approach to humanitarian problems sometimes betrayed the workings of a rigidly-controlled, coldly logical, apolitical mind. When asked once in 1921 why he was sending corn to the starving Russians instead of wheat he allegedly replied: "Because for one dollar I can buy [more] calories."[27]

Hoover at one time or other drew the criticism of almost all of Harding's cabinet officers. Unlike most of them who minded their own business, Hoover was quick to insinuate himself into their areas of operation. He was secretary of commerce and "assistant secretary of everything else." He acted as an all-around expert, a fact constantly mentioned in the press. On foreign affairs, it was Hughes "and

Hoover." On money matters, it was Mellon "and Hoover." On agriculture, it was Wallace "and Hoover." Sometimes these cabinet officers did seek Hoover's advice and support, indicating that in their reaction to him resentment and admiration often went hand in hand.[28]

The traffic problem in Washington, D. C.

April 27, 1927   *(Permission John M. Henry, Des Moines, Iowa)*

Hoover's primary adversary in the Harding cabinet was Agriculture Secretary Henry Wallace. A tobacco-chewing, golf-playing, Scotch-Irish extrovert, Wallace found Hoover "bloodless," "stuffy," and "opinionated." But more than mere personality differences were behind their frequent clashes. Wallace considered Hoover an "empire-builder" who sought to aggrandize the Commerce Department at the expense of Agriculture. Hoover's repeated raids on that department's functions gave the agriculture secretary ample reason to complain. Moreover, Hoover ardently opposed any consideration of governmental subsidies for the farmer, while Wallace inclined more and more in that direction. Further, Hoover objected to other Wallace-supported schemes for helping the farmer such as decreased freight rates, maintaining that such action would adversely affect business. Both Hoover and Wallace agreed that scientific methods and efficiency should be applied to the American farm, but Hoover, unlike Wallace, saw agriculture as simply *another* business to be encouraged and protected, not the *predominant* national economic enterprise.

Secretary Mellon had little personal or official contact with Hoover. The Pennsylvania financier regarded him as being "too much an engineer" and "too officious." One slim folder in the Hoover Papers contains all the Mellon-Hoover correspondence for the years 1921–23.[29] Like Mellon, Hoover was interested in debt reduction and in debt-funding and made a few helpful suggestions to Mellon along these lines. Usually, however, Hoover listened in silence, as did all other members of the cabinet, when Mellon spoke. Mellon's great wealth unquestionably had an intimidating effect on Hoover in these early years, causing him to hold his tongue even though he thought some of Mellon's policies, especially his tax policies, were too "rich-oriented." On at least one occasion Hoover voiced doubt about Mellon's program privately to Harding, and Harding confessed doubt about it himself, but neither of them opposed Mellon openly. Mellon, meanwhile, despite his apparent imperturbability, secretly envied Hoover's energy and his general influence with the president.

Hoover was probably closer to Secretary of State Hughes than to any other member of the Harding cabinet. But it would be too strong to call them friends. It was always "Mr. Hoover" and "Mr. Hughes" because their personalities would not permit greater intimacy. Still, Hughes was receptive to Hoover's advice and seemed more pleased by compliments from him than from anyone else in the administration except Harding. Aside from the minor differences between them over the role of commercial attachés overseas, the two men supported each other, Hughes often using Hoover's ideas in matters relating to foreign debts and loans. The two men possessed a mutual respect which, despite the formalities, bound them together. Hoover believed Hughes to be the most able man in the cabinet, next to himself.

Hoover's attitude toward some of the other cabinet members varied from disinterest to disdain. He presumed that Will Hays (postmaster general), John Weeks (secretary of war), and Edwin Denby (secretary of the navy) represented the normal surrender to political expediency in cabinet-making. He considered Secretary Davis a light-weight but harmless, and treated him accordingly. Davis, on the other hand, admired Hoover and relied on him for help in adjudicating a number of labor disputes. Harry Daugherty and Hoover had almost no contact since each had an intense dislike for the other. However, Hoover was always careful not to step on the president's sensitivity regarding Daugherty and only once—in the case of the Wilkerson anti-labor injunction—openly opposed the attorney general.

Strangely enough, the most outspoken supporter of Hoover in the Harding cabinet was Interior Secretary Albert Fall. It was Fall who suggested to Harding that Hoover be made chairman of the Colorado River Commission, and it was Fall who urged Harding to name Hoover as the administration's chief negotiator with the coal operators in the coal strike of 1922. Hoover, in turn, was curiously drawn to the New Mexican because of the latter's progressive past and his deep interest in broadening American trade overseas. Fall's prospecting and mining background also gave them a common point of reference. The flambouyant secretary of interior intrigued the stolid engineer and when Fall resigned from the cabinet in early 1923, Hoover was the first to praise his work.

In all the official family, however, there was no stronger champion of Hoover than Harding, himself. True, Hoover was difficult to handle and sometimes caused trouble within the cabinet. He was prickly and aggressive. But he *was* one of those "best minds" which Harding had promised in 1920 to seek out and place in his cabinet. Hoover's commitment to middle-class ideals and his type of "rugged individualism" ably supplemented Harding's own brand of normalcy. Hoover's belief that each individual "should be given the chance and stimulation for development of the best with which he has been endowed" was also Harding's credo. Moreover, Hoover's view of government as an umpire rather than a policeman in the economic sphere was fully compatible with Harding's own thinking. Harding especially agreed with Hoover's belief that the federal government should promote government-business cooperation and maintain an economic atmosphere in which industry could expand and flourish.

Harding's *official* contact with Hoover was greater than with any other member of the cabinet except Hughes. Harding constantly sought out Hoover for advice on a whole range of problems and quickly discovered that, unlike Hughes who was reticent to give it except on State Department matters, Hoover was prepared to voice an opinion on almost anything. "I will await your frank advice on the subject" was a common sentence ending many a Harding-to-Hoover letter.[30] Hoover, on the other hand, relied heavily on Harding to supply the political finesse which he lacked and especially to adjudicate his differences with fellow cabinet members. Most important to Hoover was Harding's steadfast support. Said Hoover later: "Harding encouraged me in everything I wanted to do. I never knew him to give a promise that he did not keep."[31] Indeed, to the time of his death, Harding retained the highest regard for his secretary of commerce and often deferred to his judgment. As he once remarked to a close friend, E. Mont Reily: "Reily, do you know, taking Herbert Hoover up one side and down the other, and taking into consideration the knowledge he has of things generally, I believe he's the smartest 'gink' I know."[32]

Despite his personality deficiencies and the animus directed at him from some quarters, by the end of the Harding administration Hoover emerged not only as one of the giants of the cabinet but as one of the president's most influential advisers. This development occurred gradually yet perceptibly. It was undeniably accelerated by Harding's growing awareness of corruption in his administration. Significantly, when the guest list was issued for the presidential pilgrimage to Alaska in June 1923, Hoover's name was prominently on it while those of many of Harding's former cronies were missing. Newspaper reporters were remarking by that time about the increasing contact between Hoover and Harding and the president's reliance on his advice and guidance. By that time also, Old Guard members were openly grumbling about the hold which the "liberal element in the cabinet" (meaning Hoover) was gaining over the president.

Hoover's relationship with Harding on the ill-fated Alaskan trip is significant. Actually, Hoover left in his papers one of the best and most reliable eye-witness accounts of Harding's last days. Hoover maintained a direct contact with the president throughout the trip, often serving as his bridge partner and several times being allowed glimpses into Harding's inner turmoil. According to Hoover, after a hot and ceremony-filled trek across the United States, Harding looked forward to the Alaskan portion of the journey and left Tacoma on July 5 with the attitude of a "school boy entering on a holiday." The president's spirits were high and he was intrigued by the majestic scenery along the inland waterway to Alaska, watching it by the hour. However, as the presidential party moved farther north and the days lengthened, Harding found it increasingly difficult to sleep and kept such irregular hours walking the deck or playing cards that it caused comment. Later, it was claimed that he was so worried he could not sleep. In reality, a worsening heart condition, the excitement of the journey, and the almost constant daylight were the primary factors. As for Harding's mental health, Hoover later remembered: "His whole outlook was forward-looking. During conversations on his Alaskan trip there was no indication of the supposed apprehension of his early end. . . . In fact conversations on many occasions [were] on the general line as to what we should undertake and what should be done as to this, that, and the other. Many of the questions discussed stretched into actual action in the future over periods of years; he sometimes put in the reservation that 'we will carry through this, that, or the other, if we are elected.' "³³

Still, there was something obviously bothering the president during the Alaskan trip because his mind was often preoccupied. Hoover recalled that on the way north from Tacoma, Harding once asked him in the privacy of the presidential cabin what Hoover would do if he were president and knew of a scandal brewing. Hoover replied: "Publish it, and at least get credit for integrity on your side." When Hoover asked for particulars, Harding said that he had discovered some irregularities in the Justice Department involving Harry Daugherty's personal aide and general factotum, Jess Smith. Harding further told Hoover that he had sent for Smith and had informed him that he was to be arrested for his crimes, but that Smith had committed suicide before this could be done. When Hoover attempted to probe deeper and asked if Attorney General Daugherty was also involved, Harding "abruptly dried up and never raised the question again."³⁴

The president's spirits continued to be good, according to Hoover, as long as the presidential party remained on the Alaskan leg of the journey. But on the trip home Harding became noticeably more morose and nervous, causing alarm among members of the president's party, especially Hoover. In Seattle, when Harding stumbled badly over a speech on the future of Alaska which Hoover had helped him write, Hoover, as well as Harding's two physicians, Dr. Charles E. Sawyer and Commander Joel T. Boone, urged him to cancel his remaining engagements and return to Washington at once. That night, en route to San Francisco, Harding suffered an attack which Dr. Sawyer first diagnosed as indigestion but Dr. Boone believed to be a heart seizure. At the request of Dr. Boone, it was Hoover who wired ahead for Dr. Ray Lyman Wilbur, president of Stanford and later president of the American Medical Association, to meet the train and bring a heart specialist with him. It was also Hoover who several months before had asked staff man Samuel Blythe of the *Saturday Evening Post* to write a favorable article about Harding, entitled "A Calm Review of a Calm Man," and it was this article that Mrs. Harding was reading to the convalescing president in his sickroom in the Palace Hotel when the end came.

Harding's sudden death on August 2, 1923, and the resultant Harding scandals ushered in a period of uncertainty and confusion for most of the president's close associates. Hoover was no exception. Along with the other "best minds" in the cabinet, Hoover soon found himself tainted by the suspicions that spilled over from the congressional investigations into the activities of such men as Veterans' Bureau Director Charles Forbes, Alien Property Custodian Thomas Miller, Attorney General Daugherty, and Secretary Fall. How was it possible, many asked, for a man with Hoover's intelligence and catholic interests not to have known what was going on? Hoover bore these suspicions stoically and, in concert with Hughes and Mellon, disclaimed not only any knowledge of the skullduggery in the Veterans' Bureau and the Alien Property Custodian's offices, but in the Departments of Interior and Justice as well. The indiscretions of Fall and Daugherty, Hoover said, were individual phenomena not touching other members of the cabinet. Certainly it was true that Harding's administrative *modus operandi,* allowing his department heads almost complete independence, encouraged corruption on the part of those who were morally weak like Fall as well as encouraging creative activity by those who were morally strong like Hoover. In any case, in these dark days Calvin Coolidge was of real value. Although he had been vice-president during the corrupt Harding administration, his known rectitude made the claims of Hoover and the others more plausible. Even so, throughout the investigation mania of the winter of 1924, Hoover, especially, remained subject to attack if for no other reason than numerous conservatives in both parties "itched" to get him.[35]

Harding's death also marked a sharp decline in Hoover's influence in the White House. Although Hoover remained secretary of commerce under Coolidge, he never achieved the same easy relationship with him that he had established with Harding. Hoover had largely ignored Coolidge during the Harding years, regarding him as having little importance for the administration. This was a feeling shared by others, including Harding. Now circumstances were changed, and Hoover was clearly not among Coolidge's favorites. Secretary Mellon, instead, emerged as the major presidential adviser within the cabinet, secretly enjoying his ascendancy over Hoover. This did not stop Hoover from remaining in the public eye or increasing his influence elsewhere. However, as he developed other bases of support, he fell even more from White House grace. Coolidge was soon referring derogatorily to Hoover as the "Wonder boy," and in a fit of pique in 1928 remarked: "that man has offered me unsolicited advice for six years, all of it bad!"[36]

Just like the innocent members of the Harding cabinet, President Coolidge feverishly attempted throughout the post-scandal years to remain clear of any possible Harding taint, even though he followed Harding's normalcy policies to the letter. In his zeal to remain disassociated, he even refused to recognize what was happening on the outskirts of the small town of Marion, Ohio, where, by 1927, the beautiful Tuscan and Ionic collonaded Harding Memorial stood completed, awaiting formal dedication. Built with the contributions of Harding's many friends, collected mainly before the onset of the scandals, this memorial represented an embarrassment, becoming more a monument to Republican political cowardice than a tribute to a dead president. Obviously, no less than a president could deliver the dedicatory address. But Silent Cal "expressed a furious distaste," as Hoover put it, at any mention of his dedicating the memorial. Coolidge remained "too busy" to do so to the end of his term.

Upon assuming the presidency, Hoover was not much better, telling Hoke Donithen, secretary of the Harding Memorial Association, that his schedule would not permit him to "suggest any date for the dedication when he might be present." Hoover's conscience, however, finally forced his appearance at Marion in June 1931, where, before a battery of microphones, he finally faced the Harding issue. After tracing the Ohioan's humble beginnings and mentioning his winning qualities, Hoover defended his former benefactor by concluding: "here was a man whose soul was seared by a great disillusionment. . . . Harding had a dim realization that he had been betrayed by a few of the men whom he had trusted, by men whom he believed were his devoted friends. . . . That was the tragedy of the life of Warren Harding."[37]

The Harding years may have been a tragedy for their namesake, but in the end they were no tragedy for Herbert Hoover. Years later, long after his own presidency and the many successes of his post-presidential career, Hoover looked back fondly on the Harding years. Hoover admitted then that his early experiences in Commerce and his activities in connection with the Harding administration were among the happiest and most satisfying in his life. Certainly they were among the most formative and crucial for his later presidential career and for the maturing of his public policy. For this, more than to anyone else, Hoover owed a great debt to Warren Harding—a weak and discredited president whose faith in Hoover from the beginning had made all the rest possible.

NOTES

1   Warren G. Harding Papers (Ohio Historical Center, Columbus, Ohio), Box 407, Folder 3118-1, various items; Herbert C. Hoover Papers (Herbert Hoover Presidential Library, West Branch, Iowa), Box AK I-7, various telegrams.

2   Harding Papers, Box 695, Folder 1, items 149279-149283; Box 701, Folder 8, items 152559-152560.

3   Frank Brandegee to Warren Harding, December 28, 1920, Harding Papers, Box 694, Folder 1, item 148691.

4   Hoover to Harding, December 22, 1920, Hoover Papers, Box AK I-7.

5   For the Dawes candidacy see Harding Papers, Box 395, Folder 4, various items. For Mellon's candidacy see *ibid.*, Box 487, Folder 3944-1, various items. Mellon's own account is in Mellon to Ray C. Harris, June 6, 1934, Ray Baker Harris Papers (Ohio Historical Center, Columbus, Ohio), Box 4, Folder 4. For Harry Daugherty's account of the Hoover-Mellon deal see Harry M. Daugherty, *The Inside Story of the Harding Tragedy* (New York, 1932), pp. 92-100.

6   Harding to Daugherty, February 9, 1921, Harding Papers, Box 368, Folder 2601-1, item 174897.

7   For Hughes's involvement see Beerits memo, "Fall Scandals," Charles Evans Hughes Papers (Library of Congress, Washington, D.C.), Box 173, Folder 45. Hoover's telegram of acceptance is in the Hoover Papers, Box AK I-7. For a complete

analysis of all the cabinet appointments and Harding's role in them see Robert K. Murray, "President Harding and His Cabinet," *Ohio History,* 75, nos. 2-3 (Spring-Summer 1966), 108-25.

8 Herbert Hoover, *Memoirs of Herbert Hoover: The Cabinet and the Presidency, 1920-1933* (New York, 1952), p. 42.

9 *New York Times,* February 25, 1921, p. 1, quoting Hoover.

10 For an excellent analysis of Hoover's publicity techniques see Craig M. Lloyd, *Aggressive Introvert: Herbert Hoover and Public Relations Management, 1912-1932* (Columbus, Ohio, 1973).

11 For a synopsis of Hoover's Commerce activities see Eugene Lyons, *Herbert Hoover: A Biography* (New York, 1964); David Hinshaw, *Herbert Hoover: American Quaker* (New York, 1950); and Joan Hoff Wilson, *Herbert Hoover: Forgotten Progressive* (Boston, 1975). For the most complete work on Hoover's Commerce years, specifically with respect to the Bureau of Foreign and Domestic Commerce, see Joseph Brandes, *Herbert Hoover and Economic Diplomacy: Department of Commerce Policy, 1921-1928* (Pittsburgh, 1962).

12 Harding to Hoover, August 24, 1921, Harding Papers, Box 285, Folder 804-1, items 122681-122683. For the best single coverage of the Unemployment Conference, see Carolyn Grin, "The Unemployment Conference of 1921: An Experiment in National Cooperative Planning," *Mid-America,* 15, no. 2 (April 1973), 83-107.

13 George B. Christian to Hoover, September 10, 1921, Harding Papers, Box 285, Folder 804-1.

14 Lyons, *Herbert Hoover,* p. 166.

15 Harding to Hoover, August 24, 1921, Harding Papers, Box 285, Folder 804-1, items 122681-122683. The conference also had roots in the report of the Economic Advisory Council which Hoover had formed in September 1921, and in the various earlier proposals of the American Association for Labor Legislation which for more than a decade had shown an interest in reform labor legislation. See Daniel Nelson, *Unemployment Insurance: The American Experience, 1915-1935* (Madison, Wisconsin, 1969), pp. 36-40, passim.

16 Lyons, *Herbert Hoover,* p. 166; Harris G. Warren, *Herbert Hoover and the Great Depression* (New York, 1959), p. 27.

17 This letter was prepared by Hoover on May 20 and was changed only slightly by Harding before he attached his signature. See Hoover Papers, Box 1-I/243. Gompers's support is found in Samuel Gompers, *Seventy Years of Life and Labor: An Autobiography* (New York, 1925), 2:521.

18 Hoover to Davis, October 4, 1921, Harding Papers, Box 285, Folder 804-1, item 122761.

19 Clinton Gilbert, *Behind the Mirrors: The Psychology of Disintegration at Washington* (New York, 1922), p. 41.

20 Hoover to Harding, April 8, 1922, Hoover Papers, Box 1-I/313; Hoover's proposed draft is in Harding Papers, Box 363, Folder 2575-1, item 172171. Harding's letter to Gary is in Harding Papers, Box 363, Folder 2575-1, items 172168-172169.

21 Hoover, *Memoirs,* 2:103.

22   For an interesting exchange of letters between Harding and Hoover over the advisability of releasing information to the press, see Harding Papers, Box 5, Folder 3-3, and Hoover Papers, Box 1-I/243 and 1-I/313.

23   For Harding-Hoover correspondence over this foreword, see Hoover Papers, Box 1-I/313, especially Hoover to Harding, November 1, 1922.

24   Hoover to Harding, June 13, 1923, Hoover Papers, Box 1-I/313; Harding to Hoover, June 18, 1923, Hoover Papers, Box 1-I/313.

25   Gary to Harding, June 27, 1923, Harding Papers, Box 365, Folder 2584-1, item 173198.

26   See various items, Hoover Papers, Box 1-I/313.

27   Gilbert, *Behind the Mirrors,* p. 132.

28   For a description of Hoover's official contacts with Harding cabinet members consult Robert K. Murray, *The Harding Era: Warren G. Harding and His Administration* (Minneapolis, 1969), passim.

29   Hoover Papers, Box 1-I/311.

30   For examples, see Harding-Hoover correspondence in Hoover Papers, Boxes 1-I/242, 1-I/243, and 1-I/244.

31   Hoover, *Memoirs,* 2:47-48.

32   E. Mont Reily, "Years of Confusion," unpublished manuscript (Ohio Historical Center, Columbus, Ohio), p. 264.

33   Alaskan Notes, Hoover Papers, Box 1-I/546, are outstanding on the Alaskan trip. These notes, written immediately after the event, differ in a number of details from Hoover's *Memoirs,* 2:48-52.

34   Hoover, *Memoirs,* 2:49.

35   Robert K. Murray, *The Politics of Normalcy: Governmental Theory and Practice in the Harding-Coolidge Era* (New York, 1973), p. 122.

36   William A. White, *A Puritan in Babylon: The Story of Calvin Coolidge* (New York, 1938), p. 400.

37   As reported in *New York Times,* June 17, 1931, p. 1.

SUMMARY OF COMMENTARY BY DISCUSSANTS AND CONFEREES

Discussion of Professor Murray's paper began with formal commentaries by Barbara Chapman of Rockford, Illinois, and Professor Peri Arnold of the University of Notre Dame. Mrs. Chapman praised the paper but wished that there had been more analysis of the roles played by Hoover's engineering mentality, his family life, and his relations with women's groups and the press. Professor Arnold took issue with Murray's depiction of Hoover as an apolitical technocrat lacking in political skills. In reality, he argued, the secretary was a skilled practitioner of the new bureaucratic or administrative politics. He knew how to mobilize administrative clienteles and use their power, and by doing so he succeeded in drastically changing the traditional role of the Commerce Department. It would later be attacked as the department that Hoover "politicized." The secretary's major weakness, so Arnold maintained, was not an inability to think and act politically. His negotiations with Harding, his sophisticated conference building, and his use of technocratic ideals for political purposes were all demonstrations of this. All indicate that he should be seen as a precursor of the bureaucratic politicians who held posts in the New Deal cabinets. His weakness lay rather in his inability to sense his own limitations and recognize situations where his opponents were solidly entrenched. He carried on losing battles too long and wasted too much energy on projects that had little prospect of ever being realized.

Subsequent discussion revolved largely around the views expressed by Professor Arnold. Hoover's central weakness, so Professor Melvyn Leffler argued, was neither an apolitical mentality nor a poor sense of his limitations. It was rather a set of ideological commitments that blinded him to the realities of business behavior and interest-group conflict. His mind, although highly creative, operated within self-imposed ideological constraints, and these, so Leffler felt, deserved fuller analysis than Murray had given them. Also pointed out in the ensuing discussion were the distinctions to be made between congressional and managerial politics, the need to see Hoover's operations as part of a larger phenomenon involving other master administrators, the roles envisioned for academics and builders of intergroup cooperation, and the weakness of interpretations viewing the Hooverian system as a creature of big business. Frequently, so Professor Joseph Brandes noted, Hoover was quite critical of large corporate structures and practices. And in Murray's view, the secretary saw almost everything as "business" and urged business measures as part of a national rather than a class program.

In addition, Professor Murray elaborated on Hoover's supporters in the Republican party, his personal relationships with Harding, and the battles that developed over the executive reorganization plans of 1921. The latter were also discussed by Professors Robert Zieger and Peri Arnold, each noting aspects of them with which he was familiar. As the session drew to a close, Professor Murray entertained and responded to questions about the Harding scandals. On these he emphasized the relatively small sums involved, the train of events set off by the presidents's decision to dissemble and cover up, and the parallel with the Watergate affair and its effects on the Nixon presidency.

Ellis W. Hawley

Herbert Hoover and Economic Stabilization, 1921–22

Editor's Introductory Note

My study of Herbert Hoover began in 1950, when Professor James C. Malin of the University of Kansas suggested that I write a master's thesis that was subsequently entitled "The Relation of Hoover's Policies to the National Industrial Recovery Act." I later turned my attention to the New Deal's business policies. But with the opening of Hoover's papers in 1966, I again became interested in his efforts to build trade associations and commit them to larger social ends. I began what I initially thought of as a study of federal trade association policy, and it was only as I became immersed in the new collections that I began to realize the extent to which Hoover's actions in this sphere had parallels in numerous other policy areas. Not only was he seeking to apply the association idea to other functional groupings but also to develop integrating institutions through which it could be applied to society as a whole. At work, it seemed, was a vision of social order resembling that being articulated by managerial corporatists in Europe. And gradually, I shifted my research focus away from industrial interest groups and toward the origins, nature, and workings of this managerial vision.

The following paper is one product of this changed focus. It examines the economic stabilization program that Hoover sought to implement during his first two years as secretary of commerce, seeking to understand both the organizational ideals involved and the difficulties encountered in realizing them. The program, I argue, was not an economic success. Recovery would probably have come without it, and the new institutions that it fostered were unable to control the forces leading to the economic debacle of 1929. But this failure, I also argue, should not be allowed to obscure the historical importance of the program. It is in 1921 and 1922, not in the 1930s, that federal officials first attempt to create tools for managing a peacetime economy. It is this experience, not the traditions of a more remote past, that serves as the model for public policy during Hoover's presidency. And it is in the development and advocacy of such a program, more perhaps than anywhere else, that Hoover and his associates stand revealed as men who have broken with and largely abandoned the laissez-faire notions of the "invisible hand." They are best seen not as champions of traditional market ideals but as articulators of an associational progressivism, developers of an Americanized variant of the neo-corporative ideal, and foreshadowers of much that would become part of the American system in the 1930s, 1940s, and 1950s.

The paper published here is essentially the one that I presented to the Hoover Seminar in 1974. I have made only a few stylistic revisions and a few changes in the footnotes. In the intervening years, however, I have become more aware of how much of the program of 1921 was anticipated by failed initiatives in 1919 and hence more inclined to view Hoover's contribution as a reassembling of these initiatives rather than a pioneering exploit. I am also less convinced than I once was that Hoover had reconciled in his own mind the tensions between individualistic and techno-corporative ideals. He had gone farther toward this than most other figures in public life, and the result was an ideology that shaped and constrained his activities. But I would now concede a residue of confusion and ambivalence, which may account in part for the fuzziness in portions of the organizational ideal, the hyper-sensitivity with which Hoover reacted to criticism, and his efforts at times to unify by proclamation rather than logic. Still, I would stand by the central arguments in the paper and its general reassessment of the stabilization program of 1921–22.

Herbert Hoover and Economic Stabilization, 1921–22

In recent scholarship the cleavage that American historians once drew between the New Deal's "managerial state" and an earlier "negativism" has seemed less and less sharp. In the new studies of progressive reform, the managerial impulse has been much in evidence, and upon re-examining the New Era, scholars have discovered a number of its leaders to be thinking in terms of macroeconomic management rather than particularistic reform or mere regulation of the money supply.[1] Like the New Dealers, such men were strongly influenced by the experiences of World War I.[2] And the more their actions are studied, the clearer it has become that New Deal interventionism had significant precedents, not only in the Hoover program of 1929 but in an earlier Hoover program, launched during the recession of 1921 and carried on under the auspices of an administration commonly associated with "normalcy" and "reaction."[3]

This is not to say, of course, that these managers of the Harding era favored the expanded public sector associated with the war government and the New Deal. Like their more conservative colleagues in 1921, they blamed a part of the nation's economic difficulties on an over-grown government and burdensome taxes; and for the most part, they went along with the type of economy measures, tax revision, and governmental retrenchment urged by business conservatives and Andrew Mellon's Treasury Department.[4] For them, however, much of the difficulty also lay in defective business organization, ill-informed decision-making, and improper uses of private power. And while they agreed that the economy must be purged of its wastes, inefficiencies, and uneconomic price-cost relationships, they believed that this could be done without putting it through the wringer of liquidation or running the social and economic risks of mass wage cuts, prolonged unemployment, and acute agricultural distress. Given the right kind of coordination and cooperative action, they argued, such painful purges were neither necessary nor inevitable. And acting on this belief, they developed a program that would foreshadow the analysis and remedies adopted after 1929.[5]

It is upon these stabilization actions, then, especially those undertaken by Herbert Hoover's Department of Commerce, that the present paper will focus. It will look, in particular, at the context in which the Hoover programs took shape, the goals and methods of the men involved, and the activities and agencies through which they hoped to short-circuit the liquidation phase of the business cycle and regularize future growth. It will also attempt to assess the significance of these actions, both in terms of their immediate impact and their influence on future governmental policy. And hopefully, by pulling together and adding to the recent scholarship on these matters,[6] it will contribute to a growing understanding of Hoover's approach to economic

management, the policies of the Harding administration, and the
paths along which the American version of the "managerial state" developed.

II

To understand the impulses behind Hoover's activities and the constraints within which his programs took shape, one must recognize the
conflicting forces at work in the immediate postwar period. For a
variety of "progressive" businessmen and their allies in the profes-
sions and social sciences, the wartime experience had strengthened an
earlier vision of managerial progress through scientific inquiry, expert
administration, and coordinated group action. Along this path, they
had come to believe, lay the nation's hope for ever increasing efficiency, harmony, and material abundance, and at war's end a number
of them had hoped to adapt the wartime machinery to this type of
peacetime development.[7] Even under war conditions, however, the
powerful traditions of anti-statism, anti-monopoly, and anti-collectivism, all deeply embedded in America's institutional and legal structure, had forced would-be systematizers to make numerous compromises.[8] And in the postwar period, as these traditions became rallying
cries for groups seeking redistributions of power or blaming their difficulties on departures from the "American way," the result was an
incoherent mixture of the war-fostered initiatives with drives for governmental retrenchment, campaigns of antitrust action, and orgies of
union-busting and red-baiting.[9] If scientific managers and enlightened
capitalists were to act as agents of progress, it appeared, they would
have to do so while making proper obeisance to these older traditions.
Under the circumstances of 1920 and 1921, it had become all but impossible to install any system managed by a "peace industries board,"
a set of formalized cartels, or the type of syndicalist arrangements envisioned by some reformers.

As these political constraints took shape, moreover, the notion had
reasserted itself that an approach blending the managerial vision with
inherited American traditions was not only possible but clearly superior
to anything being advocated by un-American "collectivists." If properly preserved, the envisioners of this "American system" argued, the
older individualistic traditions could still contribute to national progress. And building now on a set of ideas developed by pre-war
advocates of "cooperative competition,"[10] they insisted that the economy could be ordered and stabilized without creating harmful state

bureaucracies, repressive monopolies, or some type of American "soviet." The answer lay in the nation's growing network of cooperative institutions, especially its trade and professional associations, its socially-minded corporations, and its efficiency-minded labor and farm groups. With proper assistance, coordination, and delimitation, so the argument ran, these institutions could provide a new and superior type of economic system—a way whereby America could have intelligent planning and scientific rationalization without sacrificing the energy and creativity inherent in individual effort and private enterprise.[11]

Taking shape, too, particularly in the engineering societies, trade association movement, and postwar inheritors of the earlier efficiency movement, were a number of specific proposals whose implementation would allegedly help to build the new economic order. The nation, so it was argued, needed cooperative programs that would help to reduce industrial costs, allocate resources to their most productive uses, and iron out harmful fluctuations in employment, output, and demand. And government, so the argument continued, could and should play a limited role in launching and nourishing such programs. There was a need for some postwar equivalent of the wartime Conservation Division, for an expanded commercial intelligence service, for statistical assistance of the type provided during the war period, and for other agencies that could help the leaders of cooperative institutions to coordinate their activities, mobilize their constituencies, and act in the public interest. If only such agencies had been in existence and functioning, so the lament frequently ran, much of the postwar economic gyration, with its accompanying wastes and acerbation of economic and social conflict, could have been avoided.[12]

With this ideology and program, moreover, Herbert Hoover had become increasingly associated. In the postwar clashes between free-market advocates and proponents of statist direction, he had consistently sought a "middle way," a program of action that could draw on the energy and resources of private enterprise yet deploy these within the context of purposeful planning and coordination. Such had been the nature of his plans for European reconstruction and postwar trade revival.[13] And subsequently, as he concerned himself with labor conflict, agricultural adjustment, and the performance of the coal, housing, and transportation industries, he consistently called for governmental agencies that would provide "illumination, guidance, and cooperation" rather than dictation or coercive controls.[14] Clearly, he

argued, there was a need for collective initiative, overall coordination, and national planning. Left to "haphazard development" and
the workings of unrestrained competition, modern economies functioned badly. Yet when "politicized," they performed in even worse
fashion. If their potential was ever to be fully realized, it could be
done only through organizing cooperation in "the community as a
whole," providing the cooperative groups with a "national conception" of what could and should be done, and supplementing their efforts with informational aids and supportive governmental actions.[15]

As the emerging spokesman for managerial cooperativism, Hoover
was also setting forth a theory of recovery and prosperity that diverged
markedly from classical prescriptions. In late 1920 and early 1921, in
what amounted to an early version of the New Era's high-wage doctrine and the New Deal's purchasing-power theory, he was already
arguing that maintenance of labor and farm income would help to
check the economic downturn and stimulate new expansion. And this,
he maintained, was not inconsistent with lowering business costs and
restoring profit incentives. The latter could be achieved through organized campaigns of waste elimination, market expansion, and
counter-cyclical investment; and in each of these areas, he was already
moving to construct appropriate machinery. In November 1920, after
meetings with Samuel Gompers and the industrial engineer Robert
Wolf, he used his position as head of the Federated American Engineering Societies to launch a "survey of waste" that could provide a
blueprint for managerial action.[16] In December, he endorsed the newly launched Foreign Trade Financing Corporation as the key to trade
revival.[17] And throughout the period, he was considering what could
be done, especially through statistics, education, and cooperative
mobilization, to encourage counter-cyclical construction and business
planning that would serve the interests of overall stability.[18]

By early 1921 Hoover had also decided that the Department of
Commerce could be used to implement this recovery and stabilization
program. Its enabling act, he found, provided a broad charter under
which new programs could be developed. And once this realization
had dawned, he had moved away from earlier plans for private or-
chestration,[19] set aside his fears that Harding was trying to use him,
and negotiated an arrangement that would give him a free hand in departmental reorganization and a voice in financial, foreign, labor, and
farm as well as business policies. In particular, he told the in-coming
president, he wanted to strengthen the department by adding bureaus

"properly belonging in the field," establish close teamwork with the government's other economic agencies, and use the resulting structure to build cooperative programs of waste reduction, market expansion, and labor reform. These things, he was assured, would have presidential support. And having received such assurances, he joined the Harding cabinet as secretary of commerce.[20]

III

By March of 1921, then, Secretary Hoover had given some thought both to the program he hoped to implement and the role that his agency should play in the process. The task ahead was one of building the private and public institutions that could implement what he had in mind; and within days of assuming office, he was moving vigorously to bring the appropriate bureaus under his jurisdiction, staff them with men who shared his vision, and forge "a wider and better organized co-operation" with the private sector.[21] Almost immediately, claims were staked out to the statistical, marketing, transportation, and development agencies in other departments. Just as quickly, men were put to work on plans for restructuring and expanding such bureaus as Standards, the Census, and Foreign and Domestic Commerce.[22] And on March 9, in the hope of creating an advisory agency that would unify and coordinate private leadership, Hoover began consultation with some twenty-five trade and industrial associations.[23]

Despite vigorous action, however, the contemplated agencies of recovery and stabilization did not spring magically into life. On the contrary, Hoover's initiatives quickly ran into three major obstacles, all of which would continue to plague him throughout his tenure in office. One was strong resistance from established agencies who did not share his vision, had no desire to be transferred or "coordinated," and interpreted his activities as those of a bureaucratic empire-builder.[24] The second was the difficulty of fitting cooperative "stabilization" inside the framework of the antitrust laws, especially since the Department of Justice and the Federal Trade Commission seemed inclined to interpret these strictly and not to give advisory opinions on what might be prosecuted.[25] And the third was sharp criticism from business groups who were not being consulted or represented and who looked upon Hoover's scheme of public-private cooperation as amounting to an informal version of recognizing and using monopolistic chosen instruments. So sharp did such protests become that Hoover quickly backed away from the idea of a formalized economic advisory council and announced that he would work instead through monthly conferences with different business, labor, and farm leaders participating.[26]

Nevertheless, even as these obstacles took shape, some progress was being made in forging what Hoover would later call the "three legs" of his recovery and reconstruction program.[27] In Washington, one conference followed another, particularly with engineering leaders, statistical advisers, and export groups. In the confines of the Commerce Department, new desks and operations kept appearing, manned by the coordinators and trouble-shooters that the secretary had assigned to ride herd on the emerging programs. And through the swirl of activity, the outlines of the waste reduction, statistical dissemination, and trade expansion programs were taking shape, generating new institutional structures, and being sold both as recovery measures and pathways to permanent economic and social progress.[28] To support them, moreover, Hoover was lining up an impressive array of the private sector's "progressive-minded" leaders. While backing away from the idea of a permanent advisory council, he had drawn in a number of his closest associates in the earlier war government, set up both a Reorganization Committee and an Industrial Group, and was making use of these bodies to further the "upbuilding of the Department."[29]

In constructing the first "leg," that of organized waste reduction, the blueprint was still to come from the "survey of waste" being conducted by the Federated American Engineering Societies. Since January, its seventeen-man Industrial Waste Committee had been organizing and directing "assays" of six representative industries and a variety of labor, educational, health, and management factors. Riding herd on the operation was Edward Eyre Hunt, a former radical who had been caught up in the scientific-management mystique and attached himself to Hoover during the war period. And hoping now to get the "findings" into the hands of people who could act on them, Hunt arranged for preliminary summaries to be released at a meeting of the American Engineering Council in St. Louis. There on June 3, 1921, the country was told that it was suffering from immense wastes in the use of its resources—wastes that derived partly from faulty management, partly from short-sighted production restraints, partly from the failure to conserve human resources and bring harmful economic fluctuations under control. In the Waste Committee's view, moreover, more than fifty percent of these wastes were due to poor

management, and this being the case, it seemed possible to organize
economic recovery without liquidating labor and running the risks inherent in mass suffering.[30]

In business and engineering circles, the reaction was not entirely
favorable, particularly to the notion that management was chiefly responsible for the nation's economic difficulties. Hoover and the
"Taylorites," so it was charged, were trying to stir up "class antagonism." And instead of joining them in their war on waste, such groups
as the National Industrial Conference Board and the American Institute of Electrical Engineers reacted with campaigns designed to discredit the blueprint.[31] Such reactions, however, were insufficient to
derail plans for a new "waste elimination division" or for turning the
Bureau of Standards into a "super-consultant" on research and standardization problems.[32] In May, Hoover had assigned the implementation of such plans to Frederick Feiker, an engineer and publicist
long associated with the Arch Shaw and McGraw-Hill trade publications.[33] Shortly thereafter, he had persuaded a Conference of Business
Paper Editors, convened by Feiker, to conduct a survey of standardization work. And by August, armed both with the Industrial Waste
report and material gathered by the business editors, Feiker was map-
ping out programs of standardization and simplification, contem-
plating the creation of a new agency to handle them, and negotiating
with the National Paving Brick Manufacturers for what would
become the first of the department's simplified practice conferences.[34]

By August, too, some progress was being made in forging the second "leg" of Hoover's program, that designed to generate statistical
information and improve overall stability through statistically-in-
formed production planning. The possibilities here had been explored
by economists such as Allyn Young, Edwin Gay, and Wesley Mitchell,
all serving now on Hoover's reconvened version of the Advisory Committee on the Census.[35] These possibilities had then been discussed in a
series of conferences, both with individual industries and with such
groups as the Chamber of Commerce, the Business Paper Editors, and
the National Association of Manufacturers.[36] And while some businessmen seemed disinclined to share their "secrets" or put up with
more questionnaires and more "meddling,"[37] enough support had developed to set up a new government service and tie it into the informational activities of cooperating trade associations. In July 1921, the
Census Bureau launched its *Survey of Current Business,* making available on a monthly basis the production, sales, and inventory data sup-

plied by cooperating industries and technical periodicals. It was a "little service," Hoover told Frank Taussig. But he planned to build upon it. And eventually, he hoped, the statistical program could provide the knowledge and foresight necessary to combat panic or speculative conditions, prevent the development of diseased industries, and guide decision-making so as to iron out rather than accentuate the business cycle.[38]

In addition, the Commerce Department was making some slight progress in its drives to take over other statistical agencies and secure protection of the program from "unreasonable" antitrust action. Along the first line, Hoover was in the process of acquiring the Treasury Department's Bureau of Customs Statistics.[39] And along the second, he and departmental solicitor William Lamb were engaged in a series of conferences with the Justice Department, seeking to define which statistical activities were desirable and which might be used to further improper restraints of trade.[40] Along both fronts, however, resistance remained stiff. Most of the departments, Hoover lamented, were hanging on to their statistical activities like "grim death," unable, it seemed, to rise above petty bureaucratic jealousies or see how centralization in the Commerce Department could serve national interests.[41] And despite his willingness to steer clear of "open price" exchanges and condemn the type of "stabilization" that would protect inefficiencies and accentuate economic fluctuations, the Justice Department remained reluctant to spell out permissible activities. Nor was it receptive to pleas that businessmen were only doing what the Department of Commerce was urging them to do or to calls for quashing actions already begun against the activities of building-materials associations.[42]

In forging the third or trade-expansion "leg" of his program, Hoover was also encountering somewhat similar obstacles, particularly from the marketing information services in the State and Agriculture Departments and from Federal Trade Commissioners inclined toward a strict interpretation of the Webb-Pomerene Act.[43] Yet here, too, new structures and activities were taking shape. In Julius Klein, the new head of the Bureau of Foreign and Domestic Commerce, Hoover had found another energetic organizer and missionary.[44] And in well-publicized speeches, he was spelling out how a properly designed trade program could act both as a stimulant to recovery and as a permanent "balance wheel and stabilizer" yet not require such counterproductive measures as wage cuts, tariff abolition, or statist enterprise. As with the domestic economy, he argued, the answer lay in waste elimination and better marketing to reduce costs, cooperative mobilization and guidance of the needed credits, and the eventual transformation of the world economy into one producing for properly protected but ever-expanding mass markets.[45]

To help in building such a program, moreover, Hoover was moving rapidly to reorganize the Bureau of Foreign and Domestic Commerce, tie it into a network of cooperating associations, and use the resulting machinery to achieve his goals. In March and early April, he had considered a variety of plans for new commodity divisions and technical services,[46] all allegedly designed to help exporters eliminate waste and rationalize their operations. In late April, he had called the customary conference, bringing together business and academic advisers and using them to mobilize support for the bureau's expansion. And by early September, he had begun the reorganization that would eventually produce some seventeen new commodity divisions, staff them with "experts" drawn from the export industries, and regularize cooperation through parallel industrial advisory committees. "I see in my own mind," said Frederick Feiker, "a wall chart at the top of which is a horizontal list of manufacturing associations interested in export leading down through committees" and functioning "with different commodities in our own organization."[47]

As the national "exporting and selling scheme" was reorganized,[48] Hoover was also considering what could be done to provide needed credits and bring about needed adjustments in tariff rates, international debts, and foreign practices. Such actions, he had hoped initially, could be handled by special export credit corporations,[49] the transfer of tariff and debt adjustment to qualified "experts," and a properly delimited participation of the United States in the League of Nations. Efforts to secure such measures, however, had been disillusioning. The nation's banks had been reluctant to subscribe to the Hoover-endorsed Foreign Trade Financing Corporation, and its congressmen seemed bent upon collecting the war debts, retaining the traditional methods of tariff-making, and saving America from League "entanglement." Hence, by the summer of 1921, Hoover was thinking more in terms of some type of informal financial concert, linking governmental policy-makers with financial leaders at home and central bankers abroad, and using the resulting alliance to encourage American investors, press for needed reforms abroad, and reduce political irrationality to a minimum. As yet, this line of thinking had not produced specific programs, but within a few months it would begin to do so.[50]

As the summer drew to a close, then, Hoover was making progress in implementing the proposals of late 1920 and early 1921. Waste elimination, statistical dissemination, and trade expansion programs were all taking shape, and these, as Hoover visualized them, were to be the keys to a relatively painless recovery and a new era of managed and stable prosperity. Nor was this all that he had been doing. From the beginning, he had also concerned himself with a number of "problem" areas where economic "sickness" seemed to be holding back recovery and progress in the rest of the economy. And out of this concern had come special programs and plans for restoring economic health to such areas as housing, coal mining, agriculture, and the railroads.

IV

The "housing problem," as Hoover perceived it at the time, was essentially one of a backward and disorganized field of endeavor, unable to meet its obligations to the society as a whole and seemingly committed to patterns of operation that destabilized the overall economic system. Over the years, this backwardness and disorganization had left the nation with a shortage of "a million homes," blocked the modernization that could make it a "nation of homeowners," and repeatedly thrown the national economy "out of step" by subjecting it to a succession of building booms and slumps. Yet here as elsewhere, Hoover had decided, excursions into statist enterprise, detailed controls, or organized campaigns of wage reduction were likely to make things worse instead of better. The answer, he argued, lay in cooperative programs of modernization and construction planning, designed to lower costs, regularize employment, and build up construction "reserves" that could be expanded during slack periods of economic activity.[51] And shortly after assuming office, he had secured the services of housing specialist Franklin T. Miller,[52] put him to work organizing the necessary cooperative machinery, and won presidential backing for a $50,000 appropriation to support these activities. The result, when the funds became available on July 1, 1921, was a new Division of Building and Housing in the Bureau of Standards.[53]

To head the new division Hoover appointed John M. Gries, a housing specialist from the Harvard Business School.[54] And in the summer of 1921, while Hoover continued to publicize what he had in mind,

Gries moved energetically to expand upon Miller's earlier activities. On one front, the Housing Division worked with the Chamber of Commerce and the National Federation of Construction Industries to organize "community action programs," some of which quickly went "upon the rocks" over labor matters, but others of which did have some initial success in adjusting the conflicts that were paralyzing construction activities. On a second front, it worked with other Commerce officials and allies to interest the construction industries in the emerging programs of waste elimination and statistical dissemination. On a third, it proceeded to organize special advisory committees designed to work out and publicize model building codes, better zoning laws, and standardized contract specifications. And on a fourth, it began considering the problems of home financing, seasonal fluctuations, and future construction planning.[55] In each of these areas, it was hoped, some part of the "housing problem" could be solved; and once this was done, the construction field could lead the way to general recovery and contribute to future progress and stability.

Another problem area to which Hoover hoped to apply somewhat similar solutions was that of bituminous coal. Here again, as he saw it, the "problem" was essentially one of a backward and disorganized industry trapped into patterns of intermittent operation and labor turmoil that disrupted the whole economy. And again, he believed, the answer lay not in nationalization, detailed controls, or the type of union-busting that one wing of the industry was pushing. It lay rather in cooperative modernization and regularization, especially in cooperative action to reduce marketing wastes, encourage the storage of coal during slack periods, and provide the market information and statistical data needed to rationalize production, puchasing, and investment decisions. Such an approach, he had declared repeatedly, could work to the benefit of all parties concerned. And to provide the necessary stimulation and assistance, he had hoped to create a Coal Division, endow it with fact-gathering powers, and use it to organize programs similar to those being sponsored by the new Housing Division.[56]

In the case of coal, however, these plans ran into stronger obstacles and were slow to materialize. As embodied in the Frelinghuysen Bill of April 1921,[57] for example, they ran into strong opposition from the southern coal operators and their supporters in Congress. Fact-gathering and statistical dissemination, so the argument ran, was the entering wedge for government control, unionization, and removal of the South's competitive advantages. And once the southern operators had captured control of the National Coal Association's executive board the chances that Hoover could secure passage of the bill dwindled to virtually nil.[58] Nor was he able as yet to compensate for this setback by taking over existing bureaus and converting them into the agency he had in mind. Those in charge of the Interior Department's Bureau of Mines and Geological Survey were not enthusiastic about being transferred and were putting up stiff resistance to all such designs.[59]

During the same period, similar difficulties had also sidetracked Hoover's efforts to deal with another "problem" area, namely that of a depressed railroad industry unable to attract new capital and seemingly committed to rate structures that compounded the problems in housing, coal, and agriculture. The best treatment here, he felt, was one that combined cooperative efficiency measures with selective rate revision for industries that were in trouble and prompt settlement of the claims arising out of government operation during the war. This was the program that he urged upon all concerned, especially in a series of summer conferences with industry leaders, Treasury officials, and railroad regulators. Yet in implementing the program, one setback seemed to follow another. The railroads, rejecting his version of their long-range interests and social obligations, refused to consider special rate structures for coal or building materials. Anti-railroad elements in Congress blocked the bill for claim settlement. And the wage and rate cuts imposed by the Railway Labor Board and the Interstate Commerce Commission seemed designed chiefly to generate new labor turmoil and make the problem worse instead of better.[60] For railroads as for coal, it seemed, an extraordinary effort would be required to get the right kind of machinery established and operating.

Finally, as still another impetus to recovery and future progress, Hoover hoped to restore the prosperity and purchasing power of American agriculture. Like many of his contemporaries, he tended to go along with a type of agrarian corporatist thinking which looked upon farming not only as the nation's "fundamental" industry but also as basic to the general health of the whole social or national organism. And while he did not believe that extensive governmental controls could cure agricultural ills, he did see their cure as being vital and as requiring some type of remedial action along collective lines.[61] In August, in a move designed to substitute a "constructive" alternative for Senator George Norris's export subsidy bill, he helped to draft and put through the Emergency Agricultural Credits Act, authorizing the War Finance Corporation to extend credit to farm cooperatives,

foreign purchasers, and rural banks.[62] And as early as April, he began
advocating the creation of "a national food-marketing board" that
could help farmers organize themselves into cooperative associations,
provide them with "outlook" and planning data, and work with organizations of middlemen to improve marketing efficiency. This, he
thought, was the "major answer," and by the fall of 1921 he had
come to believe that most of this contemplated machinery belonged in
the Department of Commerce rather than in Agriculture. Against
strong resistance, he was trying to capture the Bureau of Markets and
use it to develop the needed programs.[63]

V

Hoover's first months in office, then, had produced a variety of efforts to "organize" recovery and progress. Yet for all the activity, the
economy was still shrinking and popular distress growing. More, it
seemed, would be necessary to check and reverse the downward cycle;
and by early August, Hoover had decided upon another major experiment in government-stimulated cooperative action. The need now, he
told the president, was for new machinery that could mobilize leadership in the "community," meet the need for temporary unemployment relief, and stimulate new consumer and investment spending.
And on August 29, two days after issuing a plea for autumn letting of
highway contracts, his department joined with the White House in an-
nouncing that the president would call an Unemployment Conference,
both to secure emergency recommendations and to study ways of less-
ening business fluctuations in the future.[64]

As the preliminaries unfolded, moreover, it became clear that this
new initiative would reflect Hoover's thinking and build on his earlier
activities. It was he who selected the conferees and arranged for preliminary study committees. And with the assistance of Edward Eyre
Hunt and an enlarged version of the earlier statistical advisory committee,[65] a program was worked out well in advance of the formal
meeting. As set forth in preliminary recommendations, it would reject
anything approaching a federal dole or governmental works projects,
ignore those calling for union-busting and wage cuts, and concentrate
on organizing a cooperative relief and recovery system working
through private groups and local communities. In particular, relief
should come through a network of emergency committees drawing
upon both private and local governmental resources and sponsoring
such things as community employment bureaus, give-a-job cam-

paigns, and share-the-work programs. Spending should be revived by encouraging industry to undertake capital improvements and governments to build needed public works. And future stability should be enhanced by educating businessmen to avoid speculative booms, providing them with improved statistical services, and establishing planning agencies that could build up construction "reserves" for the next slack period. In these proposals for long-range stabilization, the whole program was remarkably similar to the "practical measures" that the American Association for Labor Legislation had been advocating since 1914.[66]

The conference itself convened on September 26 and occasionally gave signs of getting out of hand. In the corridors, Jacob Coxey and other "ghosts of the nineties" put in an appearance, and in the closed committee meetings, unsympathetic champions of "natural law" and the "open shop" occasionally spoke out. For the most part, however, the conferees behaved according to plan, produced the unanimous committee reports that Hoover had insisted upon, and adopted a set of general recommendations that deviated only slightly from those made by the preliminary advisory group. Before adjourning on October 13, moreover, they entrusted the implementation of the program to the secretary of commerce and his lieutenants. Supervising the operation would be a Committee of Fourteen made up of the same officials and advisers who had planned and guided the conference proceedings.[67]

To head the emergency relief effort, Hoover had already enlisted the services of Arthur Woods, a former police commissioner of New York with experience in postwar demobilization activities. And during the weeks that followed, in what amounted to the most ambitious program of organized voluntarism since the war period, Woods's Committee on Civic and Emergency Measures became the coordinator, "clearing-house," and cheer leader for the charitable and job-expansion activities of some 225 local committees and a variety of cooperating organizations. At the same time, it called upon local governments and industrial groups to cooperate by undertaking needed capital improvements and public works.[68] And in the federal sphere, Hoover and his organization took the lead in urging prompt spending of appropriated funds and prompt congressional action on measures to expand road-building and reclamation work, settle the railroad claims against the government, and enlarge the work of the United States Employment Service. Through such actions, the argument ran, the pressures for liquidation could be turned into pressures for sustained expansion, and the whole matter could be accomplished without undermining America's spiritual and institutional heritage.[69]

It was only logical, too, that these new stimulants to construction should be tied into and used to reinforce Hoover's earlier activities. Special emphasis was now put on the value of statistical programs for the building and construction industries. Simplification, coordinated now by a new Division of Simplified Practice under William Durgin, focused its primary attention on the chaotic diversity of construction materials and practices.[70] And working with and through the Unemployment Conference machinery, Gries's Housing Division became the vehicle for new efforts to revise building codes, encourage home ownership, and organize the construction field for cooperative endeavor.[71] In early 1922, it lent its support to plans for a new national organization, which, as Hoover saw it, could end the "antagonism" between manufacturers, builders, and workers, unite them in an effort to "lower the cost of homes," and thus create more business and more employment.[72] The eventual result, in June 1922, would be the formation of the American Construction Council under the direction of Franklin D. Roosevelt.[73]

While mounting these new attacks on the construction problem, Hoover was also continuing to wrestle with the difficulties of agriculture, coal, and the railroads. In the first field, he was having little success in winning jurisdictional control of agricultural marketing. But he did take a keen interest in the Agricultural Conference of January 1922, strongly supported the Capper-Volstead Act of the following month, and continued to push cooperative marketing as the major solution.[74] In the second field, he used the Unemployment Conference machinery to put Frederick Tyron and a staff of twenty-five to work on a "coal stabilization" study, one that he was temporarily keeping "under cover" but hoped to "stage" later with "great effect."[75] And in the third, he continued to push for claim settlement and selective rate revision, worked out a new scheme to encourage investment through government guarantees to railroad equipment trusts, and took charge of contingency planning for and efforts to head off a national railroad strike. In October 1921, such a strike was averted when the Railway Labor Board announced that it would consider no further wage cuts for six months, and in early 1922 Hoover hoped that his action in persuading railroad and union leaders to set up regional negotiating conferences could transform the pattern of conflict into one of efficiency-minded cooperation.[76]

Trade revival, too, continued to be offered as a major facet of the recovery and reemployment drive. And here, so Hoover believed, substantial progress was being made, both in providing a "correspondence school" and "general staff" for American traders and in removing the obstacles blocking European revival and beneficial flows of credit. As reorganized, he assured Harding, the Bureau of Foreign and Domestic Commerce was becoming a highly effective instrument for generating commercial intelligence and formulating constructive trade strategies.[77] And on other fronts, the disarmament negotiations, the setting up of the debt-funding commission, the insertion of a flexible provision in the tariff, and the establishment of a loan consultation procedure designed to steer American capital into "reproductive" channels were at least partially in line with Hoover's prescriptions.[78] The task ahead was one of using such instruments effectively, and at the time he seemed optimistic about the chances of doing so.

In addition, Hoover was lending his support to programs for developing the aviation, radio, and electrical power industries, trying in each area to work out some form of public-private cooperation that could reduce investment hazards, open up large markets, and guide the development process along "constructive" lines. By early 1922, he had held conferences with both the radio and aviation industries, endorsed their efforts to set up industrial codes, and started pushing for new bureaus that could establish necessary ground rules and work with private developers.[79] And in the power field, he was now emerging as the chief spokesman for interconnected "superpower" networks, hailing these as offering an advance comparable to the first transcontinental railroad, and laying plans for regional conferences that could remove the regulatory, technical, and financial obstacles in the way of their development.[80]

Finally, as he worked to get the economy expanding again, Hoover was also following up on the suggestions for moderating future booms and slumps. In Congress, the Kenyon Bill for public works planning had his endorsement.[81] And amidst much talk of a "business service division" or "advisory planning board" to foster more and better business planning,[82] he had arranged for a quasi-public study of business fluctuations, to be conducted as an offshoot of the Unemployment Conference, but with private funds and research facilities,[83] with the results to be distributed through a prestigious private committee headed by Owen D. Young. In formal terms, this was not a planning agency, but the build-up it received, the careful coordination of its work with national trade associations, and the results expected all make it clear that Hoover and his aides hoped to use such "studies" as key tools in the future management of economic prosperity.[84]

As Hoover's first year in office drew to a close, then, his department had become the center of a complex effort to forge new tools of economic management. It was the Food Administration all over again, remarked Raymond Pearl. And the ironic thing about it, he thought, was that an administration elected to get government out of business was now "doing more interfering with business than any other administration that we have had in peace times."[85] Yet judged either in terms of economic recovery or in terms of the blueprints with which Hoover began, the effort was still far from being an unqualified success. The recession persisted, and in the process of accommodation to political realities and economic conflicts, much of the original vision had proved as yet unrealizable. Emergency relief activities were also beginning to flag as the winter wore on.[86] And of prime significance now, two major crises—one engendered by the antitrust authorities, the other by labor difficulties—were threatening to undermine the whole approach and undo what had been achieved.

VI

From the beginning, Hoover had conceded that the tools through which he hoped to improve the economy's performance could sometimes be converted into instruments of exploitation or blockades against needed readjustment. Yet given the present stage of business evolution, he insisted, this problem was marginal. Scrapping the tools because of it was like prohibiting brick houses because people were sometimes murdered with "brickbats." And it was with general consternation that he realized that the antitrust authorities and the courts seemed to be fashioning just such a prohibition. In the Hardwood Lumber Case *(American Column and Lumber Company v. U.S.)*, decided in December 1921, the Supreme Court held that the statistical program of the Hardwood Manufacturers Association amounted to a price-fixing conspiracy and, in doing so, seemed to be saying that all similar activities were *per se* illegal.[87] "The result," noted George McIlvaine of the American Trade Association Executives, "has been a 'panicky feeling' among thousands of members of national trade organizations and in many lines general demoralization."[88]

Hoover's initial response was an effort to minimize the impact of the ruling, primarily by distinguishing his programs from those of the hardwood manufacturers and urging the Justice Department to endorse these distinctions. The latter, however, remained wary of making specific commitments; and while it did agree to a public exchange of "clarifying letters,"[89] its insistence upon defining illegality in terms of economic intent and effect rather than types of activities left large areas of the Hoover program under a continuing cloud.[90] In Congress, Senator Walter Edge now agreed to sponsor "clarifying" legislation, both to define the limits of associational activities and to protect government-approved programs from prosecution.[91] And in early April, partly to mobilize support behind such legislation, Hoover called some 500 trade association representatives into conference, re-emphasized the distinctions he was making between beneficial cooperation and undesirable "price-fixing," and suggested that a revised statistical program with more of the data distributed through public channels could serve the purposes intended without running afoul of the law.[92]

In the legislative arena, opposition from antitrusters, dissident businessmen, and conservatives fearful of opening the path to new governmental controls prevented passage of either the Edge bills or the new substitutes drafted in the Commerce Department.[93] Yet as spring gave way to summer, other activities did seem to be repairing the damage done by the Hardwood ruling. To provide further "clarification," Hoover was taking two sorts of actions, one involving friendly advice to association leaders from such accommodating Federal Trade Commissioners as Nelson Gaskill, the other involving a new committee to study the subject and produce a "trade association manual."[94] In addition, he had been able to persuade those cooperating in the waste-elimination program that their activities would not be affected, particularly if they stayed within the indicated guidelines in regard to voluntarism and individual adherence to government-endorsed "recommendations."[95] And finally, he had followed up the trade association conference by commissioning David L. Wing to organize and direct a new statistical program. Under it, information that lent itself "readily" to "illegal use" was to be excluded, and associations likely to become targets of legal attack were not to participate. But with these exceptions, cooperating groups could now file their data with a special appendage of the Census Bureau and have it distributed through public channels to all who wished to receive it.[96]

If the antitrust threat had diminished, however, the one posed by labor difficulties had now burgeoned into a major crisis that threatened either to bring the economy to a standstill, force the undesirable liquidation that Hoover had hoped to avoid, or drive the public toward statist measures that, in his view, could undermine the whole basis of future progress. In April 1922, the refusal of coal operators to renew wage contracts at existing levels led the United Mine Workers to call a national coal strike, and on July 1, after the Railway Labor Board had announced further wage cuts, the walkout of the railroad shopmen produced the first nationwide rail strike since 1894. Failure to solve the coal and railroad "problems," it seemed, was about to result in national economic disaster.[97]

In the spring and summer of 1922, then, even as the Woods Committee was winding down and terminating its operations,[98] the Department of Commerce was sprouting new appendages to manage another crisis. From May through August, while Congress was considering the establishment of an emergency distribution system for coal, Hoover was organizing and operating a voluntary structure built around transportation priorities and seeking, through national and district committees, to commit the non-union operators to "fair" prices and responsible behavior.[99] At the same time, he was doing his best to set up machinery that could settle the strikes and handle future disputes.[100] And with the crisis creating a new sense of urgency, he was again working on longer-range proposals that could "solve" the coal and railroad problems. In May, he began circulating a long memorandum on coal reform, proposing now an elaborate stabilization plan featuring district cooperatives, joint-sales agencies, unemployment insurance programs, and action that would retire marginal mines and put them in a "coal reserve."[101] And in June, he began work on a railroad plan that would combine scientific rate rationalization and cooperative modernization with financial incentives to induce voluntary consolidation. The latter, he told Ernest Lewis of the Interstate Commerce Commission, was urgently needed if the railroads were to achieve "constructive leadership" and if "the almost hopeless drifting toward nationalization" was to be checked.[102]

In the railroad field, the Hoover effort to save the shopmen's union and forge a new basis for labor-management cooperation was thrown into disarray by the strike-breaking injunction that Attorney General Daugherty secured on September 1, 1922. It was not until later, with the passage of the Railway Labor Act of 1926 and the adoption of "efficiency plans" by some of the leading railroads, that elements of what Hoover had urged were adopted.[103] But in coal, the secretary of commerce was more influential, and here the settlement that emerged in August and September did bear the hallmarks of his handiwork.

Under it, union operators would maintain existing wage levels for another year; emergency controls would ease the transition from strike-induced shortages to full production; and a newly created United States Coal Commission, with Edward Eyre Hunt as secretary, would complete the "stabilization study" begun by the Unemployment Conference and hopefully lay the basis for implementing something similar to Hoover's reform plan.[104]

By late 1922, then, the two crises that had occupied most of Hoover's energies during the spring and summer months had seemingly been weathered. Although efforts to "modernize" the antitrust laws had failed, he had been successful in stemming the panic engendered by the Hardwood decision and devising strategies that kept his "stabilization" programs operating and flourishing. And while the coal and railroad problems had not been solved to his satisfaction, the threats that they had posed to national well-being had now abated and solutions, at least in the coal field, seemed closer than before. Economic activity, moreover, was picking up. It could be measured in new building starts, an expanding job market, and a rising volume of trade.[105] And like other would-be controllers of economic forces, then and since, Hoover was soon crediting his activities with having checked the forces of contraction, produced recovery along the lines desired, and provided tools that could be used to secure permanent prosperity and perpetual progress.[106]

VII

Whether Hoover's activities really had the effects with which he later credited them is at least questionable. Despite his efforts, such things as public works planning, counter-cyclical investment, balanced world recovery, and the transformation of housing into a modernized mass-production industry never really materialized in the 1920s. In all probability, too, he overestimated the effects that the new statistics and simplification programs were having on economic behavior.[107] And in the post-1922 period, the difficulties in coal, agriculture, and the railroad industry would remain as persistent "problems."[108] Recovery had come. But it was a much less balanced and stable recovery than Hoover had envisioned; and the chief forces behind it, according to economists who have studied the period, were not the Hoover activities but the liquidation of earlier inventories, the new wave of investment in the automobile and other durable consumer-goods industries, and the accumulation of enough savings to finance another burst of construction.[109] It is arguable, perhaps, that Hoover's activities contributed to these developments, or that in helping to sustain the purchasing power of labor he helped to provide the mass markets upon which the new industries would depend. But it also seems arguable that his contributions here were not such as to be crucial, that without them the course of events would have been much the same.

Nevertheless, Hoover and his associates were firmly convinced that the actions taken in 1921 and 1922 had been a great success. As they saw it, these efforts had not only vindicated the purchasing-power theory[110] but helped to shape the tools needed to optimize performance in a modern economy and save the nation from some regressive excursion into radical foolishness or bureaucratic tyranny. The whole experience, so Hoover told Will Payne in 1923, demonstrated that prosperity could be "organized" at home, even in the face of lagging exports and a persisting farm problem. It was all a matter of "organization," "intelligent cooperative effort," and "national industrial planning."[111]

These convictions, moreover, did have significant implications for the future. In the post-1922 period, Hoover would continue to build upon and utilize the tools that had allegedly brought recovery, extol them as the keys to a new and superior "American system," and take substantial credit for what he believed to be an era of unprecedented advance and remarkable stability.[112] And in the wake of a new slump in 1929, he would turn again to the strategies followed by the Unemployment Conference; organize new programs of wage-maintenance, counter-cyclical investment, and emergency relief; and tenaciously defend the notion that his type of "cooperative system" could save the nation from the triple evils of economic disorder, political radicalism, and statist regimentation.[113] In part, of course, these post-1922 policies constituted responses to new developments and pressures, but it is difficult to understand the pattern they took without taking into account the perceptions and convictions formed during Hoover's first two years as secretary of commerce.

Viewed in longer perspective, too, this period can no longer be dismissed as a time when progressive ideas went into hibernation and the country returned to "normalcy" and "laissez-faire." Intermixed with the drives for reinstating nineteenth-century Republicanism was a new vision born of the organizational revolution and the progressive and war experiences, a vision of an ordered economy guided by scientific and service-minded managers and acting collectively to translate the wonders of modern technology into ever higher levels of material abundance and social well-being. And intermixed with the policies of Mellon and Daugherty were a set of activities that did try to implement this vision and develop tools of macroeconomic management. Federal responsibilities in this field, so it now seems, began not in 1933 or 1929 but in 1921.

Again, this is not to say that Hoover and his associates were early-day New Dealers or early exponents of a formalized corporate state. Through the magic of education, voluntarism, and cooperativism, they hoped to avoid the type of statist bureaucracies, make-work endeavors, and government-backed cartelization that would later become significant features of America's "managerial state." And later, when pressures for these kinds of institutions became intense, Hoover would strongly resist them.

Yet if the Hooverites were not New Dealers or corporate statists, neither were they advocates of laissez-faire or classical economic prescriptions. In their conception of how a modern economy worked and what needed to be done to improve its performance, one can find early versions of the purchasing-power and corporatist notions that would dominate later reform thinking. And in the techniques used—especially the bringing together of established interest-group leaders for higher ends, the effort to institutionalize this through functional representation on advisory bodies, and the tendency to equate democratic progress with the participation of these private organizations in policy-making and public management—one can find an early version of the type of "corporate pluralism" that would be idealized in the 1950s and would come under attack in the 1960s.[114] In these respects, the Hoover programs of 1921 and 1922 constitute important precursors of things to come, and if one is to understand the path along which the American quest for a managed prosperity moved, it seems imperative that they receive greater emphasis and more study than they once did.

NOTES

1 Compare Richard Hofstadter, *The Age of Reform* (New York, 1955), pp. 272–328, or Carl Degler, *Out of Our Past* (New York, 1959), pp. 379–416, with Robert Wiebe, *The Search for Order, 1877–1920* (New York, 1967), pp. 111–302, James Weinstein, *The Corporate Ideal in the Liberal State* (Boston, 1968), pp. ix–xiii, 252–54,

Herbert Stein, *The Fiscal Revolution in America* (Chicago, 1969), pp. 6–38; Evan Metcalf, "Secretary Hoover and the Emergence of Macroeconomic Management," *Business History Review,* 49 (Spring 1975), 60–80, and Peri Arnold, "Herbert Hoover and the Continuity of American Policy," *Public Policy,* 20 (Fall 1972), 525–44.

2   Compare William Leuchtenburg, "The New Deal and the Analogue of War," in John Braeman and others, eds., *Change and Continuity in Twentieth Century America* (Columbus, 1964), pp. 81–143, with James Olson, "Herbert Hoover and 'War' on the Depression," *Palimpsest,* 54 (July–August 1973), 26–31.

3   See Albert Romasco, *Poverty of Abundance* (New York, 1965), pp. 24–38, 230–34; Carolyn Grin, "The Unemployment Conference of 1921," *Mid-America,* 54 (April 1973), 83–107; Robert Zieger, *Republicans and Labor* (Lexington, 1969), pp. 87–97; and Robert Murray, *The Harding Era* (Minneapolis, 1969), pp. 195–98, 231–34.

4   Murray, *Harding Era,* pp. 172–92, 381. For Hoover's praise of these policies, see his addresses of July 15, 1921, and October 17, 1922, Herbert C. Hoover Papers (Herbert Hoover Presidential Library, West Branch, Iowa), Public Statements, Nos. 164 and 264. Hoover's chief disagreement with Mellon was over the type of tax that would be most helpful. He favored lower rates on "earned income," high rates on inheritances and "unearned income."

5   Edward Eyre Hunt, "Reconstruction," 13–15, 24–25, Hunt Papers (Hoover Institution Archives, Stanford, California), Box 19; Stein, *Fiscal Revolution,* pp. 6–12. See also Hoover's addresses of February 14 and July 15, 1921, Hoover Papers, Public Statements, Nos. 128 and 164.

6   In addition to the previously cited works by Grin, Stein, Metcalf, and Arnold, see Edwin Layton, *Revolt of the Engineers* (Cleveland, 1971), pp. 189–204, Daniel Nelson, *Unemployment Insurance, 1915–35* (Madison, 1969), pp. 28–40, and Peri Arnold, "Herbert Hoover and the Department of Commerce," Ph.D. Diss. (U. of Chicago, 1972), 63–101.

7   See Robert Himmelberg, "The War Industries Board and the Antitrust Question in November, 1918," *Journal of American History,* 52 (June 1965), 59–74, and Samuel Haber, *Efficiency and Uplift* (Chicago, 1964), pp. 122–24.

8   Robert Cuff, *The War Industries Board* (Baltimore, 1973), pp. 148–90, 273–76.

9   William Moore, "Dissolution of the War Industries Board," and "Post-Armistice Industrial Developments," both in Hunt Papers, Box 10; Robert Himmelberg, "Relaxation of the Federal Antitrust Policy as a Goal of the Business Community during the Period, 1918–1933," Ph.D.Diss. (Penn. State U., 1963), 19–82; John Hanrahan, "The High Cost of Living Controversy, 1919–20," Ph.D. Diss (Fordham U., 1969).

10   See, for example, such works as Arthur Eddy, *The New Competition* (New York, 1912); E. H. Gaunt, *Co-operative Competition* (Providence, 1917); Forrest Crissey, *Teamwork in Trade Building* (1914); and Edward Hurley, *Awakening of Business* (Garden City, 1917).

11   See, for example, Glenn Frank, "Self-Governing Industry" and "The Tide of Affairs," in *Century Magazine,* 98 (June 1919), 225–36, and 102 (June 1921), 311–15; Emmett Naylor, *Trade Associations* (New York, 1921), pp. 15–31; and William Allen White to Hoover, October 18, 1920, Hoover Papers, Pre-Commerce Section, White File. These notions of "cooperative collectivism" were part of a larger postwar consid-

eration of how cooperative and "integrative" institutions could usher in a new order without sacrificing the essentials of the old. In Europe, various forms of neo-corporatism, neo-guildism, and neo-pluralism were flourishing. And in America, the proposals ranged from syndicalist designs on the left through Mary Follett's "new state" to the corporate communities envisioned by John Leitch and John D. Rockefeller, Jr. In the centrist proposals, like those of Follett, functional associations would be joined by neighborhood units and factory communities as the key regulators of the new order. See Haber, *Efficiency and Uplift,* pp. 124-27; Layton, *Revolt of the Engineers,* pp. 147-48, 179-80; and Charles Maier, "Between Taylorism and Technocracy," *Journal of Contemporary History,* 5 (April 1970), 33-46.

12   The Commerce Department under William Redfield had tried to establish such agencies, but had been largely unsuccessful in doing so. See Redfield, *With Congress and Cabinet* (Garden City, 1924), pp. 216-19. By 1921 agitation for them centered in such groups as the American Association for Labor Legislation, the American Statistical Association, the Taylor Society, the American Management Association, the National Foreign Trade Council, the Chamber of Commerce of the United States, and the American Engineering Council. See, for example, the *American Labor Legislation Review,* 10 (December 1920), 233-39, and 11 (March 1921), 47-58; the *Journal of the American Statistical Association,* 15 (March 1920), 67-75; the *Bulletin of the Taylor Society,* 5 (February 1920), 8; *Nation's Business,* 9 (June 1921), 48-52; *Industrial Management,* 61 (January 1921), 67-68; *Scientific American,* 123 (August 1920), 176.

13   See Robert Van Meter, "The United States and European Recovery, 1918-1923," Ph. D. Diss. (U. of Wisconsin, 1971), 130-31.

14   Hoover, in Senate Committee on Education and Labor, *Industrial Conference* (1920), pp. 26-38, and Senate Commitee on Reconstruction, *Reconstruction and Production* (1921), pp. 617-27; Hoover's Statement to the Kansas Board of Agriculture, James Bell Papers (Minnesota Historical Society), Box 1; Hoover, in *Mining and Metallurgy,* 159 (March 1920), 1-2; Hoover's addresses of February 17, April 10, August 27, October 12, November 19, 1920, and February 14, 1921, Hoover Papers, Public Statements, Nos. 45, 59, 84, 94, 102, 128. See also E. E. Hunt, "Notes on the Hoover Creed," Hunt Papers, Box 20, and Barry Karl, "Presidential Planning and Social Science Research," in *Perspectives in American History* (1969), pp. 351-58.

15   Hoover, in Senate Reconstruction Committee, *Reconstruction,* pp. 625-26; Hoover's addresses of August 27, 1920, and February 14, 1921, Hoover Papers, Public Statements, Nos. 84 and 128.

16   Hoover's address of February 14, 1921, Hoover Papers, Public Statements, No. 128; Hunt, "Reconstruction," 11-15, 24-25; Layton, *Revolt of the Engineers,* pp. 190-94; Metcalf, "Hoover and Emergence of Macroeconomic Management," 61-66.

17   Van Meter, "U.S. and European Recovery," 205-11.

18   Hoover to Harding, September 8, 1920, and February 23, 1921, Hoover Papers, Pre-Commerce Section, Harding File; Metcalf, "Hoover and Emergence of Macroeconomic Management," 66-69.

19   In 1919 he had felt that "a few strong men" could exert greater influence from outside the government than from within. Hoover to William Glasgow, April 12, 1919, Hoover Papers, Pre-Commerce Section, Glasgow File.

20   Hoover to Harding, February 23, 1921, Hoover Papers, Pre-Commerce Section, Harding File; E. E. Hunt, "Interview with Hoover," January 16, 1935, Hunt Papers, Box 20; Hoover, *Memoirs,* (New York, 1951), 2:36.

21 *New York Times,* March 11, 1921; Hoover's statement of March 11, 1921, Hoover Papers, Public Statements, No. 134.

22 Hoover, "Memorandum on Reorganization," and George Baldwin to Hoover, April 24, 1921, Hoover Papers, Commerce Section, Reorganization File; Hoover, "The Problem of Reorganization," May 23, 1921, Hoover Papers, Commerce Section, Reorganization of Government Departments File; "Departmental Reorganization" and "Suggestions for Expansion along Domestic Lines," Bureau of Foreign and Domestic Commerce Records (National Archives), File 160; "How the Department of Commerce Should Be Reorganized and Should Function," Hoover Papers, Commerce Section, General Government Reorganization File.

23 "List of National Organizations Prepared for Hoover," March 9, 1921, Hoover Papers, Commerce Section, Recommendations for Advisory Board File.

24 See Edward and Frederick Schapsmeier, "Disharmony in the Harding Cabinet," *Ohio History,* 75 (Spring-Summer 1966), 127-28; Joseph Brandes, *Herbert Hoover and Economic Diplomacy* (Pittsburgh, 1962), pp. 41-42; *American Federationist,* 28 (June 1921), 503-04; and Hoover to Harding, December 31, 1921, Hoover Papers, Commerce Section, Reorganization of Government Departments File.

25 Hoover, "Trade Organizations and the Law," *American Machinist,* 54 (June 30, 1921), 1147; Himmelberg, "Relaxation of Antitrust," 100-01; G. D. Goff to Hoover, March 28, 1921, and Harry Daugherty to Hoover, May 16, 1921, Hoover Papers, Commerce Section, Justice Department File.

26 Arnold, "Hoover and Department of Commerce," 86-87; *Women's Wear,* April 26, 1921.

27 Donald Wilhelm, "Mr. Hoover as Secretary of Commerce," *World's Work,* 43 (February 1922), 409.

28 Arnold, "Hoover and Department of Commerce," 121-22; *New York Times,* March 11, 15, 20, April 17, 23, 29, 1921.

29 J. W. Drake to Hoover, June 9 and 24 and July 5, 1921, Hoover to Drake, June 4, 1921, Hoover to Arch Shaw, June 29, 1921, Hoover to Charles Piez, June 4, 1921, Hoover Papers, Commerce Section, Commerce—Industrial Group File; Commerce Department Press Release, April 29, 1921, Hoover Papers, Commerce Section, Commerce—First Conference File; Hoover to Walter Tower and others, April 25, 1921, Hoover Papers, Commerce Section, Commerce—Foreign and Domestic Commerce File.

30 Federated American Engineering Societies, *Waste in Industry* (1921), pp. v, 8-16, 24-30; Layton, *Revolt of the Engineers,* pp. 201-03; Hunt, "Reconstruction," 17-21; "Purpose and Plan," February 16, 1921, Hoover Papers, Pre-Commerce Section, Industrial Waste Committee File.

31 Haber, *Efficiency and Uplift,* p. 159; Layton, *Revolt of the Engineers,* pp. 203-04. Of the groups making up the Federated American Engineering Societies, only the American Society of Mechanical Engineers endorsed the report.

32 Typical of what was being proposed and considered were George Dickson, "A Suggestion," March 21, 1921, Hoover Papers, Commerce Section, Suggestions File, and Calvin Rice to Hoover, July 26, 1921, Hoover Papers, Commerce Section, Reorganization File.

33 Craig Lloyd, *Aggressive Introvert* (Columbus, 1972), pp. 62-63. Shaw had

headed the wartime conservation agency and was now offered the post of assistant secretary of commerce. He refused, but arranged for Feiker to become Hoover's assistant.

34   Lloyd, *Aggressive Introvert,* p. 63; Conference of Business Paper Editors, "Standardization Survey," Feiker to George Babcock, July 26, 1921, Feiker to Maurice Greenough, August 8, 1921, Commerce Department Records (National Archives), File 81368.

35   Herbert Heaton, *Scholar in Action* (Cambridge, 1952), pp. 189-91; William Rossiter to Hoover, March 12, 1921, and Advisory Committee on the Census to Hoover, May 7, 1921, Hoover Papers, Commerce Section, Commerce—Bureau of the Census File. The committee had been appointed originally as an advisory body on the Census of 1920. It was chaired by the publisher William S. Rossiter.

36   Hoover's address of April 28, 1921, Hoover Papers, Public Statements, No. 149; Hoover to J. Jackson, June 1, 1921, Commerce Department Records, File 76850/1; Hoover to Harding, June 9, 1921, Hoover Papers, Commerce Section, Presidential File; Feiker to Hoover, July 8, 1921, Hoover Papers, Commerce Section, Commerce Assistants File; Nathan Williams, "Conversation with Hoover," July 7, 1921, Hoover Papers, Commerce Section, Feiker File.

37   Such opposition is discussed in the *New York Journal of Commerce,* July 2, 1921.

38   Secretary of Commerce, *Annual Report* (1922), pp. 88-89; Hoover to Frank Taussig, July 2, 1921, Hoover Papers, Commerce Section, Taussig File; Hoover to Harding, June 9, 1921, Hoover Papers, Commerce Section, Presidential File.

39   See Hoover to Mellon, April 11, 1921, Hoover Papers, Commerce Section, Reorganization of Government Departments File. The transfer finally took place in 1923.

40   *New York Times,* June 3, 1921; William Lamb to Hoover, July 11, 1921, Commerce Department Records, File 81288.

41   Nathan Williams, "Conversation with Hoover," July 7, 1921, Hoover Papers, Commerce Section, Feiker File; Hoover to George Huddleston, May 24, 1921, Hoover Papers, Commerce Section, Labor Department File; Hoover to Harding, June 9, 1921, Hoover Papers, Commerce Section, Presidential File.

42   *New York World,* June 11, 1921; Hoover to Daugherty, June 13, 1921, Hoover Papers, Commerce Section, Justice Department File; Hoover to William Jennett, September 24, 1921, and E. H. Naylor to Feiker, October 18, 1921, Commerce Department Records, File 81288; William Lamb to Feiker, August 31, 1921, Hoover Papers, Commerce Section, Feiker File.

43   Brandes, *Hoover and Economic Diplomacy,* pp. 40-42; Donald Winters, *Henry Cantwell Wallace as Secretary of Agriculture* (Urbana, 1970), pp. 222-27; A. J. Wolfe to Louis Domeratzky, March 25, 1922, and Duncan Fletcher to C. R. Snow, March 9, 1922, Bureau of Foreign and Domestic Commerce Records, File 033.

44   R. L. MacElwee, the bureau chief when Hoover took over, was dismissed for lying about material that he had fed to the press. See Hoover to Harding, March 17, 1921, Hoover Papers, Commerce Section, Commerce—Foreign and Domestic Commerce File. Klein, a protegé of Edwin Gay, had headed the Latin American division of the bureau during the war and later served as a commercial attache in Argentina. For his background, ideas, and activities, see Robert Seidel, "Progressive Pan Americanism," Ph.D. Diss. (Cornell U., 1973).

45   See especially Hoover's address before the National Shoe and Leather Exposition, July 12, 1921, Hoover Papers, Commerce Section, Feiker File.

46   See, for example, Guy Emerson to Hoover, March 15, 1921, Hoover Papers, Commerce Section, Reorganization File. See also Louis Domeratzky's "Plan for Commodity Divisions" and C. E. Herring to Hoover, April 20, 1921, Bureau of Foreign and Domestic Commerce Records, File 160.

47   Hoover to Walter Tower and others, April 25, 1921, Hoover Papers, Commerce Section, Commerce—Foreign and Domestic Commerce File; Feiker to Klein, September 18, 1921, Bureau of Foreign and Domestic Commerce Records, File 160.2; Secretary of Commerce, *Annual Report* (1922), p. 4; "Development of the Bureau of Foreign and Domestic Commerce," Commerce Department Records, Robert Lamont Collection, Box 6.

48   The phrase is used by Donald Wilhelm in *World's Work,* 43 (February 1922), 408. For a detailed discussion of the completed reorganization and the men in charge of each commodity division, see Will Kennedy, "Business Experts Make Sacrifices to Help Put the Hoover Plan Across," *Washington Star,* December 25, 1921.

49   The Edge Act of 1919 had authorized the chartering of such corporations, and Hoover had taken part in the most ambitious effort to organize one, namely the launching of the Foreign Trade Financing Corporation in December 1920. See Van Meter, "U.S. and European Recovery," 121-23, 205-11.

50   Van Meter, "U.S. and European Recovery," 212-17, 293, 317-30; Michael J. Hogan, "The United States and the Problem of International Economic Control, 1918-1928," Ph.D. Diss. (U. of Iowa, 1974), 96-99; Murray, *Harding Era,* pp. 271-74; Melvyn Leffler, "Origins of Republican War Debt Policy, 1921-1923," *Journal of American History,* 59 (December 1972), 591-96.

51   Hoover, "The Housing Problem," *Industrial Management,* 60 (December 1920), 424a-24b; Hoover to Ernest Trigg, May 16, 1921, Hoover to Harding, February 9, 1922, and "Better Homes and Decreased Costs Through Elimination of Waste in Construction," January 11, 1928, Hoover Papers, Commerce Section, Building and Housing File; Hunt, "Reconstruction," 57-62.

52   Hoover to Harding, March 16, 1921, Harding Papers (Ohio Historical Society), Box 5. Miller had directed the Senate inquiry into housing in 1919 and 1920. According to Hoover, he had "a larger knowledge of the building trades and labor conditions than anyone in the country."

53   "Better Homes and Decreased Costs Through Elimination of Waste in Construction," January 11, 1928, and Miller to Hoover, April 22, 1921, Hoover Papers, Commerce Section, Building and Housing File; Secretary of Commerce, *Annual Report* (1922), p. 7.

54   Miller to Hoover, June 7, 1921, and Hoover to Miller, July 18, 1921, Hoover Papers, Commerce Section, Building and Housing File. Gries had been in the pre-1914 Bureau of Corporations and in the wartime Division of Planning and Statistics. Since 1914 he had held the Chair of Lumber at Harvard.

55   "Better Homes and Decreased Costs Through Elimination of Waste in Construction," January 11, 1928, "Federal Activity in Promotion of Better Housing Conditions and Home Ownership" [1923], Gries to Hoover, August 16 and 24, 1921, Hoover to Joseph DeFrees, April 19, 1921, Hoover to William Calder, August 12, 1921,

and Hoover to Harding, February 9, 1922, Hoover Papers, Commerce Section, Building and Housing File; Hoover's addresses of May 12 and July 15, 1921, Hoover Papers, Public Statements, Nos. 152 and 164.

56 Hoover, in *Mining and Metallurgy*, 159 (March 1920), 1-2; Hoover to D. B. Wentz, May 18, 1921, Hoover to Joseph Frelinghuysen, June 18, 1921, Hoover to H. E. Loomis, June 27, 1921, and Miller to Hoover, May 13, 1921, Hoover Papers, Commerce Section, Coal File.

57 The original bill called for an independent coal commission to gather and publish statistics. As revised, it would authorize the Commerce Department to do so. Succeeding drafts of the bill are in the Hoover Papers, Commerce Section, Coal File.

58 "Description of Coal Conferences of June 7-8, 1921," and Hoover to Walter Smith, January 16, 1922, Hoover Papers, Commerce Section, Coal File; T. O. Busbee to C. H. Huston, May 11, 1921, W. J. Willits to Morrow Chamberlain, June 21, 1921, and E. McAuliffe to C. P. White, July 10, 1921, Commerce Department Records, File 80769. See also Ellis Hawley, "Secretary Hoover and the Bituminous Coal Problem," *Business History Review*, 42 (Autumn 1968), 255.

59 Albert Fall to Harding, November 28, 1921, and Hoover to Harding, December 31, 1921, Hoover Papers, Commerce Section, Reorganization of Government Departments File. It was not until 1925 that the Bureau of Mines and portions of the Geological Survey were finally transferred to the Commerce Department.

60 Murray, *Harding Era*, pp. 221-23; Miller to Hoover, June 8, 1921, Hoover Papers, Commerce Section, Building and Housing File; Hoover to Ernest Lewis, June 15, 1921, and Lewis's "Conference Memorandum No. 1," June 15, 1921, Hoover Papers, Commerce Section, Interstate Commerce Commission File; Hoover's memorandum of July 13, 1921, Hoover to Mark Potter, June 29, 1921, Hoover to Andrew Mellon, June 27, 1921, and Hoover to Harding, July 21, 1921, Hoover Papers, Commerce Section, Railroads File.

61 Hoover's statement before the Kansas Board of Agriculture [1920], Bell Papers, Box 1; Hunt, "Reconstruction," 66-67.

62 Murray, *Harding Era*, pp. 208-10; Winters, *Wallace*, pp. 82-86; Hoover to Harding, August 18, 1921, Hoover Papers, Commerce Section, Agriculture File; Gary Koerselman, "Herbert Hoover and the Farm Crisis of the Twenties," Ph.D. Diss. (Northern Illinois U., 1971), 130-36.

63 Hoover to Arthur Capper, April 23, 1921, Henry C. Wallace Papers (U. of Iowa), Box 2, Folder 10; Winters, *Wallace*, pp. 225-29.

64 Grin, "Unemployment Conference," 86-87; *New York Times*, August 29, 30, 1921; Hoover's letter on fall letting of highway contracts, August 27, 1921, Hoover Papers, Commerce Section, Construction File; E. E. Hunt, "From 1921 Forward," *Survey*, 62 (April 1, 1929), 6.

65 The committee was enlarged from seven to twenty members, and three subcommittees were set up, one on unemployment statistics, one on temporary relief, and one on permanent prevention of unemployment. Among the new members were Otto Mallery, Sam Lewisohn, Henry Seager, Leo Wolman, John Andrews, Samuel Lindsay, and Henry Dennison, all prominent in the development of the unemployment stabilization program being urged by the American Association for Labor Legislation. See Grin, "Unemployment Conference," 87; Metcalf, "Hoover and the Emergence of Macro-

economic Management," 62-64, 71-73; Nelson, *Unemployment Insurance,* pp. 37-38; and William Rossiter to Hoover, September 8, 1921, Hoover Papers, Commerce Section, Unemployment Advisory Committee File.

66 Economic Advisory Committee Report, September 26, 1921, Hoover Papers, Commerce Section, Unemployment Advisory Committee File. An advance summary of the report was made available on September 22. For the similarities with the earlier AALL program, compare the report with John B. Andrews, "A Practical Program for the Prevention of Unemployment in America," *American Labor Legislation Review,* 5 (June 1915), 173-92.

67 William Chenery, "Mr. Hoover's Hand," *Survey,* 47 (October 22, 1921), 107; Grin, "Unemployment Conference," 90-92; Hunt, "Reconstruction," 32-40; President's Conference on Unemployment, "General Recommendations," October 11, 1921, Hoover Papers, Commerce Section, Unemployment Conference File.

68 Grin, "Unemployment Conference," 92-96; E. E. Hunt, "Washington Conference on Unemployment," Hoover Papers, Commerce Section, Unemployment Conference File; Commerce Department Press Release, December 17, 1921, Hoover Papers, Commerce Section, Unemployment Press Releases File.

69 Hunt, "Reconstruction," 44-47; Grin, "Unemployment Conference," 97-102. Congress passed the Federal Highway Act, but delayed action on the railroad claims bill and rejected the reclamation and employment service measures.

70 Following their success in reducing the varieties of paving brick from 66 to 7, the simplifiers concentrated their attention on the face brick, refractories, building hardware, plumbing, paint, and lumber industries. Feiker to E. W. McCullough, November 19, 1921, Commerce Department Records, File 81368; Hoover to Feiker, December 9, 1921, Hoover Papers, Commerce Section, Commerce Assistants File; Secretary of Commerce, *Annual Report* (1922), pp. 138-40. Durgin, an electrical engineer from Commonwealth Edison, took charge of the program in November 1921. It was organized as a new division in January 1922.

71 Gries, "Standardization in the Building Industry," February 22, 1922, Gries to Hoover, February 16, 1922, and Hoover to Harding, February 9, 1922, Hoover Papers, Commerce Section, Building and Housing File; Gries to Hoover, March 8, 1922, Hoover Papers, Commerce Section, Construction Industries File.

72 Gries to Hoover, March 9, 1922, Hoover to R. C. Marshall, March 10, 1922, and Hoover's address to the Construction Industries Meeting, Chicago, April 4, 1922, Hoover Papers, Commerce Section, Construction Industries File.

73 Rose C. Field, "Industry's New Doctors," in *New York Times,* June 4, 1922; Frank Freidel, *Franklin D. Roosevelt: The Ordeal* (Boston, 1954), pp. 153-55; Hoover's address of June 19, 1922, Hoover Papers, Public Statements, No. 243. The new council was to bring together the leaders of ten functional groups, namely the architects, engineers, contractors, workers, materials manufacturers, financiers, retailers, government builders, utilities, and local communities (as represented by the chambers of commerce). Its job, as Roosevelt saw it, was to harmonize their work, raise their ethical standards, and commit them to "intensive national planning" in the public interest.

74 Murray, *Harding Era,* pp. 213-14, 218-20; Koerselman, "Hoover and Farm Crisis," 259-61, 309-16.

75   Hunt to Paul Kellogg, February 28 and March 24, 1922, and February 6, 1923, Survey Associates Papers (Social Welfare History Archives, U. of Minnesota), Folder 622.

76   Murray, *Harding Era,* pp. 240–42; Hoover's statements to the Railway Conference and the Interstate Commerce Commission, January 16 and February 3, 1922, Hoover to Eugene Black, February 10, 1922, Hoover to Norman Gould, February 24, 1922, Daniel Willard to Hoover, January 26, 1922, and "Federal Emergency Organization for the Movement of Necessities in Case of a Railway Strike," Hoover Papers, Commerce Section, Railroads File.

77   John Burnam, "What Hoover Is Doing," *Nation's Business,* 10 (February 1922), 16–17; Hoover to Harding, June 24, 1922, Hoover Papers, Commerce Section, Commerce—Foreign and Domestic Commerce File.

78   Hoover to Harding, January 4, 1922, Harding Papers, Box 5; Murray, *Harding Era,* 274–76, 355, 361–62; Hogan, "U.S. and International Economic Control," 97–99; Carl Parrini, *Heir to Empire* (Pittsburgh, 1969), pp. 186–88.

79   Murray, *Harding Era,* 410–11; Secretary of Commerce, *Annual Report* (1922), pp. 13–14; Glenn Johnson, "Secretary of Commerce Herbert Hoover: The First Regulator of American Broadcasting," Ph.D. Diss. (U. of Iowa, 1970), 82–88.

80   See his remarks as reported in the *San Francisco Chronicle,* September 15, 1921, and the *Boston Globe,* April 8 and 23, 1922. See also his address to the National Electric Light Association, May 19, 1922, Hoover Papers, Commerce Section, Superpower File. As part of the new development, Hoover hoped to see coal transformed into electricity at the mines and "shipped" over the wires.

81   The bill, however, failed to pass. Conservatives argued against interference with "natural law," and others opposed it because it was "fathered by big business," might be used for partisan purposes, or would give undue power to Hoover. Senator George Norris thought "we had better let God run it as in the past, and not take the power away from Him and give it to Hoover." Hunt, "Reconstruction," 46–47; President's Conference on Unemployment, *Business Cycles and Unemployment* (1923), pp. 247–48; Grin, "Unemployment Conference," 102–03.

82   See, for example, Otto Mallery to Hoover, May 5, 1922, Hoover Papers, Commerce Section, Reorganization File, and E. E. Hunt to Philip Cabot, September 13, 1922, Hunt Papers, Box 18. Symptomatic of the period was a proposal by Roger Babson in January 1922. He would eliminate "abnormal fluctuations and thus solve the problem of unemployment and social conflict" by bringing the representatives of the "great national associations" together in an "industrial capital" and having them serve as an economic council on the "nation's problems." Secretary of Labor James Davis was much taken with the idea, but Hoover did not respond. See the *New York Times,* January 23, 1922, and Davis to Harding, January 25, 1922, Harding Papers, Box 32.

83   The funds came from the Carnegie Foundation, the research staff from the National Bureau of Economic Research. Wesley Mitchell served as research director. Hunt, "Business Cycles and Unemployment," October 1, 1927, Hunt Papers, Box 28.

84   Hunt, "Business Cycles and Unemployment," October 1, 1927, Hunt Papers, Box 28; Hunt to Hoover, April 6, 1922, Hoover Papers, Commerce Section, Hunt File; Metcalf, "Hoover and the Emergence of Macroeconomic Management," 74–77.

85   Raymond Pearl to John Ford Bell, October 29, 1921, Bell Papers, Box 1.

86   Grin, "Unemployment Conference," 96–97.

87   257 *U.S.* 377; Himmelberg, "Relaxation of Antitrust," 101–02, 116; *New York Times,* June 3, 1921, and April 13 and 14, 1922.

88   McIlvaine to Hoover, February 4, 1922, Hoover Papers, Commerce Section, Trade Associations File.

89   Daugherty to Hoover, January 3, 1922, Hoover Papers, Commerce Section, Justice Department File; William Lamb to Hoover, January 16, 1922, Hoover to Daugherty, February 3, 1922, and Daugherty to Hoover, February 8, 1922, Hoover Papers, Commerce Section, Trade Associations File.

90   As trade association official Charles White put it, "Mr. Daugherty's opinion or answer to Mr. Hoover's letter has practically said nothing, and until and unless we can have some more definite statement . . . then we are just as much in the dark as ever we were, and our own people . . . will certainly not feel justified in beginning any such trade activities as are outlined in Mr. Hoover's letter." White to Hoover, February 13, 1922, Hoover Papers, Commerce Section, Trade Associations File.

91   S.J.Res. 188 and S. 3385, 67 Cong., 2 Sess., April 3, 1922, copies in Hoover Papers, Commerce Section, Trade Associations File.

92   Himmelberg, "Relaxation of Antitrust," 118–19; Conference of Trade Associations Proceedings, April 12, 1922, Lamb to Hoover, April 1, 1922, and Commerce Department Press Releases, March 17 and April 1, 1922, Hoover Papers, Commerce Section, Trade Associations File.

93   For the critique from the antitrust camp, see the exchange with Samuel Untermyer, *New York Times,* April 17, 1922. For that from the right, see the *Manufacturers' News,* April 20, 1922. For legislative action, see Edge to Hoover, April 22 and May 5, 1922, and Hoover to Edge, June 12, 1922, Hoover Papers, Commerce Section, Trade Associations File; Edge to Hoover, June 14, 1922, Hoover Papers, Commerce Section, Senate File, and David Wing to Richard Emmet, June 19, 1922, Hoover Papers, Commerce Section, Commerce—Trade Association Statistics File.

94   David Wing, Report on Cooperation Work, August 5, 1922, Hoover Papers, Commerce Section, Commerce—Trade Association Statistics File; "General Committee Cooperating on Trade Association Activities," Hoover Papers, Commerce Section, Trade Association Activities File; Feiker to Klein, December 8, 1922, Bureau of Foreign and Domestic Commerce Records, File 712.1.

95   "Report on Cooperation between Department of Commerce and the American Engineering Standards Committee," March 9, 1922, Hoover Papers, Commerce Section, Construction File; Durgin to Hoover, November 1, 1922, Commerce Department Records, File 82341; *New York Times,* May 23, 1922.

96   Wing, Reports on Cooperation Work, May 13, 23, and 27, June 19, and August 5, 1922, Wing's "Methods of Cooperation with Associations in Distributing Trade Information," and Wing to Emmet, June 7, 1922, Hoover Papers, Commerce Section, Commerce—Trade Association Statistics File; "Department's Cooperation for Distribution of Trade Statistics Gathered by Trade Associations," Hoover Papers, Commerce Section, Trade Associations File.

97   Zieger, *Republicans and Labor,* pp. 114–17; Murray, *Harding Era,* pp. 225, 243–44.

98   The Woods operation came to an end in May 1922. Harding to Hoover, May 22, 1922, Hoover Papers, Commerce Section, Unemployment File.

99   "Coal," April 16, 1922, Hoover to James Goodrich, August 26, 1922, and Hoover to Harding, August 23, 1922, Hoover Papers, Commerce Section, Coal File; Hawley, "Hoover and Bituminous Coal," 257-58.

100   Zieger, *Republicans and Labor,* pp. 123-25, 131-34; Murray, *Harding Era,* pp. 245-46, 249-50; Hoover's memorandum of July 23, 1922, Hoover Papers, Commerce Section, Railroads File; Ronald Radosh, "Labor and the Economy," in Jerry Israel, ed., *Building the Organizational Society* (New York, 1972), pp. 76-78.

101   Hawley, "Hoover and Bituminous Coal," 259-62; Hoover, "A Plan to Secure Continuous Employment and Greater Stability in the Bituminous Coal Industry," and Hoover to Julius Barnes, July 22, 1922, Hoover Papers, Commerce Section, Coal File.

102   Hoover to Ernest Lewis, June 16, 1922, Hoover Papers, Commerce Section, Railroads File; Hoover, "Railroad Reorganization" [April 1923], Hoover Papers, Commerce Section, Railroad Consolidation File; Hoover, "The Railways," November 7, 1922, Harding Papers, Box 5.

103   Zieger, *Republicans and Labor,* pp. 138-40, 202-12; Radosh, "Labor and the American Economy," 78-81; Murray, *Harding Era,* pp. 254-57, 261.

104   Hawley, "Hoover and Bituminous Coal," 258-59, 262-63; Murray, *Harding Era,* pp. 258-59; Federal Fuel Distributor's Report, December 27, 1922, Hoover to the U.S. Coal Commission, November 1, 1922, and Commerce Department Press Release, September 16, 1922, Hoover Papers, Commerce Section, Coal File.

105   Department of Commerce, "Review of Business in 1922," reprinted in *Commercial and Financial Chronicle,* 115 (December 30, 1922), 2860-61.

106   Hoover's addresses of October 17, 1922, and October 25, 1924, Hoover Papers, Public Statements, Nos. 264 and 406; Hoover, *The New Day* (Stanford, 1928), pp. 66-83.

107   For the meagerness of results in these areas, see Grin, "Unemployment Conference," 97-107; Zieger, *Republicans and Labor,* p. 96; Parrini, *Heir to Empire,* pp. 268-76; George Soule, *Prosperity Decade* (New York, 1947), pp. 172-74; and Metcalf, "Hoover and the Emergence of Macroeconomic Management," 77-79.

108   Soule, *Prosperity Decade,* pp. 160-62, 176-78, 229-34. In November 1923, Hoover still regarded coal and railroads as the "two most pressing economic problems." Hoover to Coolidge, November 22, 1923, Hoover Papers, Commerce Section, Presidential File.

109   Soule, *Prosperity Decade,* pp. 110-20.

110   "Within sixty days," Hoover noted in 1923, the "forced temporary employment" undertaken in the wake of the Unemployment Conference became "permanent employment." "The wages that the men earned on a temporary footing went into consumption and helped to make the employment permanent." Quoted in Will Payne, "Income Tax Dividends," *Saturday Evening Post,* 196 (September 1, 1923), 122.

111   *Ibid.* See also Grin, "Unemployment Conference," 92, 106-07, and Hunt, "Business Cycles and Unemployment," October 1, 1927, Hunt Papers, Box 28.

112   William Hard, "The New Hoover," *Review of Reviews,* 86 (November 1927), 478–84; Hoover to David Lawrence, December 29, 1927, Hoover Papers, Commerce Section, American Businessman File; Hoover, "The Department of Commerce" [1926], Hoover Papers, Commerce Section, Commerce Department Achievements File; Hoover, *New Day,* pp. 22–23.

113   Romasco, *Poverty of Abundance,* pp. 24–65.

114   See Arnold, "Hoover and the Department of Commerce," 217–22, and "Hoover and the Continuity of American Public Policy," 526–44. The corollary of these conclusions, of course, is that the New Deal period was far less innovative or revolutionary than once depicted. And while recent scholarship has disagreed about whether this was good or bad, it had tended to agree that such was the case.

SUMMARY OF COMMENTARY BY DISCUSSANTS AND CONFEREES

Discussion of the paper began with formal commentaries by Professors Peri Arnold of the University of Notre Dame and Alan Seltzer of the University of Maryland, Baltimore. Both expressed fundamental agreement with the central arguments, but each called for more discussion and analysis at key points. Arnold urged fuller recognition of defects in the Hooverian ideal, especially its lack of mechanisms for dealing with inequity, irrationality, and irresponsibility in the private sector and its assumption that organizations committed to conflict and clientelism could become vehicles for cooperative stabilization. He also noted how Hoover's philosophy cut across the traditional divisions between left and right, and he wondered how Hoover could fail to see that his actions were paving the way for big government. Seltzer urged further elucidation of Hoover's views on antitrust. These should be distinguished, he thought, not only from the views of Daugherty's antitrust division, the New Nationalists of 1912, and the later supporters of the NRA but also from those held by Arthur Jerome Eddy and other proponents of open price plans. In addition, he called for fuller recognition of Hoover's "naive optimism." The secretary, he noted, had once expressed strong doubts about business altruism, especially in peacetime. Yet in 1921 he relied upon the very thing he had once portrayed as weak, acted as if businessmen were or would become statesmen, and seemed willing to accept any progress as an indication that things were going well.

In a brief response to the commentaries, Hawley made several points. In Hoover's mind, he thought, there had been no contradiction between departmental expansionism and opposition to big government. The expansionism was for the purpose of erecting institutions that would save us from creeping statism; and once these were erected, governmental controls and services would tend to wither away. Hoover seemed not to doubt that they could be erected, that potentially the private sector was capable of far greater rationality, responsibility, and equity than statist institutions ever could be. Nor was this because he saw no defects in the private bodies to which he would delegate power and responsibility. It was more a matter of the greater defects he perceived in other schemes for securing economic order. As for his illusions about the effectiveness of his program, he was not much different in this regard from other men who have taken action and then witnessed the improvement of the economy. Both the New Dealers of 1936 and the New Frontiersmen of the mid-1960s fell victim to similar illusions. And as for antitrust, Hoover did not stay put to the extent that he did on most other aspects of his organizational ideal. He tried to distinguish between those statistical exchanges that contributed to general economic stability and the kind used to protect exploitive or inefficient industries. But at one time he had looked upon open price plans as belonging in the first category rather than the second, and he did support legislation widely regarded as weakening the legal barriers against open price systems and related market restraints.

The discussion following the formal commentaries revolved mostly around three aspects of Hoover's thought. One was his vision of a new business management, divorced from ownership and operating in a new institutional context as enlightened social trustees. Further comments on this were made by Peri Arnold, Robert Wood, Ellis Hawley, Robert Zieger, and Alan Seltzer, with some noting the parallels between Hoover's ideas and later managerial thought, and with others focusing on his failure to see the need for external checks and new mechanisms of social accountability. The second topic of discussion, commented on by Melvyn Leffler, Joseph Brandes, and Alan Seltzer, was Hoover's prescriptions for international stability, especially in regard to combatting radicalism and statism and developing transnational cooperation between enlightened business groups. And the third subject discussed was Hoover's "apoliticalism," a quality reflected particularly in his efforts to shift decision making into an allegedly more rational syndicalist arena where it would be less influenced by mass, interest-group, and partisan impulses. Those commenting on this agreed that Hoover had made such efforts and had called them "apolitical." But some pointed out that the actual effect was to enhance the importance of a kind of bureaucratic politics at which Hoover excelled; and others thought that "apoliticalism" was itself a political strategy, designed to strengthen a political position by insisting that it was a non-negotiable technological necessity. One commentator compared it to "solidarism" in France.

In addition, two other lines of discussion developed. One arose from Francis O'Brien's questions concerning the economic and political effects of Hoover's programs. The treatment of these, he thought, had been a bit deflating; and at his request, Hawley restated and elaborated upon the arguments as to what had brought economic recovery and how the experience of the early 1920s had shaped future policy decisions. The other line of discussion revolved around a continued debate concerning Hoover's attitudes toward open price plans. Peri Arnold argued that Hoover's renunciation of them was based on legal rather than economic considerations. Had they remained legal, they would have remained one of the mechanisms through which he was attempting to manage and stabilize market behavior. But with this view, Alan Seltzer strongly disagreed. Hoover, he insisted, came to see open price plans as being among those restraints that were contrary to the public interest, and his post-1929 position remained consistent with this perception.

Finally, as the session drew to a close, Hawley was asked to compare his interpretation of Hoover with that set forth by William Appleman Williams. In doing so, he argued that Williams had made Hoover into too much of a corporate syndicalist and had failed to bring out how corporative institutions would, in theory, work in tandem with healthy competition and individual initiative.

Robert H. Zieger

Herbert Hoover, the Wage-Earner, and The "New Economic System," 1919–29

Editor's Introductory Note

Robert H. Zieger, currently professor of history at Wayne State University, is a recognized authority on national labor policy during the interwar period. His *Republicans and Labor, 1919–1929* (1969) was the first major work to challenge long accepted stereotypes concerning federal labor policy in the 1920s; and as such it was a pioneer work in stimulating a re-examination of the labor system envisioned by Republican leaders, the role of Herbert Hoover's Commerce Department in shaping labor policy, and the relations between union leaders and Republican politicians. In the book Zieger rejected the view that Republican policy making could be understood as an anti-labor monolith. Within the party there were also pro-unionists, politicians willing to bargain with union leaders, and above all exponents of a new management-engineering vision calling for production-minded labor associations. The policy that emerged reflected the varying strengths of the competing groups. And in both *Republicans and Labor* and a series of articles published in historical journals, Zieger has traced and documented these varying strengths and the policy vacillations or compromises emerging from them. In addition, he is the author of *Madison's Battery Workers, 1934–1952* (1977) and of two major historiographical articles, one on the newer trends in labor history and the other analyzing recent interpretations of Herbert Hoover.

In the paper published here, Professor Zieger explores in detail the management-engineering vision that Herbert Hoover embraced and

Professor Zieger's paper was previously published in the *Business History Review* (Summer 1977), which controls the copyright.

the implications of that vision for labor organization and genuine industrial democracy. Hoover, he demonstrates, drew upon and attempted to synthesize four strands of a larger managerial impulse: one emanating from the aspirations of the engineering societies, a second from the new profession of personnel management, a third from promoters of shop councils and company unions, and a fourth from unionists seeking to reestablish and institutionalize their wartime status as managerial "partners." The result was his own solution for the labor problem, one that combined union recognition and responsible collective bargaining with shop councils and other agencies for securing cooperation between production-minded workers and their employers. This, he insisted, could work to the interests of all, and through a variety of actions he sought to translate the theory into reality. As Zieger shows, however, he was never able to do this. And eventually, he acquiesced in a labor system where new managerial agencies tended to enhance employer power rather than foster genuine cooperation. Productivity increased for a time. But viewed in the light of Hoover's own analysis, it rested on an unsound basis, and this would be exposed by the onset of the Great Depression.

Zieger criticizes Hoover for seeking to combine two fundamentally irreconcilable ideas concerning labor representation. But his strongest criticism is of the secretary's acquiescence in the kind of labor system characteristic of the late 1920s. Even though Hoover lacked the power to change matters, he could have exposed the unsoundness in what had developed. And since it took the New Deal labor laws to make meaningful worker participation possible, he presumably should have been among those who moved beyond voluntarism and championed such laws. Unlike some revisionists, Zieger does not find much validity in Hoover's claim that the state could not be used for such purposes without creating protected enclaves for society's parasitic, dysfunctional, and unproductive elements.

The question also arises as to which was the real Hoover: the man who responded to labor militancy by calling for meaningful participation or the one who seemed content with a solution resting on employer domination. Zieger credits Hoover with being a sincere champion of worker participation, and in support of this view he offers a good deal of evidence. But as the subsequent discussion disclosed, not all of those who read the paper or listened to its presentation were persuaded.

Herbert Hoover, the Wage-Earner,
And the "New Economic System," 1919-29*

In common with many of his generation, Herbert Hoover came to view the labor question as liberal capitalism's greatest challenge.[1] Repeatedly, in the eighteen months after his return from Europe in 1919, Hoover called for the creation of a "new economic system"[2] that would step up output and increase efficiency. He believed that unless the country could enlist workers through a system of representation in the campaign to increase productivity and eliminate waste, it could not meet the demands of the postwar world. For seven years as secretary of commerce he effectively encouraged these aims. At the same time, however, Hoover did not similarly promote effective worker representation in industry, although he had identified this goal as basic to the achievement of the others. Impressed by the apparent efficacy of welfare capitalism, proud of the prosperity enjoyed by wage-earners, and aware of the parochialism and lassitude of the AFL, Hoover muted his earlier insistence upon meaningful, democratic, and independent participation by workers in the economic system. If indeed the full realization of Hoover's goals required such participation, liberal capitalism by 1929 rested upon an unsound basis, a weakness that the onset of the depression helped to expose.[3]

Between 1919 and 1921, Hoover developed and articulated his concept of a new economic system. In speeches, press conferences, and magazine articles, he addressed himself to the economic and social challenges that would face the country in the immediate future. Unlike many Americans, he saw in the social turmoil following the war no threat of radical takeover or basic attack on "the American way." He did hold that in the interrelated problems of production, efficiency, and industrial relations lay the real challenge and the real opportunity to forge a new and modern economic system, one that would build upon the country's traditions of voluntarism, free enterprise, and democracy. To Hoover, the great strikes of 1919 were only symptomatic of deeper problems, problems that would yield to expert knowledge, sympathetic understanding of the difficulties facing workers and employers, and reliance on basic American values.

In scores of speeches and articles, Hoover hammered away at the theme of productivity. Not only did Europe clamor for America's goods, but our own citizens, including notably wage-earners, legitimately expected a rising standard of living. In Hoover's view, traditional capitalism and socialism were equally bankrupt. Society had to find a way to increase productivity and extend its benefits to the entire citizenry, not through increasing the demands on workers or through government ownership, but through the application of scientific principles of management within a setting of voluntarism and through expert leadership. Government, he held, would inevitably play a key role, but primarily as a coordinator, mediator, and information-dispenser, not as a coercive or restrictive force.[4]

While the nation's future depended on productivity, Hoover also stressed that "maximum production cannot be obtained without giving a voice in the administration of production to all sectors of the community."[5] As an engineer in touch with the maturing scientific management movement, he knew well that efforts to subject workers to arbitrary systems of production without their consent invariably ended in failure. He applauded the War Labor Board's sponsorship of employee representation as a means of insuring fairness and efficient production during the conflict. Indeed, he believed that the fair, democratic, and independent representation of working people in industry—in matters concerning production no less than in matters touching their direct welfare—was crucial to the success of the effort to step up productivity. "Industry must be humanized," he asserted.[6] Modern factories with their necessarily large-scale operations discouraged personal contact between management and employees. He insisted that American industry had to "re-establish through organized representation that personal cooperation between employer and employee . . . that was a binding force when our industries were smaller."[7] Opposing repression as a solution to labor unrest, Hoover instead proclaimed the need to enlist workers' loyalty and cooperation through recognizing their legitimate desire for a rising standard of living and through developing plans for genuine worker representation. He was convinced "that the vast majority of American labor fundamentally wishes to co-operate in production" and that workers would respond enthusiastically to efforts to increase productivity and to eliminate waste, so long as their own needs and interests were protected through representation.[8]

Hoover's views on these matters represented a synthesis of several broad streams of recent thought and action concerning the labor problem. Since the 1890s, businessmen had been experimenting with various forms of welfare capitalism. At the same time, technological change and new management techniques were restructuring traditional job classifications and patterns of shop level supervision; increasingly, the personnel manager challenged the foreman as the arbiter of employee relations. Moreover, engineers and efficiency experts contributed to the vigor and sense of change emanating from the country's shops and factories as they applied and enlarged upon the work of Frederick W. Taylor. Although American business harbored its bitter-end advocates of the open shop and its antilabor corporations, some unionists found it expedient to cooperate with businessmen through such vehicles as the National Civic Federation. With his unique international background in engineering, business, and social concern, Hoover followed these diverse trends closely; in addition, he had seen during his lengthy stay in Great Britain the need of modern societies, whether in war or peace, to mobilize and secure the loyalty of their working people. Emerging as a national leader in the postwar period, Hoover developed a synthesis of these diverse initiatives in industrial relations, one that partook of the experience of businessmen, engineers, efficiency experts, trade unionists, and wartime administrators, but one that met the exacting requirements of the American individualism upon which he based his view of postwar society as well. In 1919–20, many prominent Americans sought to resolve the problem of industrial conflict, but Hoover brought a powerful combination of experience, intellectual acuity, and boldness to the task.[9]

After his return from Europe, Hoover had two formal opportunities to develop the implications of these ideas. Late in 1919, President Wilson appointed him vice-chairman of the President's Second Industrial Conference, while in the fall of 1920 he was elected president of an engineering body dedicated to developing enlightened solutions to social problems. In both roles, Hoover energetically expounded his views, established contacts with academicians, laborites, and businessmen, and formulated concrete plans. Though these efforts bore few immediate results, they did provide him with a public forum and a body of experience upon which he could draw during his years in the cabinet.

The Second Industrial Conference

Hoover quickly emerged as the leading figure in the Second Industrial Conference. Its *Report* was primarily his handiwork, articulating his overall analysis of the economic system and focusing on the central significance of worker representation. Issued in March 1920 after three months of preparation, it asserted Hoover's view of the close connection among economic growth, reduction of waste, and worker participation.[10] Its major recommendation was an imaginative and sophisticated plan to settle industrial disputes, a plan that strongly endorsed collective bargaining and voluntary processes of implementing it, positing for government a creative and influential, but strictly noncompulsory, role. The *Report* also stressed the need for worker representation in industry, advocating secret democratic election of the workers' representatives who were to be involved in its dispute-settling machinery. Holding that the settlement of labor conflict "must come from the bottom, not the top," it called for "deliberate organization" of the relationship between workers and employers at the plant or shop level. Echoing Hoover's lament that modern industry had occasioned the "loss of personal contact," the *Report* called for "employee representation" on the shop level as a means of reintroducing the productive and mutually helpful personal relationships that had formerly prevailed.[11]

Neither the *Report* nor Hoover's subsequent public statements in its behalf was entirely clear as to the exact meanings to be attached to such concepts as "collective bargaining" and "employee representation" or "shop councils." In general, Hoover believed that the role of conflict and violence in industrial relations would diminish as rational personnel policies and expanding productivity gained ground. Labor unions had a role to play in the emerging economic system, but they would be supplemented by other forms of employee representation. The term "collective bargaining" had two meanings. As a reflection of existing reality, it entailed formal, signed contracts between labor unions and employers, arrived at through processes of negotiation that sometimes involved strikes, lockouts, and other forms of industrial conflict. Hoover favored collective bargaining in this sense as a flawed, but necessary, instrument. He frequently spoke out in behalf of unionists who sought to bargain in good faith, defended the right to strike, opposed compulsory adjudication of disputes, and castigated employers who were unwilling to enter into collective bargaining.

However, just as trade unionism was not the only form of employee representation, this conflict model of collective bargaining was not the only form of negotiation and communication between workers and managers. As Hoover saw it, in the modern factory the trade union would be supplemented, and possibly supplanted, by the shop council. It was necessary for shop committees to stand apart from the formal trade union apparatus for two reasons. First, Hoover rejected the closed or union shop as coercive; hence, inevitably there would be nonunion workers in most plants, workers whose rights to representation in company affairs had to be respected. Second, the power of craft union traditions in the American labor movement and the consistent inability of the AFL to forge instruments of mass organization insured that if organized at all, a given factory would be represented by several individual unions. Shop committees apart from the trade unions would represent workers according to their actual roles in the affairs of the company and not in accordance with arbitrary and increasingly anachronistic notions of craft. Shop committees would not negotiate contracts but rather would undertake the significant tasks of expressing workers' views about production problems, handling welfare matters, voicing grievances, and in general communicating in a constructive way on a regular basis with representatives of management. Since the application of new technologies and new methods of coordination would spur productivity and create more for all, this kind of common meeting (called by one scholar "collective dealing") would permit efficient managers to communicate to well-informed, prosperous workers the details of their growing stake in the company and the economic system.

Hoover always affirmed that labor unions had a role in the emerging economic system, especially since the American labor movement had been so loyal, conservative, and sensible in the past. Still, Hoover's response to actual instances of labor conflict revealed sharp limitations to his willingness to grant legitimacy to trade unionism. A union that sought soberly and cautiously to bargain in good faith would win his approval. However, a labor movement that turned militant or resorted to aggressive political action would forfeit its claim to be part of the new economic system. Given the passing of American industry into the hands of educated, public-minded managers, given the good sense and conservatism of Samuel Gompers and his lieutenants, and given the productivity and enterprise of "the American way," it seemed to Hoover that his notions of "collective bargaining" and "employee representation" were eminently practical and clearly realizable within the framework of existing industrial relations.[12]

After the issuance of the *Report,* Hoover served as its chief public advocate. In a series of speeches and articles, as well as in testimony before the Senate Committee on Education and Labor, he urged action on its recommendations and support for its underlying concepts.

Criticism came primarily from two sources: businessmen alarmed by its endorsement of collective bargaining and worker representation; and organized labor, whose leaders liked neither the emphasis on shop committees nor the intricate mediation plan.[13] In his defense of the *Report,* Hoover criticized the narrow-minded employers who failed to appreciate the legitimacy of workers' grievances. He reiterated his call for "open and frank relations" between labor and capital, attacking those who viewed repression as an answer to industrial unrest. He denounced employers who might endorse the notion of employee representation while seeking in fact to use it for anti-union purposes.[14]

Hoover acknowledged that organized labor had rejected the conference's recommendations. He argued, however, that labor had been hasty and imprecise in its reaction; he felt confident that many laborites would reverse their stand when they studied the dispute-settling plan more carefully. He noted that the AFL's criticisms centered on the *Report's* advocacy of shop committees and remarked that this aspect of its recommendations was "purely voluntary . . . and has no relationship to legislation."[15] When asked whether employers had in fact used representation plans to thwart unionism, he replied that on occasion the idea "has been used against organized labor." But, he added, unwittingly lending support to organized labor's fears, "I would not want to say that it has been used to the detriment of the employee,"[16] thus expressing the very dichotomy between worker and union that laborites so vehemently rejected. In none of his remarks did Hoover clarify his view of the precise nature of shop committees. He asserted their compatibility with trade unionism and scolded those who might employ them to discredit unions. But he did not respond to labor's very real fears about the challenges to its goals seemingly inherent in any system of representation that did not rest firmly and exclusively on trade unionism. Indeed, his testimony obscured the issue, for it reiterated the central importance of "trying to re-establish an intimate relationship directly between the employer and the employee," while at the same time dismissing labor's fears by underlining the "purely voluntary" nature of the shop committees that the *Report* espoused.[17]

Despite Hoover's vigorous public advocacy, the conference's recommendations received little serious public attention. None was enacted or made part of public policy. The abrupt decline of labor turbulence, the onset of the 1920 presidential campaign, and the growing prominence of the League of Nations debate, together with the tepid reception by both labor and business, all helped to shelve the recommendations. Increasingly, Hoover turned to the engineering movement in an effort to stimulate greater public awareness of economic problems and as a means of undertaking vigorous action.

The Engineering Movement

In November 1920, Hoover accepted the presidency of the Federated American Engineering Societies. For several years, a number of influential progressives in the profession had encouraged engineers to use their expert knowledge and their keen awareness of production and efficiency matters to develop rational solutions to social problems. These engineers envisaged their profession as an independent, apolitical force that could reshape public debate on major issues.[18] Hoover shared their vision. He spoke of one hundred thousand engineers who had carried forth the war effort by virtue of their technical abilities and high-minded dedication. "The problems facing America today," he wrote in 1920, "if attacked in the scientific spirit, will yield similar happy results." Established in 1920 as a kind of caucus of progressive elements in the several engineering societies, the FAES was the institutional embodiment of this enthusiasm.[19]

As president of FAES, Hoover focused intently on labor matters. Before and during the war, a number of industrial engineers had worked closely with organized labor to solve problems of production, efficiency, and labor use. While the scientific management movement had originally displayed an arrogant contempt for the labor movement, many engineers had learned that narrowly-conceived stopwatch timing and arbitrary programs of efficiency were counterproductive, since they often antagonized workers. To such engineers as Morris L. Cooke, Robert Wolf, and Robert Valentine, the labor movement was capable of intelligent adaptation to new processes if its representatives were included in planning and if the unions' interests were consulted. As a mining engineer, Hoover himself had advocated considerate and open treatment of workers, and during the war had come to value his association with Samuel Gompers. Thus, it was natural that he would see in his work with the FAES an opportunity to encourage engineers and laborites to join together to confront the economic challenges that faced the country.[20]

During the latter months of 1920 and through early 1921, Hoover sought to achieve his goals both through formal studies enlisting engineering expertise and through personal contact with labor leaders.

One of his first acts as FAES president was to establish a committee for the study of waste in industry. This body was directed by Hoover's chief aide, Edward Eyre Hunt, and formally headed by L. W. Wallace, an engineer who was, if anything, more enthusiastic than Hoover himself about the possibilities of applying technology to social problems. It set about to study waste and inefficiency in a number of industries, with a view to publishing its findings as a major document in the campaign to awaken public attention and to demonstrate the relevance of engineers' work in confronting economic problems. Hoover and his aides sought and received the cooperation of many laborites in preparing the study. For their part, a number of labor leaders participated enthusiastically, for they had come to see engineers such as those active in the FAES as potential allies.[21]

The committee's report, published in June 1921 under the title *Waste in Industry,* justified labor's cooperation. It endorsed collective bargaining and opposed wage reductions, at the time a popular expedient among businessmen pinched by postwar deflation. It attacked the notion that labor agitation fomented economic dislocation, noting for example, that over the past quarter century strikes had played only a marginal role in creating instability. Moreover, it held that the responsibility for reducing waste lay overwhelmingly with employers, thus implicitly defending workers from the common charge of inefficiency. Hoover, who played little part in the preparation of the study but whose aides worked actively with the engineers, hailed it as "carefully planned and rapidly executed." He felt sure that it would stimulate public and private efforts to raise productivity through the reduction of waste and inefficiency.[22]

Actually, public reaction to the report obscured its message. The FAES, rapidly coming under control of more conservative elements in the engineering profession, refused to sanction publication under its direct auspices. Many businessmen bridled at the leniency displayed toward labor and at the burden placed on their shoulders. Although organized labor greeted the report enthusiastically, the controversy surrounding *Waste in Industry* significantly undermined progressive influence among organized engineers.[23]

Hoover's other effort to promote his views as FAES president came through direct contacts with the labor movement and, to a lesser extent, with corporate leaders. He corresponded and conferred on a number of occasions with Samuel Gompers, while aides and associates maintained close communication with other laborites.[24] Hoover's goal was to awaken organized labor to the need for greater productivity. At the same time, he sought to convince Gompers of the value of shop committees. In addition, Hoover hoped that the engineers could help to bring about regular meetings among themselves, organized labor, and spokesmen for some of the more progressive-minded corporations. Such regular consultation would facilitate the attack on waste and would break down barriers between labor and management, while acquainting both with the work of the engineers.[25]

The highpoint of this labor-engineering collaboration was a presentation by Hoover before the AFL Executive Council on November 16, 1920. At this meeting, Hoover sought to enlighten labor leaders about productivity, efficiency, and labor representation. He decried any tendency that labor might have to restrict output as a means of saving jobs. He deplored the deadening routinization of much modern work and called for "a renewal of the creative opportunity of the individual workman." Endorsing collective bargaining and acknowledging the unique influence and importance of unions, he called for new forms of "cooperation between management and worker." This, he declared, "involves an acceptance of certain principles of shop councils." He attacked the effort on the part of many businessmen to cut wages in response to deflationary tendencies, but at the same time he suggested wage differentials and incentives to encourage workmanship and to spur productivity. He remained ambiguous about the precise role of organized labor in the "creation of a new sense of cooperation between men and coordination between groups." Earlier, he had assured Gompers directly of his dedication to collective bargaining and of his commitment to "tangible mutual guarantees . . . against violation of . . . collective agreements," but he failed to specify how to accomplish this end. In his presentation before the executive council, he called upon organized labor to lead the way toward the "new economic system" that must arise from the war. Its first step, he emphasized, was to encourage "the increase in productivity." Labor must "insist upon securing the cooperation of the employer," he affirmed, but "this the employer cannot refuse . . . when the main motive of the great organized labor movement is to create the working conditions which stimulate the productivity of the individual workman."[26]

It was an impressive performance. Gompers assured Hoover that "there was much that you advocated with which labor is in entire accord."[27] Still, nagging problems remained. Frank Morrison, secretary-treasurer of the AFL, objected to Hoover's wage-differential suggestions.[28] More serious were Hoover's allusions to shop councils, his emphasis on productivity, and his vagueness about the continuing role of organized labor. Certainly, laborites welcomed Hoover's reiterated endorsement of collective bargaining. At the same time, they remained extremely hostile toward efforts to promote separate organizations of workers dealing directly with management, especially since there was no apparent way to guarantee the forthright, democratic, and independent selection of representatives that Hoover advocated.[29] Although Edward Eyre Hunt and Robert Wolf assiduously cultivated Gompers, hoping to convince him of the value of shop committees, the AFL maintained its antagonism toward them throughout the 1920s.[30]

As with his work with the Industrial Conference, little resulted directly from Hoover's activities as president of FAES. He did help to strengthen the lines of communication between engineers and labor leaders, but at the same time the progressive influence in the engineering societies began to wane. He secured labor's cooperation with the waste-in-industry survey, but his efforts to interest corporate executives in liaison with the AFL failed. Still, his postwar activities had awakened public interest in his views and had provided him with a reputation for astute analysis to go along with his impressive record of public service during the war. For its part, organized labor found its relationship with Hoover and his associates heartening, for the engineers in effect upheld labor's position on wages and collective bargaining during a period of intensifying anti-labor feeling. When Hoover announced his decision to join Harding's cabinet, laborites could be sure of at least one sympathetic voice in the government, while Hoover could hope to continue his efforts to secure labor's endorsement for his entire economic program.

Secretary of Commerce

Hoover's acceptance of a cabinet post represented a conscious decision to seek needed social change through government. He secured from Harding the promise that he would have a voice in a broad range of concerns, including labor. Although his many pronouncements on the process of orderly social change had emphasized the activities of private voluntaristic associations and organizations, his efforts as a private citizen revealed to Hoover the necessity for energetic government action. It was clear that only through the national forum that the cabinet provided could he coordinate, facilitate, and publicize on a scale necessary to secure the innovation and cooperation among private groups needed to effect broad changes. Some of his supporters and admirers feared that cabinet service would detract from his earlier efforts and would inevitably entail sacrifice of his broad vision through political compromise. But, as the disapproving Edward Eyre Hunt remarked, "Mr. Hoover sees in the Department of Commerce a great opportunity to make the work of the engineers effective on a national scale."[31]

Throughout his tenure in the cabinet, Hoover implemented parts of his postwar program. He constantly reiterated the need for ever-greater productivity and publicized the need for efficiency and reduction of waste. Through his energetic administration, the Department of Commerce encouraged construction of highways, private building and ownership of homes, standardization of parts, and other processes designed to streamline American enterprise. The department, staffed by Hoover disciples, pioneered in the acquisition and distribution of economic information. It grew administratively in the twenties, promoting foreign trade, transportation, and new marketing and distributing methods. At the same time, the department established or strengthened its jurisdiction in such areas as radio broadcasting, aviation, highways, and flood relief. Hoover and his department continuously drew attention to the relationship between productivity and prosperity and worked hard to stimulate businessmen to revise antiquated and inefficient operations. It is true that the economy in the 1920s did have weak spots, notably certain phases of agriculture, textiles, and coal mining; but Hoover and his department were active even in these areas, although they did not claim exclusive responsibility.[32]

Under Hoover, the Department of Commerce also sought to promote the third of his postwar goals, the prosperity and representation of the wage earner. In labor matters, however, Hoover's sphere of action was limited administratively. The Department of Labor, of course, had formal jurisdiction over most areas of industrial relations, from the amelioration of disputes under the Conciliation Service to the gathering of information through the United States Bureau of Labor Statistics. In addition, a separate agency, the United States Railroad Labor Board, handled matters in a key area of concern. Still, Hoover's view of the worker as a central figure in his overall efforts to invigorate the American economy caused him to intervene in many labor matters, both as the promoter of long-range policies and as the manager of specific problems and crises. In these efforts, he was aided by the fact that Secretary of Labor James J. Davis was a man of limited experience and influence. Indeed, Davis, a businessman and fraternal order executive, devoted much of his official attention to immigration matters and cheerfully acquiesced in Hoover's ascendancy in labor policy.[33]

According to Hoover's analysis of 1919–21, there were two key elements in the achievement of justice for the American worker: a rising standard of living and a meaningful voice in the decisions that affected his working life. In general, Hoover sought to promote the first of these through general economic growth. Throughout the decade, for example, he favored tax policies that would benefit lower income groups. He actively encouraged residential construction and widespread home ownership. An enthusiastic booster of the automobile industry, he favored large-scale road construction and mass ownership of private vehicles. He encouraged the growth of the advertising and consumer-credit sectors, both so essential in a consumer-oriented society.[34]

Social scientists such as Leo Wolman and Robert and Helen Lynd noted in the twenties the spread of consumer affluence over broad segments of the population; the Lynds observed in Middletown the apparent weakening of class lines, as workers bought homes, owned automobiles, and participated increasingly in the community's recreational life.[35] In a 1928 campaign speech, Hoover heralded some of these changes: in the 1920s, he declared, national income had increased by 45%, production by 25%. "These increases," he declared, "have been widely spread among our whole people." He pointed to the construction of 3,500,000 new homes, the electrification of 9,000,000 residences, the installation of 6,000,000 telephones, the purchase of 7,000,000 radio sets and 14,000,000 automobiles. Figures developed by the Conference on Unemployment revealed that access to these labor-saving and pleasure-giving devices was reaching well into the working class.[36] Indeed, although Hoover's hope that the nation was close to eliminating poverty was premature, he could well claim in the 1928 campaign that working people had achieved under Republican auspices a standard of living and an opportunity to enjoy the delights of modern technology unprecedented in human history.

As secretary of commerce, Hoover relied primarily on the efficient workings of a revitalized economy to create and distribute these benefits. His department was extremely active in support of enterprise, in publicity and promotional work, and in efforts to insure coordination and efficiency among the various regional and functional sectors of the economy, but Hoover and his aides avoided direct governmental action wherever possible. Hoover implemented his postwar beliefs that voluntarism, private initiative, and individual enterprise, aided by an energetic but noncoercive government, held the key to economic growth and social progress.[37]

Unemployment and the Long Work Day

There were occasions, however, when social conditions demanded more forceful governmental action. If American workers were to achieve the prosperity and self-respect necessary for their full integration into the economic system, such inequities as unemployment and the long working day had to be eliminated. In neither of these matters could society rely upon purely private action: unemployment, because of its complexity and diffuseness; and the twelve-hour day, because short-sighted employers would not recognize that adoption of the eight-hour day was in their own interest. Thus, Hoover felt that both unemployment and the twelve-hour day demanded more assertive federal action than he was ordinarily willing to countenance.

"There is no economic failure so terrible . . . [as] that of a country possessing a surplus of every necessity of life in which numbers [of people], willing and anxious to work, are deprived of the necessities," he declared. From mid-1921 through early 1922, Hoover mobilized academic and engineering experts, businessmen, and labor leaders in the President's Conference on Unemployment to fight joblessness. Although these efforts did not contemplate direct federal relief, they did evolve elaborate plans for continuing coordination of private, state, and local relief efforts. Under Hoover's direction, the conference illuminated the part played by industrial waste and poor economic coordination in creating joblessness, dispelling the time-honored notion of individual inadequacy as the root cause. Although the conference in reality had little impact in producing the economic upturn of the mid-1920s, Hoover thought that his reliance on voluntarism had achieved startling results. In 1928, he hailed the work of the conference, declaring that "within a year we restored . . . five million workers to employment."[38]

Unemployment was an example of social inefficiency that Hoover thought would yield in time to improved economic techniques and better integration of functions. The long working day, however, remained in force in such important industries as steel, because of the unwise labor policies of the employers, who pointed to the peculiar technology of their industry. (Elsewhere, workdays of more than ten hours were unusual by the 1920s.) In his view, there was no excuse for the long working day. The industrial worker in the postwar era was emerging from an era of often harsh living and working conditions into a period of prosperity, self-respect, and enlightenment. Not only was this trend desirable on humanistic grounds, it was necessary if the industrial worker was to play his assigned role as a contented consumer, participant, and loyal partisan of the "new economic system."

Between 1921 and 1923 Hoover launched a shrewd and effective campaign to induce the steel industry to adopt the eight-hour day. When personal pressure from Hoover and President Harding failed to move the steel men, he drew upon the efforts of academicians, engineers, and the press in behalf of the steelworkers. Finally, after two years of carefully applied pressure, the steel magnates reluctantly agreed to move from the twelve- to the eight-hour day. Hoover was enormously proud of this accomplishment. "Owing to public opinion and some pushing on our part," he later recalled, "the twelve-hour day was on the way out in American industry."[39]

Indeed, the elimination of the long work day in steel was significant. Still, it was essentially a preliminary step toward achieving the position for the industrial worker that Hoover's "new economic system" seemed to envisage. In the steel industry itself, the companies recovered part of the financial losses that the change entailed by employing large numbers of low-paid Mexican and black workers. Moreover, Hoover's methods represented a kind of dead end for the steelworkers themselves. It would be a long time before such a combination of employer arrogance, favorable public opinion, expert engineering and academic analysis, and tenacious governmental insistence would be at their disposal again. Hoover could indeed feel proud that his efforts had been instrumental in achieving a favorable social change, but nothing in the twelve-hour day initiative did anything to encourage meaningful employee representation in the steel industry. Energetic public and private action had achieved a humane reform, but it also highlighted the inability of the steelworkers to assert themselves directly. If elimination of the twelve-hour day represented a triumph of Hoover's methods, it also underscored workers' inherent weaknesses without access to the representation that Hoover himself had earlier identified as crucial to the creative and dignified role workers were to assume in the emerging economy of modern America.[40]

Labor Representation

The problem of representation was not limited to steelworkers. Indeed, Hoover's inability to promote the participation of workers in the conduct of industry eventually weakened the general economic program that he had articulated in the postwar months. During that period he attached great importance to meaningful organization as both a right and a necessity for workers. He declared repeatedly that employers had to abandon arbitrary personnel policies. Hoover embraced the American Federation of Labor as a major factor in securing the rudiments of dignity and protection for America's wage earners. He hailed the federal government's wartime support for worker representation, whether through the trade unions or shop committees. Not only was it just and fair and democratic for workers to choose representatives to deal with management in an atmosphere free of fear and antagonism, it was vitally important for the success of the rest of his economic program. Until employers recognized the right of their operatives to representation, the old system of class antagonism, disharmony, and contentiousness would continue to characterize industrial relations. But if workers gained a voice through plant committees, the opportunity would be present for worker and employer to discuss grievances, production problems, and all other matters affecting the welfare of employees and the success of the business. With an intelligent system of representation, the new economic system could claim the loyalty of the worker and his active support in solving problems of productivity and waste. Without such a system, class antagonism, local grievances, and worker alienation would eat away at even the most progressive system of technology and enlightened management.[41]

Hoover's views on worker representation bore similarities to the views of a number of practitioners of the relatively new discipline of personnel management, and to the ideas of progressive-minded corporate executives. At the same time, but from a different angle, they came close to ideas germinating in the American Federation of Labor. The men in charge of personnel matters for such large corporations as United States Rubber, Goodyear, Standard Oil of New Jersey, International Harvester, and others involved in mass production agreed that it was essential for corporations to gain the active loyalty of their employees. To such executives and personnel specialists as Clarence J.

Hicks, Cyrus Ching, Arthur H. Young, Mackenzie King, and Alexander Legge, concern for employee welfare, including efforts to establish communication with workers through various plans of representation, made good sense. They agreed with Hoover that the long working day, the fear of arbitrary dismissal, and the subsistence wage were vestiges of the industrial past. Workers who had economic, social, and psychological ties to the corporation, they felt, performed their tasks more efficiently, were less critical of management's policies, and were less prone to absenteeism and frequent job changing.[42]

Hoover's call for representation, of course, found favor with the labor movement as well. Certainly Samuel Gompers and other laborites had always proclaimed the right of workers to free and uncoerced representation; this concept was the very essence of organized labor. Moreover, many laborites harbored hopes that in the postwar industrial milieu—a period which began with organized labor in a stronger and more influential position than ever before—the unions could expand, not only in membership, but in control over industrial processes as well. In fits and starts, inconsistently and amid other concerns, the labor movement put forth claims for consultation in the operation of the economic system. In part extending the logic of their own long term commitments, in part responding to public pressure to help boost productivity, and in part influenced by favorable contacts with progressive engineers and industrial management experts during and after the war, such laborite figures as Matthew Woll, William English Walling, Hugh Frayne, and Gompers himself asserted the need to restructure the American economy and its system of industrial relations. Workers and unions, these and other spokesmen acknowledged, should indeed be concerned about the broad problems of productivity and efficiency. At the same time, they asserted labor's right to representation and consultation in the efforts of industry to meet the postwar challenges. And, of course, the only legitimate vehicle for such representation was the American Federation of Labor and the other *bona fide* labor organizations.[43]

Fundamentally, labor's notions of representation and those of even the most progressive corporations were irreconcilable. Employee representation to a laborite meant a vigorous, independent, and active union. Employee representation to the overwhelming majority of those associated with welfare capitalism in the 1920s meant shop councils of workers chosen from within the plant. While theoretically open to the participation of members of unions, these bodies were conceived of as rival centers of activity and were often inaugurated in part to preclude or eliminate trade unionism. Although Hoover joined academicians and engineers in urging unionists and employers to resolve their differences in the matter of representation, in fact the interests of the two parties were fundamental and irreconcilable.[44]

Throughout the 1920s, organized labor retreated from its initial postwar aggressiveness and waged a rear guard defense against the employee representation/welfare capitalism movement. Many factors combined to the disadvantage of the AFL and other standard organizations. A hostile public attitude, unrelenting judicial assaults, political isolation, and erosion of the labor force in traditional areas of union strength all played their parts. In addition, organized labor's own weaknesses and confusions loomed large. When expressed by Gompers, labor's new-found interest in productivity and efficiency was plausible and not necessarily inconsistent with tough-minded trade unionism. When put forth by the meeker, less prestigious William Green, such notions smacked of blatant class collaborationism. Then too, the AFL did not organize the unorganized. Proclaim as it did its right to speak for workers as a class, its membership declined sharply. More important, its remaining strength became ever more narrowly concentrated in a few protected occupations, while the vast tides of workers manning the relatively new mass production industries remained unorganized. After the bitter defeat in steel in 1919 and 1920, the AFL could muster only one half-hearted assault on the new industries: its ill-conceived and ill-supported gesture at organizing the automobile industry in 1927.[45]

While traditional unionism declined and narrowed, employee representation under corporate auspices mushroomed. By 1929, almost 2,000,000 workers were enrolled in various plans of representation. These varied from elaborate schemes of "congressional" representation, in which spokesmen for workers, supervisory personnel, and management recapitulated the three branches of the federal government, to simple shop committees. These experiments were particularly noticeable in mass production industries and were closely intertwined with the welfare capitalism that personnel management enthusiasts promoted as a means of mobilizing workers in support of corporate loyalty.[46]

Hoover never realized that employee representation constituted a major threat to trade unionism in several respects. On the most basic level, even "enlightened" employers frequently used these schemes as part of an anti-union program. Of course, employers rarely revealed this intention explicitly; they contended that both union and nonunion workers were free to join and participate. But since the essence of American trade unionism in the 1920s was collective bargaining, and since employee representation plans by definition precluded such arrangements, it was clear that the presence of union men would be nothing more than a token gesture. During the war, the AFL had endorsed the War Industries Board's shop councils, but only because laborites expected that these bodies under government supervision would either be dominated by the union or would serve in open shops as bridges to *bona fide* organization. Shortly after the war ended, when it became apparent that employers were promoting shop councils as a means of eliminating trade unionism, the AFL condemned all forms of nonunion employee representation.[47] Hoover supported both "collective bargaining" and "employee representation" but did not acknowledge the basic divergence of these two goals in the 1920s.

On another level, representation plans threatened the labor movement because of the apparent popularity they enjoyed among some workers. The craft-dominated AFL held little appeal for workers in mass-production industries. Its jealously guarded jurisdictional satrapies made no sense to hundreds of thousands of new mass production workers. Nor did these recruits to the new industrial society find much in its combination of craft exclusivism and organizational passivity to stir their hearts. Clarence J. Hicks, personnel director of Standard Oil of New Jersey and one of the most astute proponents of welfare capitalism, remarked that the AFL's distaste for the representation of employees in the mass production industries in shop councils "was entirely consistent with its traditional slowness" in attempting to organize the unskilled masses.[48]

So effective were some representation plans in securing and retaining worker loyalty, one economist asserted, that "the battle is not so much between the unions and the employers as between groups of employees." Academic observers with close ties to the labor movement, such as William Leiserson, Leo Wolman, and George Barnett, all saw employee representation as a vigorous and plausible alternative to traditional trade unionism. Corporations using employee representation found it effective in channeling and buffering employee grievances, creating a sense of loyalty to and identification with the company among workers, and discouraging trade unionism. Although representation plans provided far more propaganda and good will value to employers than they did democratic representation to workers, the labor movement seemed unable to meet their challenge.[49]

Given his oft-repeated postwar emphasis on the importance of effective representation, Hoover was curiously silent during his cabinet years on the subject. He played a leading part in many labor controversies, helping to mediate the 1922 shopmen's strike and becoming directly involved in efforts to pacify the turbulent coal industry, for example.[50] He maintained friendly relationships with many trade unionists, who in turn listened attentively to his many pleas for productivity and efficiency.[51] However, although he verbally deplored the use of representation schemes by employers as a means of defeating trade unionism, he concerned himself hardly at all with the actual patterns of representation that developed. Thus, while organized labor thrashed about, desperately seeking ways of coming to terms with the adverse climate of affairs in the 1920s, Hoover remained on the sidelines, apparently unwilling to subject the actual functioning of the employee representation movement to the test of fairness and integrity that he had himself urged in his postwar recommendations. Forceful and articulate in his exposure of problems of production and efficiency, he was silent and acquiescent in his attitude towards representation.

Hoover did not express himself directly as to his enthusiasm for the pattern that was emerging in employee representation. Nonetheless, his lack of commentary on the issue of representation throughout the late 1920s and during the 1928 presidential campaign contrasts with the vigor and sense of commitment characteristic of his earlier utterances. Moreover, while Hoover himself did not comment directly on the decay of the AFL, several academicians closely associated with his activities in the 1920s did. Leo Wolman, who served on the Conference on Unemployment and who wrote major sections of the *Recent Economic Changes* and *Recent Social Trends* volumes, frequently expressed pessimism about the ability of the unions to cope with the changing economic system, as did Professor George Barnett of Johns Hopkins University, a consultant for Hoover-inspired projects in the 1920s. Herbert Hoover's brother, Theodore Jesse Hoover, dean of the School of Mining at Stanford, wrote in 1932 that unions were destined for replacement by "company unions, open forums, and the like" unless they rapidly adjusted to new conditions. The secretary of commerce could not express himself directly on these matters and still retain the good will of labor leaders, but his silence on the representation matter, together with the social and intellectual ambience that surrounded him, suggests that he accepted the patterns of employee representation that prevailed in company-sponsored programs as legitimate.[52]

Several factors help to account for Hoover's relative inaction. The problem of asserting rights to effective representation was, after all, organized labor's. Short of sponsoring sweeping federal involvement in the creation of a drastically innovative system of collective bargaining, he could only publicize and exhort.[53] Labor's inability to meet the challenge of welfare capitalism bespoke its anachronistic structure and its inability to change in tune with modern capitalism. Still, Hoover could and did speak out vigorously and effectively on other public issues of concern to him, in sharp contrast to his inaction in the field of representation.

Moreover, Hoover's postwar utterances were never very precise about the exact nature of representation and its relationship to unionism. While he asserted frequently the need for workers to acquire a voice in industry, he refused to specify the nature of such representation. The strong implication behind the shop committee concept was that it would function somehow separately from whatever union organization that might exist in the shop. Hoover saw shop committees as opportunities for workers and employers to meet together directly to discuss grievances, production problems, and general conditions. Such a system, while in Hoover's view fully compatible with a union agreement on broad conditions of employment, by no means required trade union organization. Hoover was never able to grasp labor's objections to shop committees as bodies inherently manipulative and destructive of solidarity. Hoover envisaged the organization of workers together with employers; organized labor regarded the organization of workers in their own unions as a requisite to any subsequent cooperation or negotiation with employers. This difference was fundamental, though never acknowledged by Hoover as such.[54]

His inability to come to grips with unionists' objections to shop committees in part reflected his background. Hoover's natural associations were not with laborites but rather with the progressive and innovative managers who ran the emerging industrial machine. He was impressed with the efforts of John D. Rockefeller, Jr., Clarence J. Hicks, Mackenzie King, and other practitioners of welfare capitalism and company-sponsored employee representation. During his service on the President's Second Industrial Conference he conferred with Rockefeller about the plan he was developing. When Mackenzie King, architect of Rockefeller's plan of nonunion representation for the Colorado Fuel and Iron Company, praised the conference's recommendations, Hoover publicly advertised King's remarks. He considered Alexander Legge, a key figure in the development of International Harvester's "model" representation system, one of the ablest and most progressive of corporate leaders. He was thoroughly familiar with the employers in the Special Conference Committee, an inter-industry body formed after World War I and designed to coordinate nonunion employee representation efforts.[55]

Hoover's high regard for the good intentions and abilities of corporate managers stemmed from his analysis of the transformation of the economy. Increasingly, ownership was separated from management, thus greatly diffusing corporate power. New managers, he declared, "are gradually coming into a new vision of their relationships" with capital, labor, and consumer. Increases in productivity and improvements in efficiency, he proclaimed in 1925, "are bound . . . to be shared with labor to secure service and contentment." The age of big business as an arbitrary and ruthlessly exploitative force was past; under the new arrangements, he declared, "labor has the opportunity to interpret co-operation with management into [sic] real gains." Apparently, to Hoover the shrinkage of organized labor's membership and its growing, partly self-imposed isolation from the new mass production industries did not impair the efficacy of this evolving industrial "regime." Hoover regarded the effective organization of workers, despite the concurrent decline of the labor movement itself, as a kind of built-in concomitant of the emerging economic order, a view that implicitly accepted nonunion employee represension programs as legitimate responses to his call for representation.[56]

In 1920, Hoover has asserted that "the friction between employer and employee in developing collective bargaining arises almost wholly over the question of representation and questions of enforcement."[57] It is true that he verbally criticized employers who resorted to shop committees for antilabor purposes, and he did sporadically attempt to bring corporate managers into liaison with AFL leaders. But when these men refused to contemplate the relinquishment of managerial prerogatives that meaningful association with organized labor would have entailed, Hoover confined whatever disapproval he felt to private expression. Throughout the 1920s organized labor declined, while thousands of workers, bereft of the experience, expertise, and financial strength that only a national labor movement could have provided, were enrolled in company unions and related plans of representation.

By 1929, the partial achievement of Hoover's postwar goals left the American wage-earner in an ambiguous position. His labors were increasingly productive and he could choose from a wide range of modern appliances and consumer luxuries. Still, wages lagged substantially behind productivity; beneath the surface of working-class life lurked the demands of assembly-line production, economic and social insecurity, and powerlessness.[58] Without an effective labor movement, American workers could only hope that the "new economic system" would continue to function with the apparent efficiency and vigor it had displayed since the mid-1920s, for they had not yet achieved their own sources of strength from which to hold the system to account.

Hoover was sharply aware that severe economic and labor problems remained. His efforts to rationalize the soft coal industry boomeranged into bitter recriminations between himself and John L. Lewis, while in 1927 the bituminous miners launched one last, desperate strike. The construction industry was hampered by jurisdictional problems, seasonal operations, and inadequate integration of supplies. Unemployment in the late twenties remained inexplicably high, while stagnation and labor strife afflicted the cotton textile industry.[59]

From his earliest days in office, Hoover had realized that as a busy administrator he could not hope fully to implement or even define clearly all of his goals. He did think, however, that he could encourage long-range study and information-gathering that would eventually supply data and recommendations for future use. To this end he encouraged the engineering studies of waste in industry and the twelve-hour day. Material developed by the engineers formed a part of the investigations of the United States Coal Commission, a body created in 1922 that Hoover hoped would point the way out of the recurrent chaos and crisis in coal mining. Through his direct support, the President's Conference on Unemployment, cooperating with the National Bureau of Economic Research, conducted three influential studies, culminating in the publication in 1929 of the two-volume *Recent Economic Changes*.[60] In dealing with economic problems in general, all of these investigations bore substantially on the place of labor in American life in the 1920s.

In this tradition, but even more ambitious, was the project begun through Hoover's initiative in the late twenties that resulted in the two volume *Recent Social Trends*. A massive survey of the state of the American people and their institutions as of the late 1920s, this study contained a major segment on labor affairs. It further documented the new affluence of the American worker, emphasizing his remarkable access to education, housing, recreation, and travel.[61] The chapters on labor, written by economists Leo Wolman and Gustav Peck, also commented on changing patterns of worker representation, documenting the decline of the standard unions and the rise of other forms of representation. Wolman and Peck suggested that the present trends might well "end in the disintegration of the labor movement in its present form." Since in their view the trend in society generally was toward democracy and assertiveness, they raised the possibility of "the rise of new labor organizations, radical in purpose and industrial in form." Noting the popularity and success of other means of representation, particularly in larger and more modern factories, the economists also held out the "possibility that the numerous plant and establishment organizations of labor, created as a rule by the initiative of the employer and surviving by his consent, will be converted by the stress of conditions into independent and autonomous unions which will serve as the nucleus of the American labor movement in the future."[62]

By the time *Recent Social Trends* appeared, Hoover was an ex-president, unable to use this massive survey directly in the formulation of public policy. But the observations of Wolman and Peck accurately delineated the options available to American workers in the years ahead, options that they would mold into the distinctive features of the American labor movement that they would create in the 1930s. Retrospectively, the economists' remarks also depicted the options available to Hoover in his contemplation of the problem of labor representation in the 1920s. Regarding militancy and radicalism as wasteful and authoritarian, but increasingly aware of the paralysis and obsolescence of the AFL, Hoover implicitly placed his hopes for effective representation in the employee representation plan. When it collapsed under the weight of the depression and its own limitations, and when American workers chose more aggressive forms of protest, Hoover could only respond with futile invective. As the depression spelled the end of his particular vision of liberal capitalist society, it also discredited his conception of the role of the worker in this "new economic system."

NOTES

*I wish to thank the Kansas State University Board of General Research for financial assistance in the preparation of this paper and Robert Wood, assistant director of the Herbert Hoover Presidential Library, for his invaluable aid in locating materials.

1   Haggai Hurvitz, "The Meaning of Industrial Conflict in Some Ideologies of the Early 1920's: The AFL, Organized Employers, and Herbert Hoover," Ph.D. Diss. (Columbia U., 1971), 20; Robert H. Zieger, *Republicans and Labor, 1919-1929* (Lexington, 1969), pp. 1-9.

2   Hoover used this phrase on November 16, 1920, in a presentation before the AFL Executive Council. Herbert C. Hoover Papers (Herbert Hoover Presidential Library, West Branch, Iowa), Pre-Commerce Files, Industrial Waste Committee—AF of L Correspondence. This document is unidentified as to authorship, but see Hurvitz, "The Meaning of Industrial Conflict," 256-58 for convincing evidence of Hoover's authorship.

3   On Hoover and labor in general, see Stephen J. Scheinberg, "The Development of Corporation Labor Policy, 1900-1940," Ph.D. Diss. (U. of Wisconsin, 1966), esp. 140-51; Ronald Radosh, "The Development of the Corporate Ideology of American Labor Leaders, 1914-1933," Ph.D. Diss. (U. of Wisconsin, 1967), esp. 81-94, 149-55, and 187-88; David Walter Eakins, "The Development of Corporate Liberal Policy Research in the United States, 1885-1965," Ph.D. Diss. (U. of Wisconsin, 1966), 158-70; and Hurvitz, "The Meaning of Industrial Conflict," passim, Scheinberg, Radosh, and Eakins were all students of William A. Williams, whose writings (e.g., *The Contours of American History* [Cleveland, 1961; page references to paperback edition, 1966], pp. 415 and 424-32; *Some Presidents: Wilson to Nixon* [New York, 1972], 38-49) have stimulated widespread reexamination of Hoover. Joan Hoff Wilson, *Herbert Hoover: Forgotten Progressive* (Boston, 1975) touches on Hoover and labor, pp. 33-34 and 94-98. See also Robert H. Zieger, "Labor, Progressivism, and Herbert Hoover in the 1920's," *Wisconsin Magazine of History,* 58 (Spring 1975), 196-208, and *Republicans and Labor.*

4   See Hurvitz, "The Meaning of Industrial Conflict" for the best overall presentation of Hoover's ideas during this period. Providing a suggestive context into which to place Hoover's views are Charles Forcey, *The Crossroads of Liberalism: Croly, Weyl, Lippmann, and the Progressive Era, 1900-1925* (New York, 1961; page references to paperback edition, 1967), pp. 35-37, 83, 157-58, 166, 183, 190; and James Gilbert, *Designing the Industrial State: The Intellectual Pursuit of Collectivism in America, 1880-1940* (Chicago, 1972), esp. chapter 4. See also Ross Thomas Runfola, "Herbert C. Hoover as Secretary of Commerce, 1921-1923: Domestic Economic Planning in the Harding Years," Ph.D. Diss. (State U. of N.Y.—Buffalo, 1973) and Evan B. Metcalf, "Secretary Hoover and the Emergence of Macroeconomic Management," *Business History Review,* 49 (Spring 1975), 60-80. The work of Ellis W. Hawley (e.g., "Herbert Hoover, the Commerce Secretariat, and the Vision of an 'Associative State,' 1921-1928," *Journal of American History,* 61 [June 1974], 116-40) is richly suggestive on the importance of Hoover's political economy.

5   Hoover, Address to American Institute of Mining and Metallurgical Engineers, November 16, 1919, Hoover Papers, Public Statements, No. 25.

6   Hoover, Foreword to *America and the New Era* by M. Friedman, February 4, 1920, Hoover Papers, Public Statements, No. 42A.

7   Hoover address, "Economic, Social, and Industrial Problems Confronting the Na-

tion," April 1920, Hoover Papers, Public Statements, No. 55A; *New York Times,* February 18, 1920.

8   Hoover address, April 1920, Hoover Papers, Public Statements, No. 55A. For other expressions along these lines, see also Hoover address before Boston Chamber of Commerce, March 24, 1920, Hoover Papers, Public Statements, No. 53; Hoover testimony, May 14, 1920, in U.S. Congress, Senate, Committee on Education and Labor, *Hearing . . . on the Report of the Industrial Conference,* 66 Cong., 2 Sess. (1920), pp. 25–42; and Hoover's remarks before the AFL Executive Council, November 16, 1920, cited in note 2.

9   In addition to sources cited in notes 3, 4, and 18, see Wilson, *Herbert Hoover,* pp. 33–43 and Gary Dean Best, *The Politics of American Individualism: Herbert Hoover in Transition, 1918-1921* (Westport, 1975), pp. v–vi and 91–107. A lucid account of the changing structure of the American factory system and attendant developments in employee relations in the progressive era is found in Daniel Nelson, *Managers and Workers: Origins of the New Factory System in the United States, 1880-1920* (Madison, 1975). Nelson's *Unemployment Insurance: The American Experience, 1915-1935* (Madison, 1969), pp. 22, 30, 36–39, 75, 129, and passim examines an important aspect of the "New Emphasis" in employee relations and indicates Hoover's place in its development and articulation.

10   For Hoover's seminal role in the conference and his authorship in its most significant items, see Hurvitz, "The Meaning of Industrial Conflict," 174–87; Best, *The Politics of American Individualism,* pp. 38–53; and Best, "President Wilson's Second Industrial Conference, 1919-1920," *Labor History,* 16 (Fall 1975), 505–20.

11   President's Second Industrial Conference, *Report of the Industrial Conference Called by the President* [dated March 6, 1920], in U.S. Department of Labor, *Annual Report for 1920* (Washington, 1921), pp. 236–71. The words quoted appear on pp. 236–38. The phraseology of the *Report* and of Hoover's testimony before the Senate Committee on Labor and Education in its behalf closely parallels the language employed by the Whitley Committee in its famous 1917 report which made similar recommendations on the future of industrial relations in Great Britain. See H. A. Clegg, *The System of Industrial Relations in Great Britain* (Oxford, 1970), 185–86.

12   The observations in these three paragraphs are drawn from an examination of the entire spectrum of Hoover's public career as it related to labor matters. See *Report of the Industrial Conference,* pp. 254–56; Best, *The Politics of American Individualism,* pp. 45–47; and Hurvitz, "The Meaning of Industrial Conflict," 174–87. The Second Industrial Conference generated a considerable amount of testimony, as well as many reports and working papers on the subject of employee representation and its relationship to trade unionism and collective bargaining. These materials are housed in the William B. Wilson Papers, Pennsylvania Historical Society, Philadelphia. Wilson was the chairman of the conference, but Hoover as vice-chairman presided over most of the meetings held while these materials were developed. The scholar quoted is Carroll E. French in *The Shop Committee in the United States,* Johns Hopkins Studies in Historical and Political Science, 41 (Baltimore, 1923), p. 53. Hoover's clearest expressions are in Herbert Hoover, "Strike Cure—And Its Critics," *Collier's* (October 25, 1920), reprint in Hoover Papers, Public Statements, No. 100; and Hoover testimony, May 14, 1920 (cited in note 8), 25–42. See also Zieger, *Republicans and Labor,* passim.

13   For opposition among businessmen, see Hoover address before Boston Chamber of Commerce (cited in note 8) and Hurvitz, "The Meaning of Industrial Conflict,"

220-21. For labor's objections, *ibid.,* 221-22; Philip A. Taft, *The A.F. of L. in the Time of Gompers* (New York, 1957), pp. 400-01; Samuel Gompers's statement of March 19, 1920, quoted in William English Walling, *American Labor and American Democracy,* 2 vols. (New York, 1926), 2:35. Hurvitz hails the *Report* as a major and innovative step toward public endorsement of unionism and seems perplexed by labor's rejection of its recommendations (Hurvitz, "The Meaning of Industrial Conflict," 222-23).

14 Hoover address before Boston Chamber of Commerce, cited in note 8; Hoover testimony in *Hearing . . . on the Report of the Industrial Conference,* pp. 33-39.

15 *Ibid.,* pp. 35-36, 38-39, 41.

16 *Ibid.,* p. 36.

17 *Ibid.,* p. 36.

18 There is an extensive literature on the engineers and their efforts to become established as a social factor. See Edwin T. Layton, *The Revolt of the Engineers: Social Responsibility and the American Engineering Movement* (Cleveland, 1971), esp. pp. 190-211; Hugh G. J. Aitken, *Taylorism at Watertown Arsenal: Scientific Management in Action, 1908-1915* (Cambridge, 1960); and William Ernest Akin, "Technocracy and the American Dream: The Technocracy Movement, 1919-1936," Ph.D. Diss. (U. of Rochester, 1971), 19-20.

19 Hoover's remarks are in his Foreword to *America and the New Era,* cited in note 6. For the background of the FAES, see Layton, *Revolt,* pp. 180-89. In 1923 Hoover remarked that engineers were uniquely suited for public service and were by definition men of high intelligence and calibre. "Through the nature of their calling," he remarked, they stand "midway in the conflicts between labor and capital." Hoover to Richard Humphrey, February 1, 1923, Hoover Papers, Commerce Section, FAES, 1922-24. Cf. Herbert Hoover, *Principles of Mining: Valuation, Organization, and Administration* (New York, 1909), p. 167.

20 See the sources cited in notes 18 and 19 above. For Hoover's comments on his role as an employer of labor while running mines, see *Principles of Mining,* pp. 162-63 and 167, as well as Hoover address before the Boston Chamber of Commerce (cited in note 8), wherein he declared that "in my own experience in industry, I have always found that a frank and friendly acceptance of the unions' agreements, while still maintaining the open shop, has led to constructive relationship."

21 On Wallace, see his undated, untitled address (ca. early 1921), Hoover Papers, Pre-Commerce Files, FAES—Industrial Waste Committee, Labor. On the Waste in Industry Survey, see Samuel Haber, *Efficiency and Uplift: Scientific Management in the Progressive Era, 1890-1920* (Chicago, 1964), pp. 159-60, and Layton, *Revolt,* pp. 201-05. On the cooperation between Hoover's aides and laborites, see the considerable correspondence between Edward Eyre Hunt, Robert Wolf, and Florence C. Thorne throughout late 1920 and early 1921. These communications appear in various folders in the FAES group, Commerce Section, Hoover Papers. See also Jean Trepp McKelvey, *AFL Attitudes Toward Production,* Cornell Studies in Industrial and Labor Relations, (Ithaca, 1952), 2:69 and 117, and Milton J. Nadworny, *Scientific Management and the Unions, 1900-1932* (Cambridge, 1955), pp. 119-21.

22 Committee on the Elimination of Waste in Industry, Federated American Engineering Societies, *Waste in Industry* (New York, 1921), pp. 8-9, 13, 16-17, 305-06,

308-17, and passim. Hoover's remarks occur on p. ix.

23 *New York Times,* June 4, 1921, p. 7; Layton, *Revolt,* pp. 195, 203–05; Nadworny, *Scientific Management,* pp. 120–21.

24 For examples of direct Hoover-Gompers contact during this period, see Gompers to Hoover, August 13, 1920; Christian A. Herter to Gompers, August 17, 1920; and Hoover to Gompers, October 23, 1920, all in Hoover Papers, Pre-Commerce Files, FAES—Industrial Waste Committee—Gompers. See also "Conference in Office of President Gompers, Friday, May 27, 1921 on the Question of Wage Theory," AFL Papers (State Historical Society of Wisconsin, Madison, Wisconsin), Office of the President Files, Box 57, Conferences, 1919–1922. This lengthy report delineates better than any published account the shrewd awareness of labor's self-interest that Gompers displayed in the AFL's association with the engineers during this period.

25 Hoover remarks before AFL Executive Council, November 16, 1920, cited in note 2; Robert B. Wolf to E. E. Hunt, January 3, 1921, Hoover Papers, Pre-Commerce Files, FAES—AFL, 1920; Hurvitz, "Meaning of Industrial Conflict," 245–50; Cyrus Ching, *Review and Reflection: A Half-Century of Labor Relations* (New York, 1953), pp. 27–28; Scheinberg, "The Development of Corporate Labor Policy," 145–46.

26 Hoover remarks before AFL Executive Council, November 16, 1920, cited in note 2; Hoover to Gompers, October 23, 1920, Hoover Papers, Pre-Commerce Files, FAES—Industrial Waste Committee—Gompers.

27 Gompers to Hoover, November 30, 1920, Hoover Papers, Pre-Commerce Files, FAES—Industrial Waste Committee-Gompers.

28 Edward E. Hunt to Frank Morrison, November 29, 1920; Morrison to Hunt, December 2, 1920; Hunt to Morrison, December 8, 1920, all in Hoover Papers, Pre-Commerce Files, Industrial Waste Committee—AF of L Correspondence.

29 McKelvey, *AFL Attitudes,* pp. 85, 89; James O. Morris, *Conflict Within the AFL: A Study of Craft Versus Industrial Unionism* (Ithaca, 1958), p. 71. McKelvey (p. 69) emphasizes that this association between laborites and engineers reached its peak just as the massive open shop campaign began making headway. See also note 24.

30 There was an extensive and rather cryptic correspondence between Hunt, Robert Wolf, and Florence C. Thorne, Gompers's administrative assistant, from November 1920 to March 1921. See, e.g., Florence C. Thorne to Hunt, December 29, 1920; Thorne to Wolf, date missing but ca. January 1921; Wolf to Hunt, January 3, 1921; exchange between Wolf and Hunt, January 8, 10, 1921, all in Hoover Papers, Pre-Commerce Files, Industrial Waste Committee—AFL, 1920–1921.

31 Hunt to Thorne, March 2, 1921, Hoover Papers, Pre-Commerce Files, Industrial Waste Committee: E. E. Hunt.

32 For some of the recent literature on Hoover's overall policies in the 1920s see Wilson, *Herbert Hoover,* pp. 283–300, and the articles by Metcalf and Hawley cited in note 4. Akin, "Technocracy and the American Dream," 111, cites figures on productivity.

33 Zieger, *Republicans and Labor,* pp. 9, 57–60, 69, 109–110; Robert H. Zieger, "The Career of James J. Davis," *Pennsylvania Magazine of History and Biography,* 98 (January 1974), 74–84; John Bruce Dudley, "James J. Davis: Secretary of Labor under Three Presidents, 1921–1930," Ph.D. Diss. (Ball State University, 1972).

34   Herbert C. Hoover, *The Memoirs of Herbert Hoover: The Cabinet and the Presidency* (New York, 1952), pp. 40-258, passim. Hoover addresses: "Reducing the Cost of Distribution," January 14-15, 1925; "Elimination of Industrial Waste in its Relation to Labor," April 11, 1925; and "The Public Relations of Advertising," May 11, 1925, all in Public Statements, Hoover Papers.

35   Leo Wolman in Conference on Unemployment, *Recent Economic Changes in the United States: Report of the Committee on Recent Economic Changes of the President's Conference on Unemployment*, 2 vols. (New York, 1929), 1, ch. 1, and 2, ch. 6; Leo Wolman and Gustav Peck, "Labor Groups in the Social Structure," in Research Committee on Recent Social Trends, *Recent Social Trends*, 2 vols. (New York, 1933), 1:801-56; Robert S. and Helen Merrell Lynd, *Middletown: A Study in Contemporary American Culture* (New York, 1929), pp. 64-65, 81-82. The Lynds' brilliant study, however, depicts the life of working class people in Middletown as declining in occupational mobility, job satisfaction, and neighborhood comradeship.

36   Hoover's remarks are reprinted in *Memoirs, Cabinet and Presidency*, pp. 183-84; Wolman in *Recent Economic Changes*, 1:13-78, esp. 59-62.

37   Among many speeches and writings reflecting these themes, see, e.g., "Reduction of Waste in Government," May 21, 1925; "State Versus Federal Regulation in the Transformation of the Power Industry," June 17, 1925; "Commercial Aviation," September 23, 1925; "Government Ownership," September 29, 1925; and "Why the Public Interest Requires State Rather than Federal Regulation," October 14, 1925, all in Public Statements, Hoover Papers. See also *Memoirs, Cabinet and Presidency*, passim, and Herbert Hoover, *American Individualism* (Garden City, 1922), as well as Zieger, *Republicans and Labor*, pp. 60-63. For a trenchant contemporary critique of Hoover's brand of localism, see Walling, *American Labor and American Democracy*, 1:210.

38   On the effort against unemployment, see Carolyn Grin, "The Unemployment Conference of 1921: An Experiment in National Cooperative Planning," *Mid-America*, 55 (April 1973), 83-107, and Zieger, *Republicans and Labor*, pp. 88-97. The words quoted appear respectively in President's Conference on Unemployment, *Report* (Washington, 1921), p. 28, and Hoover address of September 17, 1928, in Hoover, *The New Day: Campaign Speeches of Herbert Hoover* (Stanford, 1928), pp. 66-67.

39   Zieger, *Republicans and Labor*, pp. 97-108; Hoover, *Memoirs, Cabinet and Presidency*, pp. 103-05; Charles Hill, "Fighting the Twelve-Hour Day in the American Steel Industry," *Labor History*, 15 (Winter 1974), 19-35.

40   Zieger, *Republicans and Labor*, 107-08; David Brody, *Steelworkers in America: The Nonunion Era* (Cambridge, 1960), p. 274; Paul S. Taylor, *Mexican Labor in the United States*, University of California Publications in Economics, Vol. 7, 1931-1932, 2 vols. (Berkeley, 1932), 2:34-39.

41   The sources cited in footnotes 2, 5, 6, 7, and 8 above, together with Hurvitz, "The Meaning of Industrial Conflict," 172 and passim, reveal the central importance of representation in Hoover's postwar utterances.

42   The best account of welfare capitalism is Irving Bernstein, *The Lean Years: A History of the American Worker, 1920-1933* (Boston, 1960), pp. 157-89. See also Scheinberg, "The Development of Corporation Labor Policy," chapters 5 and 6; David Brody, "The Rise and Decline of Welfare Capitalism," in John Braeman, Robert H. Bremner, and David Brody, eds., *Change and Continuity in Twentieth Century America: The 1920's* (Columbus, 1968), pp. 146-78; Clarence J. Hicks. *My Life in In-*

dustrial Relations: Fifty Years in the Growth of a Profession (New York, 1941), pp. 41-84; and Cyrus Ching, *Review and Reflection,* pp. 25-31.

43   Hurvitz, "The Meaning of Industrial Conflict," chapter 2; McKelvey, *AFL Attitudes,* pp. 25-45; Walling, *American Labor and American Democracy,* 2:41-47, 82-90.

44   In addition to the works by Brody and Bernstein cited above, see Robert Ozanne, *A Century of Labor-Management Relations at McCormick and International Harvester* (Madison, 1967), chapter 7. A defense of employee representation is found in Hicks, *My Life in Industrial Relations.* See also French, *The Shop Committee in the United States,* for a scholarly contemporary account that treats employee representation as a valid, if flawed, enterprise. For indications of Hoover's interest in bringing labor leaders and progressive corporate executives together, see Ching, *Review and Reflection,* pp. 27-28; Radosh, "Corporate Ideology," 145-55, 157, 204; Morris, *Conflict Within the AFL,* pp. 68-71; Hoover to William Green, November 11, 1925, Hoover Papers, Commerce Section, AFL—William Green.

45   McKelvey, *AFL Attitudes,* pp. 45-61, 87-98; Bernstein, *Lean Years,* chapter 2.

46   Various forms of employee representation are discussed in Milton Derber, *The American Idea of Industrial Democracy, 1865-1965* (Urbana, 1970), pp. 219-63, and in Gilbert, *Designing the Industrial State,* chapter 4. The apparent success and popularity of these programs are noted in French, *The Shop Committee,* pp. 92-94; McKelvey, *AFL Attitudes,* pp. 52-61; and Brody, "The Rise and Decline of Welfare Capitalism," 162-65.

47   Shop committee advocates denied that their intent was to destroy or curtail unionism; indeed, some saw themselves as providing representation to workers ignored by the *bona fide* labor movement. See e.g., Hicks, *My Life in Industrial Relations,* pp. 78-79. Evidence of the anti-union intent and impact of the great majority of nonunion employee representation plans, however, is overwhelming. See the works by Brody, Bernstein, McKelvey, and Ozanne cited above, especially the last-named, which is based on the records of works councils at various International Harvester plants. For the AFL position, see Gompers's statement of March 19, 1920, quoted in Walling *American Labor and American Democracy,* 2:33, and McKelvey, *AFL Attitudes,* pp. 41-43, 88-89.

48   McKelvey and Brody, cited above, provide the best evidence for the real challenge that representation plans posed for the AFL. For a brilliant extension of this point into the 1930s, see David Brody, "The Expansion of the Labor Movement: Institutional Sources of Stimulus and Restraint," in Stephen E. Ambrose, ed., *Institutions in Modern America: Innovation in Structure and Process* (Baltimore, 1967), pp. 11-36. Hicks's remark is in *My Life in Industrial Relations,* p. 82.

49   The quotation is from French, *The Shop Committee,* p. 93. See also Derber, *The American Idea of Industrial Democracy,* pp. 227-29; Leo Wolman, "Industrial Relations," in Edwin R. A. Seligman and Alvin Johnson, eds., *Encyclopedia of the Social Sciences,* 15 vols. (New York, 1932), 7:715-16; William Leiserson, "Contributions of Personnel Management to Improved Labor Relations," in Wertheim Fellowship Publications, *Wertheim Lectures on Industrial Relations* (Cambridge, 1929), chapter 5; and Brody, "The Expansion of the Labor Movement," pp. 11-12.

50   Zieger, *Republicans and Labor,* pp. 110, 120, 129-30, 132-33, 137, 138, 143, 217, 227-34, 236, 247, and passim.

51   On Hoover's continuing influence among unionists, see e.g., "The Road to Industrial Democracy," *American Federationist,* 31 (June 1924), 482; Walling, *American Labor and American Democracy,* 2:32-33, 41, 91, 93, 113; and Radosh, "Corporate Ideology," 145-247, passim.

52   Theodore Jesse Hoover, *The Economics of Mining (Non-Ferrous Metals)* (Stanford, 1932), pp. 460-61. On Wolman, see Arch W. Shaw to Hoover, July 29, 1930, Hoover Papers, Presidential Subject Files, Unemployment Advisory Committee—May-July 1930, and Wolman's writings cited in notes 35, 49, and 62. On Barnett, see Brody, "The Expansion of the Labor Movement," p. 11, and L. W. Wallace to Hunt, December 24, 1920, Hoover Papers, Pre-Commerce Files, FAES—Industrial Waste Committee: Wallace, L. W.

53   Organized labor, after all, did not achieve massive organization until it secured direct federal legislative support in the 1930s. Espousal of such legislation as Section 7(a) of the National Industrial Recovery Act or the Wagner Act of 1935 was simply beyond the pale of Hoover's voluntaristic system, although it took this legislation to make possible the kind of free and fair choice that Hoover had urged after World War I.

54   See Walling, *American Labor and American Democracy,* 2:41, 93, 94, 116.

55   Hoover to Rockefeller, January 10, 1920, Hoover Papers, Pre-Commerce Files, Rockefeller; summary of Mackenzie King's remarks enclosed in Stanley King to Hoover's secretary, March 10, 1920, Hoover Papers, Pre-Commerce Files, Second Industrial Conference—General; *New York Times,* March 21, 1920. On International Harvester's reputation, see French, *The Shop Committee,* p. 41. For the Special Conference Committee, see Ozanne, *A Century of Labor-Management Relations,* pp. 156-61, and Scheinberg, "The Development of Corporation Labor Policy," 152-56. On Legge, who served as a sub-cabinet officer in Hoover's presidential administration, see Ozanne, 137, 138-39; Hoover, *Memoirs, Cabinet and Presidency,* pp. 106, 220, 255, 327; and Hicks, *My Life in Industrial Relations,* p. 44.

56   The quotations in this paragraph are drawn from Hoover's address, "Elimination of Waste in Its Relation to Labor," April 11, 1925, Hoover Papers, Public Statements. See Walling's sharp attack on these views in *American Labor and American Democracy,* 2:21-23.

57   Hoover address, November 19, 1920, Hoover Papers, Commerce Section, Federated American Engineering Societies, 1921.

58   Bernstein, *Lean Years,* chapter 1; Zieger, *Republicans and Labor,* chapter 11; Lynd and Lynd, *Middletown,* pp. 53-82.

59   Zieger, *Republicans and Labor,* pp. 234-56; Bernstein, *Lean Years,* pp. 1-43, 115-17.

60   For the work and report of the Coal Commission, see Zieger, *Republicans and Labor,* pp. 215-27. Since 1969, I have discovered a larger role for Hoover in the establishment and deliberations of the Commission, based on materials in the "Coal: USCC" file, Commerce Section, Hoover Papers. For the publications stemming from the President's Conference on Unemployment, see Herbert Heaton, *Edwin F. Gay: A Scholar in Action* (Cambridge, 1952), and the Foreword to Conference on Unemployment, *Recent Economic Changes,* vol. 1.

61   Barry D. Karl, "Presidential Planning and Social Science Research: Mr. Hoover's Experts," *Perspectives in American History,* 3 (1969), 347-409; Research Committee

on Recent Social Trends, *Recent Social Trends in the United States,* 2:825-29.

62   Wolman and Peck, "Labor Groups in the Social Structure," in *ibid.,* p. 843.

SUMMARY OF COMMENTARY BY DISCUSSANTS AND CONFEREES

Discussion of the paper began with formal commentaries by Professors George Carey of Georgetown University and George Tselos of Monmouth College. Both commended it for the new light that it shed on Hoover's activities in the labor field. Yet both also raised questions about Zieger's interpretive conclusions. For Carey the paper provided enlightening detail on the application of Hoover's philosophy to a particular policy area. It showed a creative mind working within principled commitments to productivity, decentralization, and governmental restraint; and, in Carey's judgment, the solution envisioned was definitely preferable to the kind of big labor and participation by labor bureaucracies that eventually emerged. The depression, he suggested, should be seen not as exposing an unsound solution but as creating conditions under which a sound approach lost political support, had its imperfections magnified, and was shoved aside for one creating new and greater social problems. For Tselos, the paper demonstrated that Hoover was neither a laissez-faire ideologue nor the kind of corporate society builder depicted in New Left historiography. He preached a society of corporative units yet abandoned his model for this when labor no longer seemed a threat to employer power. And for Tselos, the evidence presented by Zieger was open to other interpretations. From it, one could argue that Hoover was much more interested in achieving harmony through controlled communication channels than he was in providing weak groups with new forms of collective leverage. Or alternatively, one could argue that his real concern was with maintaining employer control and that as circumstances changed his strategy for maintaining such control also changed. As union militancy declined, the plans for participatory cooptation became unnecessary for the ends intended and were therefore shelved.

    In a brief response to the commentaries, Zieger made several points. Some writers, he noted, among them Leo Wolman, William Leiserson, and David Brody, have argued that the labor system of the late 1920s was evolving toward genuine labor participation or was at least consonant with worker values and attitudes and therefore viable so long as prosperity continued and businessmen could fulfill their promises of ever greater material benefits. Such a view, he felt, failed to take sufficient account of thwarted democratic impulses and unco-opted elements. And in regard to Hoover's motives, he could only say that the interpretation offered represented his best conjecture. Motivation was not something clearly revealed in the surviving documentation.

Much of the subsequent discussion continued to revolve around the points raised in the formal commentaries. During further exchanges concerning Hoover's motivation, Zieger agreed that Hoover's solu-tion favored his own class and Tselos was inclined to grant that the secretary had been sincere when he mistook cooptation for democratic representation. And in response to a question from Ellis Hawley, Zieger acknowledged that the drift of developments since 1950 has been toward the labor-management partnerships and corporate com-munities envisioned in Hoover's solution. He doubted, however, that this was reconciling corporate capitalism with democratic impulses, and on this point he was strongly seconded by George Tselos. The lat-ter disagreed with the view that labor was becoming more and more quiescent. The rank and file, he noted, were now rejecting numerous contracts and seemed increasingly disposed to challenge the bureau-crats in charge of what passed for collective bargaining.

In addition, Zieger answered a number of questions about other aspects of Hoover's labor policies. Hoover, he noted, favored immi-gration restriction, a child labor amendment, and scholarly studies of industrial relations. He liked the cooperative programs worked out by certain railroads and by workers and employers in the needle trades. He tried periodically to bring labor and business representatives to-gether on a national economic council. And while he signed the Norris-LaGuardia Act with some reluctance, he was outraged by the Wilkerson injunction of 1922 and worked for its modification. On this last point, Robert Murray also commented at length. Attorney General Harry Daugherty, he noted, was responsible for the injunc-tion, and at the cabinet meeting following his return from Chicago Daugherty was severely criticized. Secretary of the Interior Albert Fall had opened the attack, and Hoover, Secretary of State Charles Evans Hughes, Postmaster General Will Hays, and Secretary of Labor James J. Davis had all then lined up against Daugherty.

Finally, two other matters came in for some discussion. One was Hoover's tendency to downplay or suppress statistics showing per-sistent unemployment, increasing corporate concentration, and distributive patterns involving much larger gains for capital than for labor. This was commented on by Melvyn Leffler and George Tselos and was discussed by Zieger, who pointed out that Hoover had reasons for distrusting some of the statistics and that his perception of the modern corporation led him to discount fears of industrial concentration. The other topic of discussion was the degree of concern in the 1920s about union-corporation alliances against the consuming public. These existed, so Zieger noted, in some sectors of the construction industry, and agriculturalists often felt that high wages meant high prices. But arguments against union power tended to stress its resistance to productivity measures rather than its use to maintain monopolistic price levels.

JOAN HOFF WILSON

Herbert Hoover's Agricultural Policies, 1921–28

EDITOR'S INTRODUCTORY NOTE

Joan Hoff Wilson, currently professor of history at Arizona State University, has published extensively in the fields of American diplomatic and political history. Her *American Business and Foreign Policy, 1920–1933* (1971) was a path-breaking work in challenging established views of New Era diplomacy, exploring the period's tensions between business nationalists and internationalists, reconstructing the ideological framework embraced by New Era policy makers, and showing the extent to which Herbert Hoover had been the architect of the period's diplomatic visions and activities. Her *Ideology and Economics* (1974) offered a reinterpretation of American-Russian relations between 1918 and 1933, and in *Herbert Hoover: Forgotten Progressive* (1975) she synthesized the new scholarship on Hoover and argued that he was best understood as a progressive activist, opposed to statism and globalism yet embracing and seeking to realize progressive social ideals. In addition, she is the author of numerous articles and essays and coauthor of *Sexism in the Law: A Study of Male Beliefs and Judicial Bias in Britain and the United States* (1978).

In the paper published here, Professor Wilson traces and evaluates Hoover's efforts to find a solution for the farm problem of the 1920s, focusing particularly on how these efforts interacted with those undertaken by Secretary of Agriculture Henry C. Wallace and the sponsors of the McNary-Haugen bills. She sees both lines of action as representing a search for order and profitability through corporative institutions. Both envisioned the development of a business collectivism

Professor Wilson's paper was previously published in *Agricultural History* (April 1977), which controls the copyright.

within the agricultural sector, the differences between them being less a matter of clashing social ideals than of differing perceptions as to how the state might be used to nurture and protect the new institutions. In advancing this interpretation, Wilson breaks sharply with the older views of agricultural politics in the 1920s, views that put Hoover and Wallace on opposite sides of clashes between the "people" and the "interests" or between industrial profiteers and virtuous agriculturalists. And in evaluating the competing strategies for achieving order and profitability, she breaks with those who have credited McNary-Haugenism with being the wiser and more realistic approach. In comparison with Hoover's solution, she argues, it was simplistic, narrowly oriented, and unmindful of the problems it could generate in the international sphere. Nor was it the solution most likely to alter established patterns of power and privilege. On this point, Wilson accepts the revisionist scholarship of Gary Koerselman and concludes that those interested in maintaining the status quo were more concerned about Hoover's initiatives than about the McNary-Haugen movement.

The picture that emerges from Wilson's analysis is of a coherent and realistic solution pushed aside by rural provincials who were able to mask their interest-group orientation behind pseudo-populistic rhetoric and thus win the public relations battle. But for a number of those at the seminar, her exposure of McNary-Haugenism seemed more persuasive than her arguments concerning Hoover's coherence, realism, and progressiveness. The Hoover approach, it was argued, also had its contradictions, its misperceptions as to what was realizable, and its tendencies to accept and reinforce illiberal institutions. What it might have achieved had it won greater political support in the 1920s can only be a matter of conjecture. But one wonders if agricultural order and profitability were not unattainable without the kind of governmental interventionism that eventually came with the New Deal.

Herbert Hoover's Agricultural Policies, 1921–28

Herbert Hoover's agricultural policies have been doubly damned. First, he himself admitted that he was less than successful in solving the postwar problems of American farmers as secretary of commerce and president. Second, most agricultural studies of the 1920s have not only accepted this personal assessment of failure, but have also sided with Hoover's contemporaries who opposed his handling of the farm crisis between 1921 and 1933.[1]

Some of this opposition on the part of historians is due to a partisan attempt of liberal Democrats to justify the farm policies of Franklin Delano Roosevelt by contrast. Most of it has simply been the result of the absence until recently of serious, scholarly research into the 1920s —a period sandwiched in between the seemingly more important events that immediately preceded or followed it: the Progressive Movement and World War I; the New Deal and World War II. Ending as it did in the nation's worst depression, the decade was first repressed by many who had lived through it and then later portrayed by social scientists as frivolous at best and reactionary at worst.

Another factor contributing to the largely negative appraisal of Hoover's economic policies in general and his agricultural ones in particular is more complex and abstract. It is related to the general search for a new political and economic order undertaken by the executive branch of government, individual corporations, interest groups, and all types of American reformers—a search, semiconscious at best, that had begun in the 1880s. The first phase of this quest for more efficient governmental and economic organization climaxed in the United States just before and after World War I with the appearance of federal regulatory agencies and departmental restructuring, along with the revitalization of specialized trade associations and such broadly based, influential national economic groups as the National Association of Manufacturers, the American Bankers Association, the Chamber of Commerce of the United States, the American Farm Bureau Federation, the Farmers Union, and the National Livestock Producers Association.

It was an agonizing search for a new sense of order among human values and for more efficient organizational and industrial techniques. And it took many different forms among government officials, businessmen, farmers, and social reformers, especially during the Progressive Era. Viewed as part of the pervasive thrust toward greater rationalization of society, which was common to all industrialized nations at the turn of the century, this search for a new order in the form of socioeconomic organization, followed corporatist lines in the United States.[2]

There were two major ways in which reformers could introduce corporatist elements into the American economy in the early twentieth century. One stressed completely cooperative economic organization and regulation along neoguildist and voluntary associational lines. The other stressed federally directed and enforced organization along rigidly bureaucratic and statist lines. Progressives did not usually follow either course exclusively as indicated in the election of 1912 with the New Freedom of Woodrow Wilson and the New Nationalism of Theodore Roosevelt.

Consequently, the apparatus that emerged from this search for order was an ambiguous and often contradictory structure of federal regulatory agencies and antitrust procedures purporting to preserve liberal democratic concepts about private property, individualism, voluntary effort, and local control. Concurrently, there was a significant increase in monopolistic or oligarchic economic practices and large-scale national economic organizations at all levels of society; these often came to dominate and utilize the federal regulatory and service apparatus in their own interests. This phenomenon even occurred in the agricultural sector of the economy, which was one of the most disorganized and chaotic of all the natural resource industries.[3] It is against this background of a general search for order through progressive, corporatist reform[4] that all of Hoover's attempts at national economic planning must be viewed.[5]

Beyond any doubt agriculture more than any other "sick" sector of the economy seemed to defy his New Era economic theories. In the last half of the 1920s Hoover regretfully admitted that it had proven next to impossible to integrate the agricultural industry into his comprehensive plans for eliminating the contradictions between the domestic and foreign policies of the United States. He attributed his lack of success to the "extreme individualism" of the American farmer "which persistently keeps individuals competing with the [farmers'] cooperatives, and the natural inability of the farmers themselves to provide the large sums of working capital" to build more cooperative associations. He also believed that the agricultural industry in general lacked "skilled direction" in establishing marketing cooperatives and diversifying crop production.[6]

Hoover thought that the American farm problem was aggravated by what he called the socialist ideas of the secretary of agriculture in Harding's cabinet, Henry Cantwell Wallace. While the charge of socialism was exaggerated, it is true that before his death in 1924 Wallace and his Farm Bloc friends did more than any other single group to thwart Hoover's plans for expanding the powers of the Department of Commerce at the expense of the Department of Agriculture. They not only persistently interfered with the creation of voluntary marketing cooperatives, which Hoover regarded as the equivalent of trade associations for farmers, but also irrevocably tarnished his postwar image as a Progressive.[7]

The clash between Hoover and Wallace was a classic one of personality and ideology that had begun during World War I. Convinced that Hoover was an "exceptionally big-brained business man" who did not understand the unique problems of the farmer when he was wartime food administrator, Wallace opposed the presidential boom for Hoover, throwing his support at the GOP convention of 1920 to Illinois Governor Frank O. Lowden. Nonetheless, Hoover recognized that Wallace was "admirably fitted for the work" of secretary of agriculture. Therefore he refused to oppose the nomination of the fiery farm editor when he learned that Harding was considering him. However, Hoover steadfastly refused as secretary of commerce to turn the Food Administration files over to the Department of Agriculture because he did not want to continue their dispute over wartime price supports.[8]

These two Iowa-born cabinet members immediately disagreed about which department should have exclusive authority to send agricultural attachés abroad to obtain information needed to broaden the foreign market for American exports. As a part of a general reorganization of the executive branch proposed by Hoover, the Jones-Winslow Bill would have given such authority to the Department of Commerce, but Wallace forces in Congress finally defeated it in June 1924. As a result this jurisdictional conflict was never resolved. In fact it was exacerbated by the respective reorganizational efforts of both secretaries during the first half of the decade. Hence, the two departments often duplicated one another's domestic and overseas work in a perfect example of the kind of inefficient, bureaucratic "overlap" that Hoover so detested.[9]

Their major confrontation, however, occurred over the best way to bring the American farm industry out of its postwar decline. The secretary of agriculture favored direct government intervention in the form of a federal export corporation established for the purpose of purchasing surplus agricultural commodities and selling them abroad. Variations of this idea appeared in various congressional bills throughout the decade, most notably in McNary-Haugen legislation which embodied the so-called two-price system—a high domestic price and a low export price. The former would have been artificially determined by the United States government without relation to actual domestic supply and demand in order to stabilize the purchasing power of the farmers; while the latter would automatically be determined by the current world price.

In contrast, the secretary of commerce opposed such federal tampering with domestic prices and the natural laws of supply and demand. He also feared foreign retaliations against such large American agricultural exports in the form of trade embargoes or prohibitive tariffs. So Hoover urged instead that the government develop a system of voluntary marketing cooperatives to reduce "waste of materials and motion between the farmer and the consumer . . . and thus give a larger part of the consumer's dollar to the farmer." Such cooperatives, according to an address to the American Dairy Federation on October 1, 1924, also would have encouraged greater diversification of crops among farmers who found themselves suffering from "continuous over production," conversion of "occasional seasonal surpluses" into alternative by-products, and standardization of quality subject to government certification. "Generally," he said later in the same year at the President's Agriculture Conference, "the fundamental need is the balancing of agricultural production to our home demand."[10] These ideas constituted the underlying philosophy of both the Cooperative Marketing Act of 1926 and of the Federal Farm Board Hoover finally created as president.

On April 8, 1924, Wallace presented his most specific objections to Hoover's legislative suggestions for creating a Federal Marketing Board and system of marketing cooperatives, in a four-page letter to President Coolidge.[11] Arguing that the Capper-Williams Bill backed by the Secretary of Commerce unnecessarily altered the previous relationship of government toward agricultural cooperatives, Wallace said his department's traditional policy of simply providing information to farmers about cooperatives was satisfactory. From Wallace's point of view, dissemination of information about cooperatives was enough because he did not think they represented adequate means for solving the farm problem. Furthermore, he accused those who did of confusing the marketing of agricultural products with industrial products. (This latter argument was, of course, an indirect reference to Hoover's presumed identification with big business and inability to understand agricultural problems, a point that later pro-Farm Bloc historians accepted as fact.)[12]

By thinking more of the "particular crop than the individuals who grow it," Wallace told the president, they made the organization of marketing cooperatives an end in itself when it was at best only one of many ways to help the American farmer. He also opposed the Hoover-endorsed hierarchy of farm boards contained in the Capper-Williams Bill because it would create unnecessary overhead expenses. According to Wallace, the Department of Agriculture already did or could begin to do the work of these boards by simply using existing personnel. In addition, he predicted that such federally sponsored boards would not command the "confidence, loyalty, and whole-hearted voluntary support of the individual member" of the average cooperative. Although Wallace admitted that the federal government could do more to encourage farmers' cooperatives, he wanted this done through additional appropriations to his department, not to Hoover's.[13]

At the end of 1924 the *Annual Report* of the Department of Agriculture contended that the cooperative movement in agricultural areas had actually been "somewhat retarded in recent years by over-enthusiastic persons who have held it up as a panacea for all the ills from which the farmers are suffering." Like Wallace's earlier letter to Coolidge, this report overstressed the danger of government controlled cooperatives. Sounding curiously similar to Hoover's own philosophy of federal guidance rather than federal dictation, the Agriculture Department said: "The relationship of the Government to cooperation should be one of service. It should help the farmers market their crops just as it helps them to produce crops not by doing the work but by supplying information which the farmers cannot get for themselves. To go further would be to injure rather than aid the cooperative movement."[14]

Hoover in turn apprised President Coolidge of his detailed criticisms of Wallace's attempt to subsidize agricultural production through various export aids and the two-price system. First he questioned the constitutionality of the "equalization fee" which would be charged either producers or processors under the two-price system to make up for any loss to the government for selling surpluses at world prices. Hoover also opposed price-fixing by the United States government on the basis of his wartime experiences. "I have done more of it than any other man who lives . . . ," he once stated, "and I would not propose price-fixing in any form short of again reentering the trenches in a World War."[15] He also disagreed with Wallace and other advocates of McNary-Haugenism, who cited the marketing operations of the United States Grain Corporation during the war as precedent for establishing a federal Export Corporation. Hoover dismissed this as an illusory comparison because the Grain Corporation had succeeded in time of crisis through the voluntary and patriotic efforts and "personal influence of a small group of leading grain merchants," while the Export Corporation would now be opposed by those same private exporters. Citing examples of foreign agricultural pools established after the war, he argued that such pools usually led to strict government control of prices and production and that this would be resisted by American grain producers as contrary to their best interests in time of peace.[16]

In addition, Hoover personally thought that most farm prices had been "fixed" too high during the war and as a result had encouraged the very overproduction from which farmers were then suffering in the 1920s. Although this position was very unpopular among farmers, he remained absolutely certain from his experiences as food administrator that even greater surpluses from overproduction would result if the government established artificially high domestic prices for a select group of agricultural commodities. (Based on the "parity" principle these prices were designed to give farmers the purchasing power they had in the years before 1914.)[17]

Hoover and his agricultural advisers also foresaw that diplomatic complications would arise if these surpluses were "dumped" on foreign markets by the proposed Export Corporation in violation of the antidumping laws of many countries, including the United States. They said, among other things, that nations which normally exported agricultural products were bound to initiate economic retaliation in the form of remission of taxes, export bonuses, subsidies in shipping, and higher tariff barriers. But even more serious than this, according to Commerce Department reports, was the fact that all export debenture plans represented direct "government interference in international commercial affairs."[18]

In developing his economic foreign policy for the United States, Hoover repeatedly opposed government control of private traders. This was one of his arguments against foreign cartels and against Soviet-controlled marketing agencies. Accordingly, Dr. Alonzo E. Taylor, one of Hoover's experts on farm policy and head of the Stanford Food Research Institute, reiterated in his criticism of the first McNary-Haugen Bill a common Hoover principle of international economic relations: "Government interference in international commercial affairs tends in the direction of international trade wars." Finally, these intradepartmental reports asserted that larger American agricultural exports would hinder those debtor nations which also happened to be grain surplus-producing nations in their payment of international debts, especially to the United States, the world's leading postwar creditor.[19]

Hoover's supporters aimed their strongest criticisms of McNary-Haugenism, however, at its domestic, rather than foreign, economic and political ramifications. Although the two-price system was popular in agricultural areas because it offered "sure fire methods of getting farmers more money," it was at best a temporary expedient and not a remedy for the basic problems of the industry. By arbitrarily raising commodity prices, it would produce "sharp increases in wholesale and retail prices of food." Then, their argument continued, "organized consumers, particularly the labor unions, would react with demands for wage advances." If granted they "would promptly reappear in the prices of finished goods," and parity commodity prices would have to be readjusted upward once again. "We would thus have inaugurated," said one critic of McNary-Haugenism, "the same vicious circle of pyramidding [sic], of which we have had so many illustrations in Europe since the war." In the process "the exportable surplus might become so large that actual losses would result to the Government" unless the equalization fees were indefinitely raised, which he thought unlikely.[20]

All of these potentially negative political and economic ramifications of McNary-Haugenism finally prompted Hoover to predict that since there were six times as many families (18,000,000) who "are solely consumers of wheat" as there were wheat farming families (3,000,000), "sooner or later this vast majority would force action of government officials against the farmers' interest." "In any event," he said, "if we are to go into socialism I prefer that we should do so by the front and not the back door." In 1925 he was most pessimistic about the "justice or ability of government officials" to act fairly under such circumstances "no matter how hard they try."[21] After two more years of trying against impossible odds to change the character of Washington's bureaucratic structure, he was more convinced than ever in 1927 that the federal government was not fit to run a business.

I can't see how this Government of ours could expect, with its loosely knit system and all the political activity we have, to expand its activities into buying and selling without complete disaster. The loosely knit character of local government against federal government and its entanglements, to say nothing of the character of our election system give it no adaption [sic] whatever to the administration of business. No one can sit in the middle of the Federal Government and watch this operation of bureaucracy, even in its best sense, and have any confidence whatever as to its ability to buy, sell, and distribute commodities and services.[22]

In summary, Hoover believed that McNary-Haugen legislation would: (1) possibly disrupt harmonious economic relations with certain foreign nations; (2) create uncontrolled inflation in food prices and correspondingly inflationary demands for increased wages by organized labor; (3) encourage the same type of overproduction in agriculture that the war had; (4) benefit primarily the large agricultural producers rather than the small, traditionally independent and stubborn farmers and thus possibly produce oligopolistic control of the industry; and (5) prompt other industries to propose that the federal government aid them in a similarly direct fashion. This, of course, would mean the politicizing of the American economy with Congress becoming the focal point of extensive lobbying by major interest groups.

"I hesitate to contemplate the future of our institutions, of our government, and of our country," Hoover once remarked, "if the preoccupation of its officials is to be no longer the promotion of justice and equal opportunity but is to be devoted to barter in the markets." Thus, to Hoover, enactment of McNary-Haugen legislation meant the ultimate destruction of an American agricultural system based on informal guildist corporatism. His worst fears about statist corporatism began to come true when Wallace's son, Henry Agard Wallace, incorporated the basic philosophy of McNary-Haugenism into New Deal agricultural programs.

This is not to say that Henry Cantwell Wallace always agreed with his son's views and would have supported the same course of action in the 1930s had he lived. For example, they differed in the early 1920s over the value of high protective tariffs for farm products and the need for the government to redirect agricultural production. The elder Wallace and his son did, however, perceive differently from Hoover the use of federal power during World War I. Their opposing interpretations of wartime efforts to control farm prices lie at the heart of their socioeconomic differences in the 1920s over McNary-Haugenism and other farm measures. In particular, the depth of the Hoover-

Wallace disagreement over the way the Food Administration had handled the supply and price of pork during and immediately following the war explains much of the petty personality clashes in which they became embroiled in the early 1920s.[23]

Recent research has concluded that Hoover as food administrator did indeed make every effort to keep price supports for hog growers through the spring of 1919. He achieved this over the opposition of Secretary of the Treasury Carter Glass by obtaining a liberal interpretation of Liberty Loan provisions for extending credit to the former Allied powers, by successfully lobbying for a 100-million-dollar congressional appropriation enabling neutral and newly liberated areas to purchase American agricultural products at established wartime prices, and by working to end the Allied blockade of other potential European markets.[24] Even Wallace's son privately admitted in 1944 that when he had joined his father in criticizing Hoover in 1919 he "was not familiar with other aspects of the situation. . . . Looking back on it now I feel that the plan which I recommended to the Food Administration, while undoubtedly effective in bringing about increased hog supplies, also had inflationary possibilities of a serious nature."[25] These possibilities Hoover recognized at the time and he vowed never again to place himself in the position of guaranteeing specific prices to farmers for their products. Although he had regarded the United States Grain Corporation after World War I as "purely a commercial operation in the promotion of the sale of American [surplus] commodities," and relief organizations as "purely commercial customers of the Grain Corporation," he did not want to continue to use federal corporations or relief food purchases as a means of price support.

Hoover and Wallace were never able to resolve their personal differences over their wartime experiences with price supports. The secretary of commerce viewed price-fixing as at best a necessary evil in time of war and wanted no more of it in the twenties, while the secretary of agriculture wanted price-fixing utilized as a temporary measure to help farmers make the transition to a peacetime economy. Wallace was more than willing, therefore, to use the vast power and financial resources of the federal government to establish and maintain a two-price system and an Export Corporation, yet he exhibited an excessive fear about government influence over farmers' marketing cooperatives. Hoover, on the other hand, opposed government price-fixing, but not government-encouraged and financed cooperatives. In

essence, both secretaries proposed solutions for agricultural marketing problems. They disagreed over whether federal power should be
used *to force cooperation* from independent farmers in the marketing
of basic commodities by having them all pay the equalization fee (to
make up for any loss incurred when the government sold surpluses at
low world prices), or *to elicit voluntary cooperation* from them in following federal guidelines not only for marketing purposes, but also to
control production (which would have meant alienating some of the
largest producers and cooperative marketing associations, groups
whose interests lay in maintaining the existing system and whose
power was not threatened by the various McNary-Haugen proposals.)[27]

The other irreconcilable factor in their relationship as members of
Harding's cabinet was Hoover's conviction that the Department of
Commerce, and not the Department of Agriculture, "can materially
assist in the economic settlement of our foreign relations." With respect to American agriculture this meant several things to Hoover.
First, the exportation of farm products could not "be separated from
the other great issues of commodity movement such as transportation,
foreign tariffs, foreign exchange, credits, foreign purchasing power,
economic conditions, foreign commercial law, exchange of imports,
etc."[28] Second, in view of the traditional significance of agricultural
exports for the country's economic foreign policy, the "Department
of Agriculture should tell the farmer what he can best produce based
on soil, climatic, and other cultural conditions, and the Department of
Commerce should tell him how best to dispose of it."[29]

Aside from these two basic disagreements Wallace and Hoover
agreed on a limited number of solutions to the farm problems, even if
their most vociferous supporters did not. It is unfortunate that they
never cooperated with each other in a joint effort to help the farmer.
Such cooperation would not have solved the postwar agricultural
crisis, which was complex and worldwide,[30] but it might have eliminated some of its least admirable characteristics. Instead, even when
Hoover and Wallace agreed on a particular farm problem, they usually managed to disagree over its solution. At most, they often ended up
supporting one another's worst ideas and opposing each other's best
ones.

Both, for example, recognized that the fundamental problem of
American agriculture after World War I was overproduction. Neither,
however, was willing to support plans for federally enforced acreage
allotments. Hoover did advocate voluntary methods for curtailing

farm output, and gave strong support to ideas for converting marginal lands to pastures and for diversifying traditionally one-crop areas like the grain belt. However, he usually denied in public that he was for production control, i.e., economic scarcity for agriculture, for he knew this idea was very unpopular among most farmers. Ultimately Hoover did not think there would be a surplus problem within ten years because the "growth of population would overtake the production of non-marginal lands and when that situation arrived and increase in marginal lands was required, then farmers' prices would rectify themselves upon a tariff protected domestic market." On this question of surpluses Wallace, just as simplistically, insisted that they had to be exported by the government, regardless of rising postwar European agricultural production.[31]

Because Hoover and Wallace saw the relationship between this surplus problem and tariff protection for the American farmer, they both supported high import duties on foreign agricultural products.[32] But as long as there was a domestic surplus, high tariff rates on wheat, for example, did little for wheat farmers because their surplus drove the domestic price down to the world market level. Hence they did not dispute the fact that unless the surplus was eliminated tariff protection could never be as effective for the farmers as Republican politicians had been telling them since the 1890s. It was a question of how to eliminate the domestic surplus. Should it be through voluntary production control, crop diversification, more efficient interstate distribution methods, and increased home consumption, as Hoover advocated, or by government purchase and indiscriminate sale abroad, as Wallace proposed?

In addition, the two secretaries believed that farmers needed low interest rates and short-term credit. Yet they never participated in a joint effort to obtain such legislation. Consequently their lack of cooperation contributed to the woefully inadequate Agricultural Credits Act of 1923. Both further agreed that more facts were needed to properly analyze the farmer's problems, but each questioned the reliability of the data gathered by their respective departmental agents in the field. They were particularly suspicious of each other's statistics on agricultural conditions in foreign countries and the purchasing power of postwar American farmers. (The Commerce Department generally pegged the latter higher than the Agricultural Department.)[33] Finally, both men were considered "progressive" on the farm question by their followers, but by the middle of the decade Hoover's well-publicized (and often misrepresented) opposition to McNary-Haugenism had alienated him from some of the leading Progressives in the Congressional Farm Bloc and among the leaders of most of the national agricultural associations.

In large measure this represented the loss of a public relations battle, which the Wallace forces simply waged much better than Hoover's supporters because they successfully capitalized on misleading populist-sounding rhetoric. Nonetheless, Department of Commerce records and the *Congressional Record* clearly indicate that Hoover retained throughout the decade the support of a number of individual small farmers and some congressional Progressives. This was because the failure of the initial Farm Bloc program to solve the postwar farm crisis by 1922 increased dissension and dissatisfaction among agricultural groups, including Farm Bloc members themselves.[34]

Ironically, it was under the leadership of George N. Peek, successful midwestern farm-implement executive and president of the American Council of Agriculture, a powerful lobbying organization, that hostile relations between the country's agrarian interests and the secretary of commerce temporarily escalated after Wallace's unexpected death in October 1924. Peek could scarcely qualify as an unselfish spokesman for the common "dirt" farmer and yet that is exactly how standard agricultural studies have portrayed him. At the end of 1924, Hoover privately accused Peek, who was the chief architect of the two-price system, of distributing a memorandum containing "gross misrepresentations" about the Department of Commerce. It included the charges that Commerce officials were "invading the functions of the Department of Agriculture in foreign trade," and that Hoover personally was "endeavoring to secure the transfer of the Bureau of Markets from the Department of Agriculture."[35]

Hoover categorically denied both charges. With respect to the first one, he maintained that the Department of Agriculture was encroaching upon the long-established and legitimate promotion of United States trade abroad by Commerce officials, citing the longer experience and greater number of his personnel engaged in aiding the export of foodstuffs. On the second charge, Hoover's case was considerably weaker because the transfer of the Bureau of Markets had appeared in his first reorganization plan.

As early as 1921 Hoover had asserted that the "functions of the Department of Agriculture should end when production on the farm is complete and movement therefrom starts, and at that point the activities of the Department of Commerce should begin."[36] Subsequently, when under attack in 1924 he argued that this proposed transfer had originated in 1921 with Walter F. Brown, chairman of the Joint Committee on Reorganization. Admitting the logic of this suggestion, he said that he had "strongly advised against the transfer on public grounds." However, Hoover wrote Brown a letter and memorandum on October 20, 1921, which left little doubt that since Wallace's Bureau of Markets was sending trade promotion representatives abroad to compete with those of the Commerce Department, Hoover strongly favored the transfer at that time. He simply found it impossible to effect in 1921–22 and therefore expedient to deny in 1924–25. So he switched his emphasis to gathering data on foreign sources of raw materials and on potential agricultural export markets, which less obtrusively encroached on the existing functions of the Bureau of Agricultural Economics of the Department of Agriculture. This ended up in an inconclusive congressional fight in 1924 over which department should be the sole agency for investigating and reporting on the overseas economics and commercial aspects of American agriculture.[37]

When Peek refused Hoover's private requests to cease his propaganda campaign, Hoover insisted on a thorough investigation from Wallace before his death and then specifically requested an official denial of the charges from the interim Secretary of Agriculture Howard M. Gore at the end of 1924. Reiterating that the memorandum being distributed by Peek and the American Council of Agriculture "was a gross violation of the Cabinet confidence and deliberately intended to mislead," Hoover went out of his way to exonerate the late Secretary Wallace of the whole affair by saying "he was too great a gentleman to have had any part in such transactions," although Wallace had officially complained to Brown in January 1923 about Hoover's transfer ideas.[38]

A legal brief and detailed report prepared for Hoover on May 25, 1925, stated that Peek's memorandum had been drafted and run off by Agriculture personnel who copied almost verbatim from an editorial published in the *St. Paul Dispatch* on November 18, 1924. The information upon which the editorial was based had originally come from a mimeographed memorandum in the files of the Department of Agriculture summarizing data compiled between May 1921 and June 1924 on the subject, "Encroachments of the Department of Commerce upon the Department of Agriculture." The evidence was such against

Peek, other officials of the American Council of Agriculture, and certain junior members of the Department of Agriculture, according to this thirteen-page account, that Hoover could prosecute them under Sections 19 and 37 of the Conspiracy Statutes for attempting to discredit him and his department in the minds of other government officials and the agricultural population of the country.[39]

No legal action was ever taken against Peek, however, and the entire squabble ended unsatisfactorily for all concerned. Hoover never received the personal vindication he wanted from the Department of Agriculture, and through the summer of 1926 he continued to complain privately about Peek's attempts to smear him. "As you know," he wrote to a fellow Iowan, "I would like to find some way out of the agricultural situation just as much as would anyone in the United States but so long as the farmer is busy chasing rainbows set up by such people as George Peek, he will not listen to reason. Any suggestion advanced only brings a storm of protest that one is a criminal trying to swindle the farmer. I have made up my mind, therefore, that I will take no part in agricultural problems until I am requested to do so from a responsible section of the industry." In the Peek camp there was also little evidence of satisfaction, for the Farm Bloc in Congress was not able to overcome two presidential vetoes of McNary-Haugen legislation, and the attempt to deliver eleven midwestern food-producing states to Al Smith in 1928 failed, although farm leaders campaigned against Hoover as the "arch enemy" of farm relief.[40]

Despite his running battle with Peek, Hoover's relations with the Department of Agriculture in general improved perceptibly after Wallace's death in the fall of 1924. Hoover even joked with the interim secretary, Howard M. Gore, about how he was "not trying to absorb the activities" of that department. Most important, however, after President Coolidge appointed William M. Jardine to take Wallace's place, Hoover felt freer to explain his ideas and programs to aid the farmer in greater detail than ever before. Jardine's ideas, according to Hoover, were "sane and in line with the declared principles of the Republican party." Translated this meant Jardine supported cooperative marketing and voluntarily controlled agricultural output.[41]

Always denying that he was trying to dictate or determine farm policy, Hoover wrote to Jardine and others during 1925–26 elaborating at length the proposals for national legislation that he had been making for over two years. In particular he carefully pointed out to the new secretary of agriculture how his farmers' cooperatives were in actuality intended to be "farm marketing organizations rather than the narrower interpretations sometimes applied to cooperatives." It was absolutely necessary, he said, to get "sound . . . marketing organizations started" with government advice and financial assistance, but not government control, before individual solutions for each commodity problem could be worked out.[42]

In the short run Hoover wanted to assist farmers in forming these new organizations by creating a Federal Cooperative Marketing Board and Farm Advisory Council representing all farm commodities on a geographical basis. He estimated that federal working capital for such a nationwide endeavor would amount to ten or fifteen percent of the entire cost, or approximately $100 to $150 million. After this initial investment by the government, other sources of private credit could be drawn upon. Ultimately Hoover envisaged the creation of Central or Regional Marketing Associations "with wide power and based on the membership of existing Farmers' Marketing Organizations having the liberty to act also for non-members." These Central Marketing Associations would work to "lessen competition between [local cooperatives] and eliminate waste in distribution."[43]

"I believe," Hoover wrote in June 1926 to a midwestern cornbelt farmer, "that progress toward the elimination of agricultural booms and slumps lies in this direction . . . to regulate in greater measure the supply to the demand is consonant with the development of all forms of industry and is a necessity if the farmer is to have an equal voice in bargaining." Above all Hoover stressed that his cooperative approach for alleviating farm distress would not put the "government into the business of buying and selling. It is not government price fixing. It does not impose political control over farmers' marketing. It places entire direction of farmers' marketing within his own control."[44]

Hoover always asserted that his plans for the American farmer, unlike McNary-Haugenism, were based on economic, not political, thinking, and he logically followed up his pleas for legislation to create a system of marketing cooperatives with a call to exempt these organizations from the "restraint of trade laws." His argument here did not contradict the defense he made of antitrust legislation in connection with trade association activity because, as he stated in several addresses and press releases in 1925, "agricultural products differ from other products in that an excessive price cannot be fixed and maintained in the event a cooperative obtained a monopoly of a product." In other words, Hoover believed that there can be no continuous organization of the farmers in the marketing of their product which will militate against public interest. The reason is simply that if the production or combination of producers of any farm product demands more than his fair proportion of the total national income he will at once stimulate competition and real overproduction which will overwhelm him. . . . All of the alarm that has been expressed at the possible combination of the farmer to override the consumer against public interest is to my mind entirely unnecessary and not worthy of consideration.[45]

Even though he outlined his farm policy in greater and greater detail after 1925, most of Hoover's public statements as secretary of commerce on the question show an uncertainty that cannot be found in his pronouncements about the economic problems of other industries. Indeed, the ingrained individualism of the average farmer seemed to defy his scientific as well as his cooperative solutions. It was almost as though he unconsciously recognized that all his talk about applying the standards of the factory system to the farm did not quite ring true, or at best applied only to those farmers dealing in perishables, like the dairy and citrus fruit industries, where marketing cooperatives had been most successful. On more than one occasion, he frankly admitted that he did not know of any panacea for the farmers' dilemma, but he always qualified this admission with the idea that the right kind of conference could find the answer. "I confess I do not know how to go about it at the moment," he wrote J. G. Mitchell, a Des Moines lawyer on July 3, 1926, "but if we could get 25 sensible men in a room together without the pressure of either publicity or politics I believe the agricultural industry of the United States could be put on a basis more stable than any other industry."[46]

Hoover's most candid remarks about the agricultural problem were made two years before he became president during an off-the-record question-and-answer session at the Business Man's Conference on Agriculture in April 1927. In forty-three pages of transcript Hoover talked extensively about some of the "external issues" which complicated the farm problem such as the land boom in sections of the Midwest, the financial problems of the average farmer and how businessmen could help alleviate them, what his department was doing outside of promoting cooperatives to aid agriculture, and the relationship of the protective tariff to the farmer.[47] Hoover's frankness at this conference simply confirmed that the Commerce Department under his leadership generally recommended solutions for agriculture problems similar to those for other "sick" industries; that is, tariff protection

combined with more efficient and economical production and marketing systems, resulting in lower costs and higher wages for all Americans. The major differences between Hoover's economic policies for
agriculture and for the mining or manufacturing industries was that he
did not anticipate a growing foreign market for American staples, as
he did for American manufactured products. Hence, he placed more
emphasis on providing short-term agricultural credit and on crop
diversification than on staple production or refined food products for
export in the belief that population growth in the United States would
expand the domestic market until it absorbed the bulk of farm crops.[48]

The degree to which Hoover believed that international relations affected American agriculture cannot be overestimated. But he was
never able to convince opponents of his farm policies that the United
States had to consider the production capabilities and export needs of
foreign nations as well as its own. He had demonstrated his willingness to export food products for famine relief abroad, especially if the
American market were suffering from a surplus, as was the case in the
early 1920s. Under his direction the American Relief Administration
in Russia did just this between 1921 and 1923 and even sold a certain
percentage of the 1922 U.S. wheat crop to the Bolsheviks, whom
Hoover would not deal with under any other circumstances. He also
deliberately expanded the foreign offices of the Bureau of Foreign and
Domestic Commerce (BFDC) not only to aid the sales of manufactured goods abroad, but also to gather information and data on possible foreign agricultural markets as well. Consequently, Hoover refused to view the farm problem as an isolated domestic issue and
always dealt with it in terms of tariff policy, international loans, and
balance of payments, and the rate of postwar reconstruction taking
place in various European nations. In particular he refused to operate
under the illusion of Wallace, Peek, Norris, and others that the United
States could permanently replace Russia as the grain supplier of postwar Europe.[49]

Above all else, Hoover feared making farm profits dependent upon
any extensive foreign marketing schemes (illusory or otherwise) because of his belief in establishing as much economic self-sufficiency
for the United States as possible. He already thought that manufacturing profits were too dependent upon overseas sales. But he worried
more about how foreign debtor nations which produced the same agricultural surpluses for export as the United States would be able to
meet their balance of payments, if they had to compete with American

farmers, than he worried about those debtor nations which were trying to sell manufactured goods in direct competition with the United
States. This seeming inconsistency possibly reflects what Wallace and
Peek (and later historians) thought was Hoover's unconscious businessman's bias against farmers. Hoover personally denied this, insisting that such markets would be much more limited in the future than
those for American manufactured products, and that manufactured
exports would not obtain the same degree of dependence on foreign
markets as was the case with agriculture.[50]

His critics notwithstanding, during his eight years as secretary of
commerce, Hoover exercised considerable influence on the
agricultural administrative policy, if not popular agricultural attitudes. Despite the less than successful President's Conferences on
Agriculture in 1922 and 1924, and the Business Man's Conference on
Agriculture in 1927, the business community in general endorsed
Hoover's cooperative marketing approach rather than subsidy plans
based on a two-price system or export debenture corporations.
(However, the annual National Agricultural Conferences called by the
Wallace-Peek forces during the decade invariably supported plans for
subsidizing farm production.) Hoover exerted his greatest influence
over agricultural policy when, largely upon his advice, President
Coolidge vetoed two consecutive McNary-Haugen bills passed by
Congress in 1927 and 1928.

It is also often overlooked how much Hoover's agricultural policies
affected some of his other domestic programs. This was particularly
true in the area of transportation because he believed that the distribution problems so many farmers faced was a matter of eliminating
waste—in this case inefficient or inadequate transportation systems.
So directly or indirectly he related his railway, waterway, highway,
subsidized ship-building, and even airway projects to the agricultural
problem. The same is true of Hoover's activities in the field of conservation and his attempts to make notes from farm cooperatives
"eligible for rediscount with Federal Reserve banks." But little credit
has been given to the comprehensive view that he took of the farm
crisis or of the general services that his department rendered to the
agricultural industry.[51]

Hoover estimated in his *Memoirs* that inquiries from farmers' organizations and agricultural commodity exporters to the Commerce
Department asking for assistance increased from 42,000 in 1922 to
400,000 by 1927. Although a few of these were critical of Hoover or

represented quack propositions, most indicated that Hoover's reputation for honest, efficient business advice and objective statistical data was respected by agricultural exporters within the farm community, despite their opposition to some of his specific proposals for ending the farm crisis.[52]

Despite Hoover's less-than-positive reputation among organized farm interest groups, President Coolidge offered him the position of secretary of agriculture upon Wallace's death. Hoover refused without hesitation, as he had the year before declined to become secretary of the interior, because he believed he was in the process of creating a Department of Commerce that could best serve all the major economic needs of the country. By remaining where he was he thought that he could continue to aid the American farmer, albeit indirectly, by combating waste, unemployment, and widely fluctuating business cycles with his cooperative and scientific methods, by developing waterways and generally improving national transportation systems, by generally promoting a high standard of living for all Americans through tariff protection, and by expanding foreign exports. Hoover also explained to Coolidge in refusing to take Wallace's place that while he was no "technologist on agricultural production," he would continue to support all sound proposals for alleviating the surplus problem which was at the heart of the depressed condition of the postwar farmer.[53] It is possible, however, that he left unstated a major reason for refusing to replace Wallace: he had no solution for solving the complex problems of American agriculture.

There is no doubt that Hoover's ideas about agricultural policy evolved in the course of the decade. In 1920 he simply recommended that foreign purchases of American surpluses be facilitated through private loans abroad, although both during and after the war he had attempted whenever possible to use these excess food products in his relief operations. Then he proceeded to develop his cooperative marketing theories and between 1920 and 1925 cooperative farm sales increased 85% in volume. By the end of the decade almost 2,000,000 farmers belonged to cooperatives which distributed about two billion dollars in farm products annually. But this still represented only a small fraction of agricultural production for the country. Soon Hoover saw the need for voluntary crop reduction—a proposal that even his enemies later admitted was ten years ahead of its time—and finally suggested a federally financed system of agricultural cooperatives and stabilization corporations to achieve both reduced output and higher prices for farmers. This finally became a reality in the Agricultural Marketing Act of 1929 which established a Federal Farm Board. It has been called an "almost perfect illustration" of Hoover's decentralized corporatist approach to voluntary regulation of the American economy.[54] Unfortunately it became one of the first of many legislative victims of the Great Depression.

We know that farmers ended up accepting federal production controls in the 1930s under the New Deal, and one wonders why they would not do so voluntarily in the 1920s when Hoover suggested it. According to agricultural historian Gilbert C. Fite, farmers naturally resisted the idea of economic scarcity for agriculture, especially when it came from someone their leaders told them was trying to sell agriculture out to industry by advocating unlimited production and exports for manufacturers, but not for farm interests. Also, Hoover's insistence on voluntary production limits seemed too complex, too long-term, when what the average farmer wanted was an immediate price-lifting solution guaranteed by the government. In writing about the economic history of this period, George Soule once said that a "better solution" to the farm problem than McNary-Haugenism or later New Deal measures "would have been to increase the purchasing power both of the consumers of food throughout the world and of the American farmers themselves, by larger production and lower prices of manufactured products. But this solution would have involved extensive reform in the nonagricultural sections of the economic structure."[55]

As an integrated part of his comprehensive economic plans for the United States, Hoover's multifaceted agricultural policy represented a "better solution" according to the terms outlined by Soule. Hoover was one of few national leaders in the 1920s who struck at the root of the surplus problem by calling for a change in the negative attitude of farmers about cooperative production control. From the beginning of the decade Wallace and Peek insisted that it was impossible to re-educate farmers along the lines of cooperative individualism, because they were too insulated from normal publicity tactics and public pressure. Possibly so, but in taking this position Wallace and Peek ignored recent developments in mass communication and thus refused to participate in any long-term educational program aimed at changing the values of farmers. One wonders if a less traditional and expedient attitude would have resulted in a more successful handling of the post-World War I agricultural problem.

Finally, the charge that Hoover deliberately sacrificed the American farmer on the altar of big business in the 1920s is patently false. Hoover's comprehensive planning and belief in preserving American economic self-sufficiency did not tolerate such short-sighted tactics. This is not to say that all of the assumptions upon which he based his agricultural and other economic theories were correct, but in retrospect many of them made sense. With one-third of its population living on farms in the 1920s, he never suggested that the United States should "submerge agriculture under industrial domination," as England did with the repeal of the Corn Laws in 1846. Hoover simply thought that foreign nations could not absorb our postwar agricultural surplus, as they could our manufactured goods, because of their own production capacities. Accepting this unpleasant fact, he tried to devise a long-term solution for the farm dilemma based on integrating farmers into the modern technological economy of the United States, rather than keeping them on the periphery of it.

It has been evident since the New Deal that there is little hope of reconciling domestic farm policy with promotion of unlimited American economic expansion abroad. As long as the agricultural program is aimed at keeping tariffs high and at establishing governmental control for output and prices, it contradicts international trade policies which have moved, until recently, in the direction of lower tariff barriers and equal opportunity to compete for world markets.[56] Unlike most public figures in the 1920s, Hoover anticipated this basic contradiction. Thus, he devised tactics to avoid it by bringing farm production in line with what he overestimated to be an ever-increasing domestic demand, and by including a system of high tariffs for American agriculture and manufacturing which would promote qualitative as well as quantitative expansion abroad. Although the depression destroyed his farm policy before it was ever adequately tested, he correctly predicted that surplus production and over-dependence on foreign markets would remain major farm problems despite all the government controls instituted after 1933.

NOTES

1 Following the trend of Hoover's contemporary critics, the first scholarly works on agricultural policy in the decade following World War I began to appear in the 1950s with a negative interpretation of his relationship to the agricultural industry. They include: Theodore Saloutos and John D. Hicks, *Agricultural Discontent in the Middle*

West, 1900-1939 (Madison, 1951); Murray R. Benedict, *Farm Policies of the United States, 1790-1950* (New York, 1953); Gilbert C. Fite, *George N. Peek and the Fight for Farm Parity* (Norman, 1954); James H. Shideler, *Farm Crisis, 1921-23* (Berkeley, 1957); James G. Patton, *The Case for the Farmers* (Washington, 1959); Murray R. Benedict and Elizabeth K. Bauer, *Farm Surpluses: U.S. Burden or World Asset?* (Berkeley, 1960); Edward L. and Frederick H. Schapsmeier, *Henry A. Wallace of Iowa: The Agrarian Years, 1910-1940* (Ames, 1969); Donald L. Winters, *Henry Cantwell Wallace as Secretary of Agriculture, 1921-1924* (Urbana, 1970).

Many of the following studies do not deal exclusively with farm policy, but nonetheless are critical of Hoover's, and antedate or were influenced by the above monographs: George Soule, *Prosperity Decade: From War to Depression, 1917-1929* (New York, 1947); Arthur M. Schlesinger, Jr., *The Crisis of the Old Order, 1919-1933* (Boston, 1957); William E. Leuchtenburg, *The Perils of Prosperity, 1914-1932* (Chicago, 1958); John D. Hicks, *Republican Ascendancy, 1921-1933* (New York, 1960); Robert K. Murray, *The Harding Era: Warren G. Harding and His Administration* (Minneapolis, 1969); Gene Smith, *The Shattered Dream: Herbert Hoover and the Great Depression* (New York, 1970).

A few books discussing Hoover's agriculture policies have broken with this completely negative pattern, including: Grant McConnell, *The Decline of Agrarian Democracy* (Berkeley, 1953); Harris G. Warren, *Herbert Hoover and the Great Depression* (New York, 1959); Joseph Dorfman, *The Economic Mind, 1919-1933* (New York, 1959); Joseph Brandes, *Herbert Hoover and Economic Diplomacy: Department of Commerce Policy, 1921-1928* (Pittsburgh, 1962); Albert Romasco, *The Poverty of Abundance: Hoover, the Nation, the Depression* (New York, 1965); J. Joseph Huthmacher and Warren I. Susman, eds., *Herbert Hoover and the Crisis of American Capitalism* (Cambridge, 1973), and almost all of William Appleman Williams's writings, especially *The Tragedy of American Diplomacy* (New York, 1959) and *The Contours of American History* (Cleveland, 1961). The most positive reevaluation to date of Hoover's agricultural policies is Gary H. Koerselman, "Herbert Hoover and the Farm Crisis of the Twenties: A Study of the Commerce Department's Efforts to Solve the Agricultural Depression, 1921-1928." Ph.D. Diss. (Northern Illinois U., 1971).

2   For discussion and documentation of this search for a new order through corporatism see: Joan Hoff Wilson, *Ideology and Economics: U.S. Relations with the Soviet Union, 1918-1933* (Columbia, 1974), pp. vii-xii, notes 3-6; Ellis W. Hawley, "Herbert Hoover and American Corporatism, 1929-1933," in *The Hoover Presidency: A Reappraisal,* ed. Martin L. Fausold and George Mazuzan (New York, 1974); Eugene Golob, *The Isms* (New York, 1954), pp. 541-97; Robert Wiebe, *The Search for Order, 1877-1920* (New York, 1967), passim.

3   Hoover considered agriculture one of the "sickest" natural resource industries in the 1920s along with lumber, petroleum, and bituminous coal because of their practice of destructive and wasteful competition. He never gave up hope that he could convince them that less disorganization and more associationalism was the way to maximize profits. Even within these atomistic industries, however, there were a few strong organizations and pressure groups. A good example within agriculture was the way in which the five powerful meat-packing companies backed by such groups as the congressional Farm Bloc, the American Farm Bureau Federation, the National Grange, and the Illinois Agricultural Association were able to transfer federal regulation of the packing industry from the Federal Trade Commission to the Department of Agriculture where it would be more lax. This occurred with passage of the Packers and Stockyards Act of 1921. See Koerselman, "Hoover and the Farm Crisis," 237-51. The same interest-group defiance of federal regulation can be seen in the relationship between the Chicago

Board of Trade and the implementation of the Grain Futures Act of 1922, and the way in which that legislation benefited primarily the large wheat producers. See William R. Johnson, "Herbert Hoover and the Regulation of Grain Futures," *Mid-America,* 51 (July 1969), 155-74, and Koerselman, "Hoover and the Farm Crisis," 252-58.

4   For discussion and documentation of neoguildist and statist versions of progressive corporatism see: Joan Hoff Wilson, *American Business and Foreign Policy, 1920-1933* (Lexington, 1971), pp. 2-7; Wilson, *Ideology and Economics,* pp. xi-xii, note 6; Wilson, *Herbert Hoover: Forgotten Progressive* (Boston, 1975), pp. 36-44, 66-74; Otis L. Graham, Jr., *The Great Campaigns: Reform and War in America, 1900-1928* (Englewood Cliffs, 1971), pp. 1-51, 97-169; Ellis W. Hawley, essay and rejoinder in *Hoover and Crisis of Capitalism,* pp. 3-34, 115-20; Hawley, *The New Deal and the Problem of Monopoly* (Princeton, 1966), pp. 189-223; Louis Galambos, *Competition and Cooperation* (Baltimore, 1966), pp. 199-202; James Olson, "The End of Voluntarism," *Annals of Iowa,* 41 (Fall 1972), 1104-13; John A. Garraty, "The New Deal, National Socialism, and the Great Depression," *American Historical Review,* 77 (October 1973), 907-36.

5   While Hoover believed that the American economic potential was nearly limitless, he was proud of the fact that the United States exported only 6 to 10% of its total productivity, and confident that even this remarkable level of domestic economic self-sufficiency could be surpassed with careful planning of domestic consumption. So he argued that because "we consume an average of about 90 percent of our own production of commodities," the United States could boost domestic consumption so that 97% of all agricultural and manufacturing products, regardless of economic conditions in Europe, would be marketed internally, making the United States "more self-contained than any other great nation." See: Hoover, draft of letter, January 10, 1922, Herbert Hoover Papers (Hoover Presidential Library, West Branch, Iowa), Commerce Section, Economic Recovery in Europe; Hoover addresses of May 16, 1922 (to the U.S. Chamber of Commerce) and January 7, 1925 (to the National Council of Cooperative Marketing); Hoover, "Business Depression and Policies of Government in Relation to It," June 15, 1931; State of the Union Message, December 8, 1931, all in Hoover Papers, Public Statements, Nos. 228, 431, 1587, and 1729. For the impact this concept of economic self-sufficiency had on his foreign policy views, see Wilson, *Hoover: Forgotten Progressive,* pp. 170-71, 244-45.

6   Hoover, transcript of remarks to Business Man's Conference on Agriculture, April 15, 1927, Hoover Papers, Commerce Section; Hoover address to U.S. Chamber of Commerce, May 12, 1926, Hoover Papers, Public Statements, No. 579.

7   James H. Shideler, "Herbert Hoover and the Federal Farm Board Project, 1921-1925," *Mississippi Valley Historical Review,* 41 (March 1956), 721; Edward L. and Frederick H. Schapsmeier, "Disharmony in the Harding Cabinet: Hoover-Wallace Conflict," *Ohio History,* 75 (Spring/Summer 1966), 134-35; Koerselman, "Hoover and the Farm Crisis," 2-8; Winters, *Wallace,* pp. 217-45; Wilson, *Hoover: Forgotten Progressive,* pp. 84-85, 103-10.

8   Schapsmeier and Schapsmeier, "Hoover-Wallace Conflict," 128; Winters, *Wallace,* pp. 31-33, 244; Fite, *Peek,* pp. 126-27; Herbert Hoover, *Memoirs, The Cabinet and the Presidency, 1920-1933* (New York, 1952), p. 109; Gary Dean Best, *The Politics of American Individualism* (Westport, 1975), p. 109; Hoover to Wallace, February 25, 1922, Hoover Papers, Commerce Section, H. C. Wallace—1922. The Food Administration files I consulted for this paper are housed at the Hoover Institution on War, Revolution, and Peace, Stanford, California.

9 As secretary of commerce, Hoover attempted not only to reorganize his own department, but also the entire executive branch to improve efficiency and avoid duplication of work. For details of his successes and failures see: Wilson, *Hoover: Forgotten Progressive,* pp. 80–90; Ellis W. Hawley, "Herbert Hoover and the Expansion of the Commerce Department: The Anti-Bureaucrat as Bureaucratic Empire-Builder," paper delivered at the Organization of American Historians convention, April 1970. Wallace's reorganization of his department began on July 1, 1921, with the merger of the Bureaus of Markets and Crop Estimates. Finally, on July 1, 1922, the Bureau of Agricultural Economics (BAE) was established, incorporating all of the economic functions of the Department of Agriculture into a single division. It was in this area of gathering statistical data for marketing American agricultural products abroad that the two departments most often clashed and duplicated one another's work. See Winters, *Wallace,* pp. 116–25, 222–45.

10 Hoover, "Advancement of Cooperative Marketing," address to the American Dairy Federation, October 1, 1924, Hoover Papers, Commerce Section, H. C. Wallace —1923–24; Fite, *Peek,* p. 129; *Some Long Views for Improvement of the Farmers' Profit: A Condensation of Statements by Herbert Hoover* (Washington, 1925), pp. 5–6; Hoover address to the National Council of Cooperative Marketing, January 7, 1925, Hoover Papers, Public Statements, No. 431.

11 Wallace to Coolidge, April 8, 1924, Hoover Papers, Commerce Section, H. C. Wallace—1923–24. Wallace was obviously satisfied with the Capper-Volstead Act of 1922, which had exempted farm cooperatives from prosecution under the anti-trust laws and which was administered by his department. The Hoover-sponsored Capper-Williams Bill of 1924 went far beyond what Wallace thought necessary and was Hoover's attempt to counter the early McNary-Haugen bills pending in Congress.

12 For the standard references to Hoover's anti-agrarian and pro-business attitudes, see the works cited in the first paragraph of note 1. Hoover repeatedly denied this charge and carefully distinguished in many statements between the problems of agriculture and the problems of industry—all to no avail because he continued to advocate associationalism for both. For example, he clearly told the American Dairy Federation in 1924 that "we should not mislead ourselves into thinking that cooperation is the complete solution to the problem of marketing all agricultural produce. Nor is the form of cooperative organization the same in any two commodities." Part of this problem of communication was that Hoover always viewed the farm crisis as an international rather than simply a domestic problem, unlike his critics. While they believed the agricultural depression was simply a temporary result of the dislocation caused by World War I, Hoover knew that some of the basic economic maladjustments between nations in the postwar period were being caused by worldwide overproduction in agriculture and that simplistically nationalistic plans for exporting American meat and grain surpluses, like the 1921 Norris plan for creating a Federal Farmers Export Financing Corporation, would not remedy what was a long-term international problem. However, his substitute counterproposal did not solve the problem either. It resulted in the Agricultural Credits Act of 1921, which financed the sale of agricultural surpluses through a continuation of the War Finance Corporation and made up for weaknesses in the Federal Reserve System's agricultural loan policy. Nor was the subsequent passage of the Intermediate Credit Act of 1923 any more successful. They were simply less aggressively nationalistic attempts by Hoover to develop a comprehensive national agricultural policy, rather than stopgap measures as so many of the Farm Bloc proposals were. See: Koerselman, "Hoover and the Farm Crisis," 111–41; Hoover addresses of January 7, 1925, and August 11, 1928, Hoover Papers, Public Statements, Nos. 431 and 878; Hoover to Harvey Ingham, September 19, November 4, 1925, Hoover Papers, Com-

merce Section, Harvey Ingham; and Wilson, *Business and Foreign Policy,* pp. 8-14, esp. notes 17 and 18.

13   Wallace to Coolidge, April 8, 1924, Hoover Papers, Commerce Section, H. C. Wallace—1923-24.

14   Department of Agriculture, press release, November 11, 1924, and *Annual Report* (December 8, 1924), both in Hoover Papers, Commerce Section, Agriculture. It should be noted that these appeared after Wallace had died in October 1924.

15   Hoover, transcript of remarks to Business Man's Conference on Agriculture, April 15, 1927, Hoover Papers, Commerce Section.

16   Alonzo E. Taylor, "Analysis of Senate Bill 2012," 13, Hoover Papers, Commerce Section, Agriculture; Johnson, "Hoover and Grain Futures," 155-61, 167-74.

17   Hoover, transcript of remarks to Business Man's Conference on Agriculture, April 15, 1927, Hoover Papers, Commerce Section; Fite, *Peek,* p. 126; Hicks, *Republican Ascendancy,* p. 199.

18   Taylor, "Analysis of Senate Bill 2012," 16-17, 19, Hoover Papers, Commerce Section, Agriculture; Theodore D. Hammatt to Hoover, November 21, 1927, Hoover Papers, Commerce Section, Agriculture.

19   *Ibid.*

20   *Ibid.*

21   Hoover to L. J. Keating, March 5, 1925, Hoover Papers, Commerce Section, Keating.

22   Hoover, transcript of remarks to Business Man's Conference on Agriculture, April 15, 1927, Hoover Papers, Commerce Section.

23   Donald L. Winters, "The Hoover-Wallace Controversy During World War I," *Annals of Iowa,* 34 (Spring 1969), 586-97; Winters, *Wallace,* pp. 98-99, 150; Russell Lord, *The Wallaces of Iowa* (Boston, 1947), pp. 193-200, 211-15, 221, 265-66, 275-80; Arno J. Mayer, *Politics and Diplomacy of Peacemaking* (London, 1967), pp. 270-73; Gary Dean Best, "Food Relief as Price Support: Hoover and American Pork, January-March 1919," *Agricultural History,* 45 (April 1971), 79-84.

24   Best, "Food Relief as Price Support," 81. Confusion and bitterness had arisen between the Wallaces and Hoover over the 13-bushel-of-corn ratio that the former insisted was necessary to encourage enough corn to go into hog production. This meant that the farmer could count on getting for each 100 pounds of pork ready for market thirteen times the average cost per bushel of corn fed each hog. Hoover reluctantly proclaimed this as a *statement of intention* in November 1918, only to finally peg the price at a $17.50 minimum, which was in effect a ratio of 10.8 bushels. Moreover, his international activities were aimed at prices paid to meat packers who in turn were supposed to meet the price supports set for pork by the Food Administration. These middlemen did not always honor their commitment to the government and Hoover.

25   Lord, *Wallaces of Iowa,* pp. 279-80.

26   Hoover to Food Administration, February 1919, in Suda L. Bane and Ralph H. Lutz, *Organization of American Relief in Europe, 1918-1919* (Stanford, 1943), pp. 238-39.

27   Fite, *Peek,* pp. 61, 128–29; Koerselman, "Hoover and the Farm Crisis," 312–25, 340–56.

28   Hoover to Adolph C. Miller, February 11, 1925 (with enclosed letter of December 19, 1924, to George Peek), and Miller to Hoover, February 25, 1921, both in Adolph Miller Papers (Hoover Presidential Library), Board of Governors, FRB File.

29   Hoover's testimony before the House Agricultural Committee, 68 Cong., 2 Sess., 1923, Hoover Papers, Public Statements.

30   For reasons behind the postwar farm crisis and the details of its magnitude see: Winters, *Wallace,* pp. 61–71, 246; Koerselman, "Hoover and the Farm Crisis," 50–90.

31   Fite, *Peek,* pp. 128–30, 137; Hoover address to National Council of Cooperative Marketing, January 7, 1925, Hoover Papers, Public Statements, No. 431; Hoover to *Journal of Land and Public Utility,* n.d. (contained in enclosures sent to J. G. Mitchell, August 7, 1926), Hoover Papers, Commerce Section, Mitchell; interview with Hoover in *Baltimore Sun* by John F. Sinclair, March 31, 1925, Hoover Papers, Commerce Section, Achievements of the Department of Commerce.

32   They did not in fact support tariff protection of American agricultural products for the same reasons. A high level of agricultural duties was one of Wallace's original postwar demands and was considered an end in itself by him, but not by Hoover. For Hoover understood that the Emergency Tariff Act of 1921 had not benefited farmers as its supporters claimed it would and viewed tariff policy in general as simply one part of a very complex foreign and domestic program for transforming "the whole superorganization of our economic life." Tariff protection was necessary, according to Hoover, to maintain an expanding domestic market for agricultural and manufactured goods; that is, it was a means for increasing American consumption of homegrown products, not an incentive to farmers to increase production for foreign exportation as Wallace and most farm organizations viewed it. See Wilson, *Business and Foreign Policy,* pp. 71, 87–98.

33   Hoover to Wallace, October 7, 1921; Wallace to Hoover, October 17, 1921; Gray Silver to Hoover, April 24, 1923; Hoover to Silver, April 26, 1923, all in Hoover Papers, Commerce Section, H. C. Wallace—1921–24.

34   In particular the Farm Bloc began to disagree in 1922 over the effectiveness of tariff protection because the bloc comprised high-tariff western Republicans and low-tariff southern Democrats; rural credits also created dissension. Most important, however, in the decline of the Farm Bloc was the formation of a new congressional bloc of Progressives which siphoned off the more radical members of the original Farm Bloc like LaFollette, Norris, and Edwin F. Ladd. See Winters, *Wallace,* pp. 89–90. For other difficulties of the Farm Bloc and for those who supported Hoover's agricultural policies or at least questioned those of his opponents see: Leroy Ashby, *The Spearless Leader: Senator Borah and the Progressive Movement in the 1920s* (Urbana, 1972), pp. 36–37, 218–37; Koerselman, "Hoover and the Farm Crisis," 255–61, 274–91.

35   Hoover to George Peek, December 19, 1924, Hoover Papers, Commerce Section, Peek.

36   Fite, *Peek,* pp. 127–28; Hoover to Walter F. Brown, October 20, 1921, Hoover Papers, Commerce Section, Brown.

37   Christian Herter (for Hoover) to editor of the *Cleveland Leader,* January 19, 1922, with attached correspondence over reorganization plans of the Department of Com-

merce, and Hoover to Brown, March 3, 1925, Hoover Papers, Commerce Section, W. M. Jardine; Hoover's review of his own reorganizational plans in relation to Peek's charges, November 24, 1924, and December 23, 1924; Hoover to Peek, December 19, 1924, all in Hoover Papers, Commerce Section, Agriculture; Winters, *Wallace,* pp. 225–41.

38 Hoover to Howard Gore, November 26, 1924, Hoover Papers, Commerce Section, H. M. Gore; Hoover to Peek, December 19, 1924, Hoover Papers, Commerce Section, Peek.

39 Legal brief and memorandum, "On Attempt to Discredit Hoover by Peek," May 25, 1925, Hoover Papers, Commerce Section, Agriculture and Commerce Departments Propaganda.

40 Hoover to William M. Jardine, October 13, 1925, April 1, 1926, Hoover Papers, Commerce Section, Agriculture Department; Hoover to Peek, June 25, 1926, Hoover Papers, Commerce Section, Peek; Hoover to Eugene Funk, February 5, 1926, Hoover Papers, Commerce Section, Funk; Gilbert C. Fite, "The Agricultural Issues in the Campaign of 1928," *Mississippi Valley Historical Review,* 37 (March 1951), 46–64; Hicks, *Republican Ascendancy,* p. 213.

41 Hoover to Howard M. Gore, February 11, 1925, Hoover Papers Commerce Section, H. M. Gore; Hoover to Walter F. Brown, March 5, 1925, Hoover Papers, Commerce Section, W. M. Jardine; Winters, *Wallace,* pp. 242–43.

42 See letters to Jardine cited in note 40.

43 *Some Long View Policies for Improvement of the Farmers' Profit: A Condensation of Statements by Herbert Hoover* (Washington, 1925); Hoover to (no name, but presumably a midwestern farmer), June 25, 1926, Hoover Papers, Commerce Section, Agriculture—Corn Belt.

44 *Ibid.*

45 Hoover press release, July 17, 1925, Hoover Papers, Commerce Section, Agriculture; Hoover address to National Council of Cooperative Marketing, January 7, 1925, Hoover Papers, Public Statements, No. 431. For details of Hoover's evolving position on the application of anti-trust legislation to trade associations and marketing cooperatives, see Robert F. Himmelberg, essay and rejoinder in *Herbert Hoover and the Crisis of American Capitalism,* pp. 59–85, 128–32, and Wilson, *Hoover,* chapters 4 and 5. There is no doubt that Hoover was willing to accommodate a greater degree of relaxation of anti-trust laws and, hence, encouragement of cartel development in "sick" natural resource industries like agriculture than he was in other sectors of the economy. In retrospect it is clear that his suggestions for greater cooperation and associationalism failed to take hold in those industries which were the most disorganized and whose profits were below the national average. In these instances he was willing to allow for less strict application of anti-trust legislation if that would result in their economic stabilization.

46 Hoover, "Advancement of Cooperative Marketing," address to American Dairy Federation, October 2, 1924, Hoover Papers, Commerce Section, Agriculture; Soule, *Prosperity Decade,* p. 245; Hoover to J. R. Howard, editor of the *Homelands Farm* (enclosing all correspondence with J. G. Mitchell), July 2, 1926; Hoover to J. G. Mitchell, August 7, 1926, all in Hoover Papers, Commerce Section, Mitchell.

47 Hoover, transcript of remarks to Business Man's Agricultural Conference, April

144 AGRICULTURAL POLICIES, 1921-28

15, 1927, Hoover Papers, Commerce Section.

48 Theodore D. Hammatt to Hoover, November 21, 1927; W. H. Cowles to Hoover, December 20, 1927; Hoover to Cowles, January 4, 1928 (with enclosed critical responses by Hammatt and the *Spokesman Review* to Cowles's agricultural plan), all in Hoover Papers, Commerce Section, Agriculture; Hoover address to National Council of Cooperative Marketing, January 7, 1925, Hoover Papers, Public Statements, No. 431.

49 Hoover to Representative John C. Ketcham, February 14, 1925, Hoover Papers, Commerce Section, Ketcham; Benjamin M. Weissman, "The American Relief Administration in Russia, 1921-1925: A Case Study in the Interaction Between Opposing Political Systems," Ph.D. Diss. (Columbia U., 1968), 325-32, passim; George W. Hopkins, "The Politics of Food: United States and Soviet Hungary, March-August 1919," *Mid-America*, 55 (October 1973), 245-70; Koerselman, "Hoover and the Farm Crisis," 117-22, 152-233. It is usually forgotten that the United States was *not* the leading grain exporter in the 1920s and 1930s that it has become since World War II. See Sterling Wortman, "Food and Agriculture," *Scientific American*, 235 (September 1976), 37, and Henry D. Fornari, "U.S. Grain Exports: A Bicentennial Overview," *Agricultural History*, 50 (January 1976), 142-47.

50 While these commercial calculations were not entirely correct, they did significantly affect Hoover's foreign-policy views both as secretary of commerce and president because of their relationship to economic self-sufficiency. This becomes an even more evident factor in his foreign-policy views after 1933. See: Hoover, "Economic Prospects of 1924," Hoover Papers, Commerce Section, Economic Situation in the U.S.; Hoover, "The Future of Our Foreign Trade," March 16, 1926, Hoover Papers, Commerce Section, Foreign Trade; Hoover, "Our Future Economic Defense," September 18, 1940, in *Addresses Upon the American Road, 1940-1941* (New York, 1941), pp. 23-24.

51 Wilson, *Hoover*, chapter 4; Koerselman, "Hoover and the Farm Crisis," 369-71. For his early FRB correspondence about farm cooperatives, see Hoover to Miller, June 29, 1921; Miller to George C. Jewett, June 23, 1921; and Miller to Hoover, June 30, 1921, all in Miller Papers, FRB File.

52 Arthur March to Hoover, February 2, 1925, Hoover Papers, Commerce Section, Agriculture; Hoover, *Memoirs*, p. 110; Koerselman, "Hoover and the Farm Crisis," 167-69.

53 Hoover, statement refusing the secretaryship of the Department of the Interior, January 6, 1923; statement refusing the secretaryship of the Department of Agriculture, January 16, 1925, Hoover Papers, Public Statements, Nos. 278 and 436; Hoover to General E. H. Woods, January 1, 1925, Hoover Papers, Commerce Section, Woods; Hoover, *Memoirs*, pp. 110-11.

54 Fite, *Peek*, p. 16; Ray Lyman Wilbur and Arthur M. Hyde, *The Hoover Policies* (New York, 1937), p. 147, 150; Soule, *Prosperity Decade*, p. 245; Romasco, *Poverty of Abundance*, p. 23; Hoover, memorandum on Farm Board Organization and Possible Procedure, Hoover Papers, Presidential Subject Files, Farm Matters; Hoover, Message to Congress, April 16, 1929, Hoover Papers, Public Statements, No. 1011.

55 Fite, *Peek*, p. 130, 137; Soule, *Prosperity Decade*, pp. 248-49.

56 John M. Leddy, "United States Commerce Policy and the Domestic Farm Program," in *Studies in United States Commercial Policy*, ed. William B. Kelly, Jr. (Chapel Hill, 1963).

Summary Of Commentary By Discussants And Conferees

Discussion of the paper began with a formal commentary by Professor Robert H. Zieger, who was then affiliated with Kansas State University. This started on a facetious note, expressing Zieger's surprise that he had not learned more about Kansas State's William Jardine. But it then became more serious, expressing fundamental agreement with most of Wilson's interpretation but challenging a few aspects of it. It took issue, first of all, with those sections of the paper stressing conflict between Hoover and the big business establishment. In reality, Zieger pointed out, Hoover was a great admirer of the modern corporation and the "new" big business, with close ties to the centers of corporate power and especially on agricultural matters to Alexander Legge of International Harvester. In addition, Zieger disliked the term "corporatism," primarily because of the connotations it had acquired through its association with fascism. Wilson, he thought, was on target in seeing the Hoover and Wallace activities as part of a larger "search for order." But he preferred to discuss this under the rubric of progressivism and would go even further than Wilson in viewing Hoover as a synthesizer of such progressive ideological strains as positivism, corporationism, the New Freedom, and the New Nationalism.

The second formal commentary came from Professor Gary Koerselman of Morningside College. Like Zieger, he expressed basic agreement with Wilson's interpretation and especially with the way she had made sense of a complicated subject and explored the alternatives that had existed in the 1920s. Unlike Zieger, however, he called for an even greater emphasis on Hoover's efforts to reform the organization of cooperative marketing, get it out of the hands of large promoters, and create structures characterized by greater internal democracy and better business practices. To achieve these ends he had advocated federal certification based on continuing audits, and on this there had been conflict between Hoover and agri-business leaders. They had attacked him for urging new forms of governmental interference in business. In Koerselman's view, Wilson had also failed to bring out the full implications of Hoover's battle with Wallace. Hoover was right, he thought, in seeing the Department of Agriculture as a tool of vested interests and would-be builders of a political capitalism, and he astutely anticipated the kind of welfare-warfare state that could emerge from the growth of such a bureaucracy.

Subsequent discussion revolved largely around challenges to the view that Hoover's solution was wiser and more realistic than the one associated with Wallace and the McNary-Haugenites. Alan Seltzer, for example, found it difficult to distinguish between Hooverian prescriptions and the "decline of agrarian democracy" that Grant McConnell had described in his history of the American Farm Bureau Federation. Melvyn Leffler failed to see how a cooperative marketing system, even if realized, could have coped with the kind of agricultural overproduction characteristic of the 1920s. And others pointed to contradictions in Hoover's market development proposals and to his support for reclamation projects that could only aggravate the problem of overproduction. In response, Professor Wilson again emphasized how cooperative marketing was seen not as the solution but as one part of a complex and multifaceted program designed to cope with a complex and multifaceted problem. She also argued again that the feasibility of cooperative marketing could have been greatly enhanced by a properly designed and properly executed educational program. Peek and Wallace argued otherwise, but they were remarkably effective in educating farmers to support the McNary-Haugen solution.

During these exchanges, Wilson and Koerselman also responded to a number of questions about those facets of the Hoover program that had not been emphasized in the paper. They elaborated, in particular, on Hoover's efforts to secure cheaper transportation for farm goods, on his support for diversification measures and programs, on the new farm credit system that he helped to establish, on his hopes for the China Trade acts as developers of a new market, and on his attempts to foster land-use planning and alternative uses for marginal lands. He did not, to Wilson's knowledge, seem much concerned with the growing tenancy problem. But his designs for rural development anticipated those of the 1960s and 1970s, and following the Mississippi River flood in 1927 he tried to develop a program through which share-croppers might acquire their own farms.

Finally, there was some discussion of two other matters. One was the decline of true agrarian radicalism in the 1920s, a decline that Koerselman and Wilson attributed to the successful organizing and propaganda campaigns of the Farm Bureau Federation and the McNary-Haugenites. In effect, they diverted class discontent into support for interest-group activism. The other topic discussed was Hoover's political success vis-a-vis the McNary-Haugenites. On this, Robert Murray and Robert Zieger argued that he was more successful than Wilson seemed to think. He, after all, had won and maintained control of the executive branch, had got the Republican nomination despite strong opposition from the McNary-Haugen leaders, and had won most of the farm vote in 1928.

Melvyn P. Leffler

Herbert Hoover, The "New Era," and American Foreign Policy, 1921–29

Editor's Introductory Note

Melvyn P. Leffler, professor of history at Vanderbilt University, is an authority on French-American relations and a scholar whose work has done much to alter established perceptions of Republican diplomacy in the 1920s. In *The Elusive Quest: America's Pursuit of European Stability and French Security, 1919–1933,* he traced and analyzed the American programs for reconciling German prosperity with French security, noting particularly how these were circumscribed by political and fiscal considerations, how they lodged power and policy making in the hands of private agencies and unofficial experts, and how their weaknesses eventually led to diplomatic failure. These were also the themes in pioneering articles published in *The Journal of American History* and *Perspectives in American History.* In these, Leffler stressed the continuities between Wilsonian and Republican diplomacy, especially in regard to perceptions about and efforts to achieve European stability. But unlike some revisionists, he also stressed the unwillingness of American policy makers to compromise domestic priorities or incur binding strategic commitments. And probing into areas usually ignored by diplomatic historians, especially the interrelationships between government agencies, private bankers, and unofficial experts, he illuminated new aspects of the policy-making process.

In the paper published here, Professor Leffler focuses on the economic diplomacy of Herbert Hoover as secretary of commerce. This, he argues, had many of the same features that characterized Hoover's domestic programs. Although not globalist in orientation, it rested on managerial and functionalist assumptions, recognized the interdependence of the modern world, sought solutions combining apolitical expertise with cooperative action, and envisioned a promotional and coordinative role for government. It was anything but a return to isolationism and laissez-faire. But like Hoover's domestic programs, it had serious weaknesses, both in conception and in application. It assumed more enlightenment and solidarity in the private sector than actually existed. It underestimated the power of political and strategic considerations, and it was being applied by a man who tended to become increasingly complacent, increasingly political, and increasingly disposed to ignore the real experts and their warnings. It recognized the twin dangers of irresponsible isolationism, on the one hand, and of dangerous overcommitment on the other. But in operation it failed, and in doing so it paved the way for the isolationism of the 1930s and the globalism of the 1940s.

As with other spheres of Hooverian activity, some historians still question the degree of coherence and the ideological dimension that Leffler finds in those aspects of New Era diplomacy dominated by the Commerce Department. The crucial determinants, they continue to argue, were material interests, pressure groups, and concerns with immediate and pressing problems. And on the other side, as shown by the discussion following the paper, a number of historians remain more impressed with Hoover's achievements than Leffler does. They credit him with seeking to develop an informed and realistic internationalism, with having sound reasons for ignoring some experts, and with at least seeing the problems inherent in capitalist pressures for continued growth and sustained profitability. With both groups the debate seems likely to continue.

Herbert Hoover, The 'New Era,' and American Foreign Policy, 1921–29

In recent years there has been a continuing reappraisal of the career of Herbert Hoover placing him in the domestic progressive tradition from which he stemmed. No longer is Hoover portrayed as the reactionary and callous conservative reluctant to use governmental powers to alleviate distress and to cope with the problems of the depression. Instead, he increasingly appears as a twentieth-century enlightened manager and scientific reformer engrossed in the problems of stabilizing modern industrial society, involved in the effort to promote harmony between capital and labor, devoted to the task of fostering cooperative competition among businessmen, committed to the use of systematic approaches to solve national problems, and inclined to accept limited governmental responsibility in the struggle to manage the business cycle and eradicate poverty. Hoover, of course, carefully placed constraints on the functions of government. Moreover, he loathed the proliferation of bureaucracy, extolled the principles of self-help and voluntary cooperation, and glorified the virtues of equal opportunity and individual initiative. His significance, therefore, rests in his being a transitional figure in American history in his effort to adapt traditional American principles and values, such as individual opportunity and free enterprise, to a new era which he correctly recognized was underway.[1]

Hoover's emphasis on recognizing the interdependence of the modern world, on fostering the use of experts, on finding apolitical solutions, on encouraging private voluntary and cooperative action, and on enlarging but circumscribing the role of government characterized his approach to foreign policy no less than his attitudes toward domestic policy. Indeed the transference of Hoover's assumptions and methods from the realm of domestic policy into the arena of international diplomacy was remarkable. And just as his domestic policies provide a bridge between the New Freedom and the New Deal, so do his foreign policies constitute a critical link in the evolution of American foreign policy in the twentieth century. In other words, Hoover's "New Era" approach to foreign policy took notice of America's important place in world economic affairs, but did not make the functioning of the world economy the primary responsibility of the United States government; it acknowledged the interrelationships between the American economy and the international economy, but did not consider the survival of American liberal capitalistic institutions contingent upon overseas expansion; it accepted the fact that events elsewhere affected American interests, but did not call for political and military action to protect those interests; it took cognizance of the impact of World War I on international economic and social affairs, but did not call for the military suppression of revolutionary movements; it postulated the superiority of American institutions, but did not call for their forceful imposition upon others. This orientation toward international affairs distinguished Hoover from post-World War II globalists and identified him with those World War I functionalists inside and outside the peace movement who called for a managerial approach to world order and world peace.[2] Yet, despite the balance and perspecuity that characterized Hoover's approach to foreign policy, it ultimately failed because of its own inherent inconsistencies and because of Hoover's personal failure to live up to the high standards he set for himself. These themes can be elucidated by briefly examining Hoover's view of international relations and by more closely analyzing his managerial approach to European affairs.

I

Hoover realized that the advancement of science, the progress of technology, the revolution in transportation and communication, and the migration of capital had bred worldwide economic interdependence. The Great War had magnified the social consequences of this economic interdependence by unleashing new social philosophies and ideological movements that competed for the support of peoples everywhere. Referring to the chaos in Europe in 1920, Hoover stated that "Every wind that blows carries to our shores an infection of social disease from this great ferment; every convulsion there has an economic reaction upon our own people."[3] Indeed the forces of technology had bound together the fate of all peoples and had knit together the economies of all nations. During his goodwill tour of Latin America in 1928, Hoover explained to his listeners in Rio de Janeiro:

> A century ago, our countries could and did live a more primitive life without the exchange of products of the Temperate Zone for coffee, rubber, and a score of other articles. Today, however, but for the products which we exchange, not a single automobile would run; not a dynamo would turn; not a telephone, telegraph, or radio would operate; a thousand daily necessities and luxuries would disappear. In fact, without these exchanges of commodities, huge masses of humanity who have now become dependent upon an intensive and highly attuned civilization could not be kept alive.[4]

Given his view of the unified structure of the modern world economy, Hoover often stressed the importance of maintaining international peace and world stability. He firmly believed "that the delicate machinery of social organization, of production and commerce upon which our civilization is founded [could] not stand such a shock [as the war] again."[5] Moreover, he assumed that if world peace and international stability could be maintained, world demand would tend normally to grow.[6] This assumption was of great importance because

Hoover postulated a close interrelationship between world purchasing power, American exports, and the overall economic well-being of the United States. Economic recovery and financial stability abroad meant prosperity at home. In 1928 Hoover described the workings of the business cycle on an interdependent world economy in the following way:

> The forces of credit, communications, transportation, power, foreign relations, and whatnot must all be kept in tune if steady employment is to be assured. A failure in any part imposes a penalty upon labor through unemployment. Break this chain of relationship at any point and the whole machine is thrown out of order. . . . Cease exporting automobiles to South America or Europe, and automobile workers are thrown out of work in Michigan. The suffering does not stop there. It only begins. The steel mills slacken in Pennsylvania and Indiana. The mines employ fewer workers at Lake Superior. And every farmer in the United States suffers from diminished purchasing power.[7]

Hoover, as an enlightened business manager in the progressive tradition, felt that it was entirely possible to cope with the problems of the worldwide business cycle through the application of human intelligence, the utilization of expertise, and the institution of cooperative action. In 1920, he called upon his fellow engineers to take a more active interest in solving national and international problems and he urged all Americans to adopt "the attitude that marks the successes of America, the attitude of the business man, of the engineer, and of the scientist." The great problems of the day, he proclaimed, were susceptible to solution through quantitative analysis and cooperative action.[8] And subsequently, he repeatedly urged the accumulation of statistical information that would enable the United States to play a more intelligent role in world affairs. At the Geneva Economic Conference in 1927, for example, American representatives suggested that one means of coping with the world agricultural crisis was through the better collection of data pertaining to production, markets, prices, consumption patterns, and costs of production. This was the essential prerequisite for possible subsequent cooperative efforts to regulate agricultural production and land utilization on an international scale.[9] Through such methods of scientific investigation and voluntary cooperative action, Hoover believed much progress was possible.

In domestic affairs Hoover had little faith in the ability of political institutions or legislative enactments to settle complex modern problems. In 1924 he wrote that "Regulation and laws are of but minor effect on . . . fundamental things. But by well directed economic forces, by cooperation in the community . . ." substantial progress was possible. Accordingly, he hoped to establish close ties between the administrative side of government and associational forces in the community.[10] Similarly, in foreign affairs he had little confidence in the efficacy of international political agreements and sought to avoid accords that were based on coercion. Instead he was willing to rely on "seasoned public opinion. . . . Its mobilization at home and the cooperation in its use with other nations abroad is our contribution to peace. . . ." Thus, Hoover could be satisfied with arms limitations and consultative agreements (for example, the Washington treaties and the Kellogg-Briand pact) that did not provide for inspection and enforcement. This was the corollary of voluntarism on the domestic level. "[T]he essence of accomplishment in government," and in international relations Hoover might have added, "lies in that threadbare expression—cooperation," not compulsion.[11]

By advocating the application of business principles to international relations, Hoover desired to take international questions out of the hands of politicians where they often were treated on the basis of emotion and to put them into the hands of experts where they would be analyzed according to the dictates of fact. Domestic and international political factors, in his opinion, only confused and obscured what were admittedly complex, but nevertheless, soluble international questions. These questions, Hoover contended, were more predominantly economic than at any time in American history. For this reason, he considered them susceptible to the type of empirical investigation and systematic management that he so greatly cherished. Consequently, after World War I, Hoover sought to develop viable institutional mechanisms that would provide for the settlement of international issues in an impartial way and on an objective basis. And for those disputes that did not lend themselves to solution by economic experts and financial analysts, he advocated the use of legal formulae and juridic principles. These, too, supposedly had the advantage of underscoring the importance of apolitical considerations and impartial examination.[12]

Hoover maintained that the American government still had an important but circumscribed role to play in the resolution of great international questions. Its legitimate obligation was to sponsor empirical studies, to encourage private cooperative action, to cultivate apolitical institutions, and to promote a modified open door.[13] He warned, however, that it was economically unconstructive and politically destabilizing for the government to enter directly into international business transactions or to assume political commitments. Government credits and state monopoly controls politicized international business affairs, aroused national sentiments, and bred international animosity. In addition, such direct state economic intervention stifled constructive competition and generated inefficient production.[14] Thus, Hoover's conception of the New Era in American foreign policy was one in which the United States government played a continuous and constructive, but carefully delimited role in helping to preserve world peace, prosperity, and stability.

II

Since Hoover believed that modern civilization was complex, organic, and ever-changing, he disdained comprehensive solutions to international questions and advocated piecemeal and systematic efforts to cope with pressing world problems.[15] In 1923, he maintained that "Wisdom [in international affairs] does not so much consist in knowledge of the ultimate; it consists in knowing what to do next." He praised the Harding administration, of which he was a leading member, for the success of the Washington Disarmament Conference and for the current recommendation to join the Permanent Court for International Justice. Emphasizing that these were only initial steps toward the ultimate goal of preserving world peace, he chided the critics of the administration. "Those who condemn the proposal [for joining the World Court] because it is merely one method are the ones who would have complained on the Wednesday night of Genesis, and would have gone to bed with a grouch because the Creator had not yet made a finished job of the sun and moon, and would have called a mass meeting on Thursday morning to demand more forward action." Such forward action, Hoover indicated, would be forthcoming. "[T]he rejection of one particular device [the League of Nations]," he stated, "does not mean that America has lost interest in finding a solution" to world peace and international cooperation.[16]

Indeed, Hoover had supported the League of Nations in 1919, not because he considered it an ultimate answer to the turmoil wrought by the war, but because it provided an institutional framework, that is a World Council, where grievances could be raised, uncorrected wrongs discussed, cooperative action cultivated, and the "intelligence of the world'' mobilized. He had not viewed the League as a mechanism for permanently embroiling the United States in the world's political and military affairs. Quite the contrary, he had hoped that the League would "forever relieve the United States of the necessity to again send a single soldier outside of our boundaries.''[17] Precisely because he had considered the League a means to an end rather than an end in itself, he was prepared, when the Senate rejected the League, to seek other mechanisms and instruments that would enable the United States to contribute to world stability and prosperity without incurring political entanglements. But these means had to be based on the use of expertise, the promotion of voluntary action, and the subordination of political factors.

Before accepting the position of secretary of commerce in 1921, Hoover requested and was granted authority to deal with all aspects of the American economy.[18] He immediately set to work to cope with the severe economic slump that was then underway. Like most businessmen of the day, Hoover believed that the expansion of foreign trade would improve the domestic economic situation. But the revival of commerce itself depended upon constructive efforts to solve pressing international economic questions, especially those pertaining to European economic reconstruction.[19] Therefore, Hoover began examining solutions to such problems as unstable currencies, excessive armaments, unsettled war debts and reparations, unproductive foreign loans, and depressed foreign trade.

In 1921 the international issue causing most alarm amongst American businessmen was the instability of currencies. Hoover considered this to be virtually the greatest impediment to foreign trade. In the immediate postwar years, fluctuating exchange rates and depreciating foreign currencies generated uncertainty, retarded exports, and enhanced the competitive ability of foreign products in the American market.[20] Hoover immediately sought to find ways to stabilize currencies and restore the gold standard as a means of facilitating worldwide economic rehabilitation and of promoting American overseas sales. During the summer of 1921, he turned his attention to the commercial and financial problems besetting Central European nations. He asked Benjamin Strong, Governor of the Federal Reserve Bank of New York, whether private banking institutions here and abroad could not take responsibility for formulating a plan of financial cooperation aimed at rehabilitating currencies. Claiming that constructive political measures were unlikely, the commerce secretary urged that recovery depended upon divorcing economic from political action. He contended that the central banks of Europe and the Federal Reserve Bank of New York could bring about the stabilization of currencies through the mobilization of private capital and thereby avoid the political pitfalls inherent in governmental action.[21]

In the short run, the stabilization of currencies and the restoration of the gold standard were not achieved through central bank cooperation. But in the mid-1920s cooperation between central banking institutions became a primary instrument for fostering international currency stability as the essential prerequisite for the expansion of international commerce. Central bankers crisscrossed the Atlantic in their continuous attempts to keep in touch with foreign developments, to reconcile monetary policies, and to cooperate voluntarily in restoring a modified gold standard. In 1925, the Federal Reserve Bank of New York began extending credits to England and other major European nations to facilitate their return to a gold exchange standard. Subsequently, the Federal Reserve Board managed discount rates and engaged in open market operations with a close eye on European monetary developments. Adolph Miller, a member of the Federal Reserve Board, later recalled that this was regarded "as a brilliant exploit in central bank policy and as a demonstration of the reasonableness of the belief, that through well-conceived and well-timed monetary policy the terrors of the business cycle could be largely if not wholly removed and price stability and economic prosperity be insured. It will not be forgotten that by many the opening of the year 1928 was heralded as the beginning in these respects, as well as in many others, of a new era."[22]

Republican officials applauded these developments. Treasury officials, in particular, kept in close contact with Strong and his associates at the Federal Reserve Bank of New York. They encouraged, supported, and sometime even guided specific actions.[23] By delegating the task of restoring the gold standard to the central bankers, government officials (in the United States and abroad) hoped to remove this goal from political considerations. Indeed, Strong always insisted that in return for Federal Reserve credits, central bankers abroad had to achieve full independence from their respective governments. It was hoped that if central bank policy were insulated from the political process, then national and international monetary policies could be molded intelligently on the basis of economic and financial criteria.[24] This informal collaboration of assumedly disinterested experts was not accompanied by any binding commitments and simply resulted from the bankers' common appreciation of their mutual interests.

Central bank cooperation conformed to Hoover's standards of enlightened action. It utilized "expertise"; it called for voluntary action; it was "apolitical." It proceeded with the approval of the administrative side of government, the Treasury Department. Therefore, though the secretary of commerce had misgivings about the utilization of discount rates and open market operations to accommodate European financial needs, in the mid-1920s he did appreciate the importance of Federal Reserve efforts to maintain currency stability. His criticisms of Federal Reserve policies stemmed from his belief that Strong was over-emphasizing the international basis of American prosperity and underestimating the importance of sound internal financial conditions. But, in general, he acquiesced to Federal Reserve policies because he believed that the ultimate goal, the reestablishment of the prewar gold standard, would institutionalize a process of automatic adjustments between national economies and thereby diminish the prospect that national or international political considerations might interfere with financial developments.[25]

During 1921, however, the secretary of commerce quickly realized that before much progress could be made toward stabilizing foreign currencies, matters such as armaments and reparations had to be handled constructively. In May 1921, he wrote President Warren G. Harding:

> There is nothing that would give such hope of recovery in life and living as to have this terrible burden and menace [arms expenditures] taken from the minds and backs of men. As Secretary of Commerce, if I were to review in order of importance those things of the world that would best restore commerce, I would inevitably arrive at the removal of this, the first and primary obstruction.[26]

Hoover, like many of his contemporaries, viewed armaments as an impediment to economic rehabilitation because arms expenditures weighed so heavily on government finances, thus contributing to budgetary deficits and to currency instability. Naturally, then, he was a strong supporter of the Washington Conference of 1921.[27] And insofar as that conference limited naval armaments, reaffirmed the open door, and provided for consultation in East Asia, all without imposing political commitments, the treaties accorded with Hoover's emphasis on dealing with international issues on their merits through voluntary and cooperative international action.[28]

To Hoover, the progressive organization of peace demanded military retrenchment not only in naval armaments but also in land armaments. He was particularly upset with the French because of their large military expenditures and substantial standing army. French armaments constituted an unbearable strain on French finances, affected France's capacity to meet her wartime obligations, and caused economic dislocations throughout Europe.[29] France, of course, would not voluntarily agree to limit land armaments without firm guarantees of her security. In other words, she refused to cooperate in the settlement of what Hoover liked to consider economic issues without interjecting political and strategic factors. As a result, the secretary of commerce sought other means to influence French behavior. Within the cabinet, he became the leading advocate of using financial leverage to force other nations to curtail arms expenditures.[30] Such proposals reflected his continuing preoccupation with organizing the forces of peace, as he defined them, when economic arguments were rejected and when appeals to international voluntarism were ignored.

In the early 1920s, the secretary of commerce maintained that the reparations issue was the other great impediment to European currency stability, world prosperity, and American well-being. The enormous reparations burden imposed upon Germany contributed to the fluctuation of European exchange rates, the depreciation of European currencies, and the consequent weakening of European purchasing power. In addition, Hoover, like many bankers and businessmen, feared that the precipitous depreciation of the mark might enable German exporters not only to flood the American market with German goods, but also to outstrip their competitors in the quest for world markets. Therefore, the commerce secretary carefully estimated what Germany was capable of paying without disrupting world commercial and financial conditions.[31] But in the view of American officials even more important than specific figures was the creation of some mechanism that would enable the United States to cooperate unofficially in the resolution of this problem, that would divorce the issue from political considerations, and that would facilitate the voluntary mobilization of the beneficent forces in the private banking community.[32]

The creation of committees of businessmen and bankers to study the reorganization of Germany's finances and to determine Germany's ability to pay reparations served as an ideal means to cope with the reparations crisis. The appearance of so-called experts dealing with the problem on a "business" basis raised the possibility of removing the issue from domestic politics in all nations and of facilitating an accord that politicians might accept without certainty of political retribution. Moreover, policy makers in the United States anticipated that the American experts would remain in close contact with government officials. Therefore, Republican officials assumed that the American experts could be relied upon to present the American program for a settlement based on economic, not political, considerations. At the same time, the experts were expected to stifle all proposals linking the war debt issue to a reparations settlement. They could do this without impairing American bargaining power because any reparations accord depended upon the flotation of an international loan in the United States.[33]

The Dawes Plan, however, did not entirely satisfy the secretary of commerce or his subordinates. The Commerce Department officials who served behind the scenes as technical advisers to the American experts complained that the Dawes annuities were too high, that the controls were too cumbersome, and that political factors had not been sufficiently disregarded.[34] But Hoover decided to support the Dawes Plan, as agreed upon in London in August 1924, because there was no constructive alternative. In his *Annual Report* for 1924, Hoover wrote that the plan was "the first effort to solve the reparations question purely on a commercial and economic basis." Moreover, it had won the voluntary support of prominent banking institutions. And perhaps most significant to the secretary of commerce, the plan had "within itself machinery for correction or alteration of details as difficulties arise in its execution." By establishing the office of Agent General with extensive powers to regulate transfers, to oversee the entire Dawes machinery, and to recommend eventual revisions, the plan created the most apolitical machinery that could be expected to deal with such an emotion-laden issue. It was hoped that with the return of currency stability and the free flow of private capital, salutary economic forces might eventually permit additional constructive action.[35]

Hoover recognized that the problem of war debts was unavoidably linked to the other questions of reparations, arms limitation, and currency rehabilitation. As in the case of these other issues, he avowedly sought to divorce the war debts question from political considerations, to resolve it according to economic criteria, and to use it as an instrument to manage the determinants of European stability. Like other members of the Harding cabinet, he would have preferred to tackle the war debts controversy through the administrative side of government. But when Congress refused to relinquish control over this matter, Hoover accepted the World War Foreign Debt Commission as an appropriate institutional means to handle the debt settlements.[36]

Hoover, however, rejected the harsh terms set by Congress. Instead he urged that the War Debt Commission, of which he was a leading member, demand the full payment of principal, but adjust interest payments according to the capacity-to-pay formula. Interest payments, the secretary of commerce rightly contended, were of much greater quantitative significance over the long run than the return of principal. By adjusting interest payments according to the capacity of nations, he hoped to secure the largest possible return to the American people without disrupting currency stability and international commerce. He recognized that nations could make international transfers only through the export of gold, commodities, or services. And he realized that since there were limits on the ability of nations to export, adjustments had to be made to meet individual circumstances.[37] The capacity formula provided a means to study particular cases on their merits and to dispense with political criteria. "In other words," Hoover wrote, "we slowly get ideas established into a practical economic basis, more and more stripped of the purely emotional side."[38] Accordingly, the interest payments of Italy, Belgium, and France were substantially reduced. Hoover insisted that these accords took accurate account of foreign economic conditions. But if the facts warranted greater remissions, Hoover intimated that he might still be more conciliatory. He told Thomas Lamont of J. P. Morgan and Company that he was willing to examine periodically the interest component of the debt agreements in light of changing economic circumstances.[39] He thereby acknowledged the need for continuous review in the complex task of negotiating debt settlements on the basis of the capacity formula.

According to Hoover, the capacity formula could be used not only to secure financially viable debt settlements, but also to extract concessions in other areas that would have a salutary impact on the European economy. Since the capacity formula was flexible, Hoover was willing to use it to elicit foreign concessions on such matters as arms limitation and budgetary reform. Debtors that reduced military expenditures, curtailed deficits, and stabilized currencies, Hoover argued, should receive favored treatment. This approach contradicted the notion of the capacity formula serving as a statistical means of determining what debtors could pay. But it provided Hoover with leverage in world affairs so that he could progressively organize the forces of peace.[40]

Hoover wanted to manage American capital outflows, in the same way that he adjusted war debts, to promote European stability and American prosperity. He had little doubt that experts could distinguish between productive and unproductive uses of capital and therefore he advocated foreign loans for "reproductive purposes." In fact, the "reproductive" criterion in foreign loans was the corollary of the "capacity" formula in war debts. It could be used systematically both to reconcile internal and external demands for capital and to apply pressure on foreign nations to make concessions on vital international issues. In general, Hoover insisted that the making of foreign loans was "an economic blessing to both sides of the transaction" and that therefore the government had a moral obligation to guide American capital outflows into productive channels. He wrote Secretary of State Charles Evans Hughes in April 1922:

> We are morally and selfishly interested in the economic and political recovery of all the world. America is practically the final reservoir of international capital. Unless this capital is to be employed for reproductive purposes there is little hope of economic recovery.[41]

The United States government could effectively channel American loans into productive purposes, Hoover maintained, by securing the voluntary cooperation of the private banking community. He denounced proposals for direct governmental extension of loans and credits, claiming that they would be based upon political criteria rather than economic fact, that they would be influenced by ethnic groups in the United States, that they would lead to undesirable international political entanglements, and that they would invite congressional meddling.[42] The objective, Hoover insisted, was not only to help mobilize private capital for reproductive purposes, but also to insulate the government from responsibility to intervene abroad to protect private lending. This could be accomplished if the private banking community agreed voluntarily to set productive loan standards in consultation with the administrative side of government.[43]

Hoover worked diligently to secure this private voluntary cooperation, while simultaneously trying to avoid government responsibility to protect private loans. The bankers were asked to inform the State

Department regarding all proposed foreign loans. Then State, Commerce, and Treasury officials decided whether such loans conflicted with national policies. If they did, the bankers were so informed and were in essence requested not to partake in the loans. Hoover wanted to define national policies in a broad way and to ask the bankers to cooperate in barring loans to nations with large military establishments, unbalanced budgets, and unsettled war debt obligations. Such nations, he claimed, constituted a menace to international stability and world commerce.[44] He also disapproved of loans to government sponsored monopolies and cartels because he considered them inefficient, uneconomic, and unsafe.[45] Furthermore, he frowned upon any loan that did not generate sufficient capital for repayment, such as loans to foreign municipalities.[46] Loans of the above types, he maintained, would eventually lead to transfer difficulties, defaults, and political entanglements. In essence, Hoover hoped to secure the voluntary cooperation of the American banking community and to apply financial leverage in his struggle to bring about European economic and financial stability. Since his Cabinet colleagues often objected to such informal cooperation with private bankers lest it generate undesired political entanglements abroad, Hoover was able to utilize American financial power only in a few instances, for example, in behalf of war debt settlements.[47]

Hoover's concern with currency stability, arms limitation, reparations, war debts, and foreign loans reflected his broader interest in maintaining international economic equilibrium in general and European financial stability in particular. He realized that if American exports were to expand without disrupting this equilibrium, foreign nations had to have sufficient dollar exchange. In order to cope with the liquidity problem, Hoover and his colleagues began to analyze the workings of the international economy and to study the flow of international payments. Recognizing that the United States had become a creditor nation, they were especially interested in the meaning and importance of invisible items in the nation's foreign economic relations. Hoover maintained that "A full comprehension of the invisible items and their approximate value is not only a profound importance in assessing our international balance sheet, but no sound conclusion can be made concerning the effect of foreign trade movements upon our credit structure or upon the ability of foreign countries to purchase our commodities or to pay their debts, or upon exchange rates, or upon the movement of gold, or the ultimate trend of price levels . . .

without some comprehensive balance sheet including the invisible items.''[48]

''Scientific'' studies both of the invisible items in the American balance sheet and of the triangular nature of American trade eventually convinced Hoover that the United States could both maintain the protective principle and collect the war debts without endangering European financial stability. Capital outflows, tourist expenditures, and immigrant remittances, Hoover argued, would enable European nations to continue to buy American goods while repaying old debts. Therefore, he discounted the importance of the very favorable merchandise balance that the United States had with major European nations. But he also pointed out that those nations could expand their exports and secure dollar exchange in the tropical areas of the world where the United States had an unfavorable merchandise balance. Moreover, many European nations could go on receiving enormous sums of dollars as a result of their direct or indirect ownership of the raw materials in many tropical areas. Given these facts, Hoover argued that anyone who contended that the protective principle was irreconcilable with world prosperity simply ignored the findings of modern science.[49]

These claims, however, did not mean that Hoover or his subordinates in the Commerce Department were unaware of or indifferent to the need to expand merchandise imports. Indeed they recognized that a smaller favorable balance of merchandise exports provided a sounder basis to carry on foreign trade. They acknowledged the need to increase imports and they stressed that such increments, especially of noncompetitive raw materials, would inevitably accompany domestic industrial development and material advancement. Throughout the 1920s, they noted that imports were increasing more rapidly than exports. This increase was sufficiently impressive, especially if measured in quantitative terms, that prominent economists and Commerce officials began to believe that the nation's economic growth and improving standard of living would generate a large enough demand for foreign raw materials and luxury items to constitute a viable international equilibrium regardless of American tariff barriers.[50] In fact, Hoover and his colleagues took particular pains to demonstrate statistically that the tariff did not greatly influence foreign purchasing power. They mustered data revealing that most imports were duty free, that a significant percentage of imports were luxury goods unaffected by duties, that essential dutiable imports came in regardless of rates, and that American customs barriers were not appreciably higher than those of other comparable nations.[51]

Hoover, therefore, never ceased to support the protective principle. In his view, it insured American producers and workers against competition from low wage areas and enhanced American prosperity, thereby augmenting the nation's demand for foreign goods, increasing immigrant remittances, enlarging American overseas tourist expenditures, and contributing to international financial stability. But while vigorously supporting the protective principle, he nevertheless emphasized that the setting of tariff rates had to be taken out of the political process, where they were subject to congressional logrolling, and placed in the hands of experts where they could be managed on a "scientific" basis, according to the principle of equalizing the costs of production. He supported the Tariff Commission as an appropriate apolitical institutional device to mold tariff policy, and he urged it to make more vigorous use of the flexible provisions of the Fordney-McCumber Act.[52] And he sympathized with William Culbertson's efforts within the Commission to make it a more politically independent body capable of formulating tariff policy not only according to its impact upon American industry but also with regard to its influence on international trade and finance.[53]

In general, then, Hoover's approach to foreign policy in the New Era focused on the need to develop "scientific" and "apolitical" mechanisms and formulae capable of fostering world order, European stability, and mutual cooperation. The War Debt Commission's use of the capacity formula, the Tariff Commission's adoption of the "costs of production" principle, the Commerce Department's championing of the "reproductive" loan criteria, the central banks' commitment to the gold standard, and the reparation experts' emphasis on Germany's "ability to pay" all reflected an effort to progressively organize the forces of peace by mobilizing expertise, generating voluntary action, and minimizing political imperatives. Hoover hoped that such tactics would enable the United States to play a continuous and constructive role in world affairs, to restore the free flow of private capital, and to remain independent of political and military commitments. In theory, it was a grandiose vision. But practically it failed because of Hoover's own departure from its rules, and because of flaws within its conception.

III

Hoover prided himself on being the enlightened manager liberated from antiquated assumptions, committed to the empirical method, and indifferent to political factors. In 1928, he confidently exclaimed: "It has been no part of mine to build castles of the future but rather to measure the experiments, the actions, and the progress of men through the cold and uninspiring microscope of fact, statistics and performance."[54] Such rhetoric sounded reassuring, but was far from accurate during the latter part of the 1920s. By the middle of the decade, Hoover became complacent, overestimated the soundness of the American economy, exaggerated the extent of world progress, and began operating in political arenas where fact often succumbed to expediency.[55]

Though by 1925 initial efforts had been undertaken to deal with many of the major international economic questions, few of them had been permanently resolved. Many prominent businessmen, bankers, and government officials, whom Hoover would have been inclined to call "experts" had they not disagreed with him, realized that readjustments would have to be made continuously if permanent stability were to be achieved. Owen Young wrote Hoover in January 1926 that he was troubled by national policies that demanded large payments from debtor nations, and then not only excluded their goods from the American market but also broke up their raw material monopolies which were instrumental in securing foreign exchange. Young was certainly not alone in recognizing that American tariff barriers, war debts collections, and loan policies strained the entire international economic system, jeopardized the gold standard, and threatened European stability.[56]

As the enlightened manager and supporter of apolitical machinery to handle such problems, Hoover might have been expected to encourage progressive steps to ameliorate existing difficulties. But he tended to remain inflexible and to disregard arguments and statistical evidence that conflicted with his own basic assumptions. For example, he often acknowledged that a closer balance between American merchandise exports and imports constituted a sounder basis for world trade, but he belittled the significance of the growing disparity between exports and imports in the latter 1920s.[57] Though he emphasized the need to increase imports in order to provide the rest of the world with dollar exchange, he combatted government controlled raw material monopolies abroad that boosted prices and foreign exchange earnings. He justified this by claiming that monopolies undermined efficient production,[58] but he supported both the protective principle and the costs of production formula which, as applied, contradicted the whole concept of comparative advantage and efficient international specialization. He maintained that "invisible" imports and foreign loans would provide the basis for a continued equilibrium in the balance of international payments, but he never developed an effective means of systematizing the extension of reproductive foreign loans;[59] nor did he analyze the growing quantitative importance of American earnings from previous investments abroad.[60] He often claimed that the triangular pattern of world commerce (American exports to Europe, European exports to the tropics, tropical exports to the United States) was the solution to Europe's balance of payments difficulties. But he overlooked the fact that the American campaign to expand exports to South America and Asia was deranging the triangular nature of international commerce.[61]

Despite mounting evidence that the protective principle could not be reconciled with the nation's commercial and financial position in the world economy, Hoover would not abandon his commitment to it. During the 1928 presidential campaign critics charged that both Hoover's support of the protective tariff and his willingness to accept upward revisions were politically inspired. Though his campaign rhetoric suggests that political factors were not inconsequential, his vigorous support of the protective principle was based on the assumption that protectionism was vital to American prosperity and compatible with international financial equilibrium. As already indicated, he marshalled considerable evidence to show that protective tariffs did not significantly affect imports, but he usually failed to take into consideration the international payment difficulties stemming from simultaneous policies of import protectionism and export expansionism in a period of declining raw material prices. Fundamentally, protectionism was an article of faith for Hoover, conceived in advance of the evidence, rationalized by selective use of the "facts," and illustrative of his primary preoccupation with the domestic economy and his unabashed pride in the American system. All in all, his approach to the tariff question and the international liquidity problem, engendered legitimate questioning about Hoover's reputation as an apolitical manager and farsighted economist.[62]

The same might be said about Hoover's attitudes and actions on the
war debts issue. He proclaimed his willingness to examine this question on the basis of fact, not emotion. But he usually suspected that
the foreign debtors were trying to dupe the American war debt commissioners. Consequently, he almost always took a hard line approach
and defined "capacity" in the most exacting way possible. Lenient
members of the War Debt Commission often were exasperated by his
opposition to more liberal concessions. Treasury officials, like Garrard Winston, who studied the debt problem most intensively, believed the "facts" warranted larger remissions than Hoover thought
advisable.[63]

In isolation the debt issue was not of great significance, but it assumed larger importance because it was very closely related to efforts
to revise the Dawes annuities and to maintain European currency stability. Throughout 1927 and 1928, central bankers, the agent general
for reparations, and other prominent international figures gave considerable attention to European financial problems. They recognized
that Germany's reparations burden had to be lightened and England's
financial strain relieved. Yet it was difficult to attack these problems
without interjecting the war debts issue.[64]

Hoover, however, manifested little inclination to be helpful. Though
he had acknowledged the possibility of revising the war debt accords,
he refused to support any such action during the late 1920s. In fact, he
praised the financial viability of the debt settlements and claimed that
they imposed no financial hardships on debtor nations. He gathered
an impressive array of statistics demonstrating that annual war debt
payments were only a small percentage of budgetary expenditures,
that they were an insignificant item in the total foreign trade of any
nation, that they constituted less of a financial burden than armaments expenditures, and that they were often exceeded by annual
American tourist expenditures abroad.[65] Though these statements
were for the most part true, they disregarded the additional burden
that war debt transfers placed on an international monetary system
that already was under considerable strain. The invisible import items
in America's balance sheet may have greatly exceeded war debt payments, but they were not large enough, not constant enough, to provide debtors with easy and steady access to dollar exchange.[66] Therefore, war debt payments did exacerbate, if not cause, the liquidity
problem. In failing to place the war debts issue in the context of the
myriad problems afflicting the international monetary system,

Hoover used factual information not to enlighten the American people about the realities of that situation, but to distort that reality. This was totally contrary to his previous emphasis on studying a problem objectively, on mobilizing the public for voluntary action, and on managing the issue according to the best advice of experts.

Hoover's failure to abide by the tenets of the New Era was especially apparent during the reparation negotiations of 1929. Once again international "experts" (businessmen and financiers) convened to resolve the reparations dilemma. As part of a final settlement they hoped to establish an international bank, the Bank for International Settlements, that would facilitate international transfers and that would foster currency stability. During these negotiations, the Hoover administration bitterly denounced any linkage between the war debt and reparation issues, opposed any official American connection with the proposed international bank, and initially objected to any American financial sacrifices on behalf of army costs or mixed claims. This negative attitude complicated the work of the experts and threatened to retard a constructive step toward international monetary stability. Hoover justified his actions on the basis of past American precedent (of separating the war debt and reparation issues), on the grounds of saving taxpayers' dollars, and on the merits of remaining aloof from Europe's political problems.[67] These reasons had a traditional ring, but they defied the best advice of the "experts," reflected a cowardly attitude toward breaking precedent, and illustrated a sensitivity to domestic political rather than international economic factors. Hoover's reaction to the Young Plan negotiations was certainly not in the best tradition of innovative management and apolitical statesmanship. The experts accused him of playing politics, but other factors played a role as well, including his emotional antipathy to the Old World, especially France, and his minimizing of international financial problems.[68]

Hoover's inability to jettison political considerations, to reappraise fundamental assumptions, and to properly manage internal and external economic variables indicated his personal failure to live up to the rigorous tenets of the New Era. But there also were flaws within the New Era approach that made constructive action on the international scene difficult. Hoover's emphasis on mobilizing voluntary and cooperative forces within the private sector, rather than extending governmental powers, had many merits, but also suffered from conceptual weaknesses. He relied upon private bankers to cooperate with his policy of extending loans for reproductive purposes only. But in their struggle to utilize available capital and to reap large profits, bankers disregarded his advice to refrain from loans to German municipalities. Hoover's theory of voluntarism postulated that when private groups were informed of the "facts," they would concur with the government on what constituted appropriate action. When the bankers disregarded his warnings, Hoover's limited conception of what constituted legitimate government action precluded more forceful measures to prohibit these loans. As a result, American capital continued to flow into Germany and the American financial system became increasingly intertwined with European financial developments. Hoover and his assistants looked upon this with great dismay. They expected a crisis to arise during which the bankers would pressure the government to insist that loan service receive priority over reparation payments. This foreshadowed not only an uncertain financial future, but also political entanglements in Europe. Yet Hoover presented no effective means of dealing with the situation. The secretary of commerce did not advocate direct government prohibition of unproductive loans even to German municipalities lest it be interpreted to mean that the government was assuming responsibility to safeguard all loans it did not bar.[69]

The bankers' refusal to accept the government's guidelines regarding the "reproductive" nature of German loans illustrated another flaw in Hoover's New Era approach to foreign policy. He maintained that all critical issues could be studied in an objective way, systematically quantified, and then expertly managed. But most foreign policy issues inescapably involved political, emotional, and psychological factors that made "rational" decision-making difficult, if not impossible. For example, not only was there much discord on what constituted a productive loan, but even when agreement could be reached among government officials, it was hard to implement policy and direct the outflow of American capital.[70] Likewise, the capacity formula, as the Treasury Department pointed out, was "not subject to mathematical determination," but was "largely a matter of opinion." Despite the enormous amount of statistical data that was collected by the War Debt Commission (and the reparations experts), subjective judgments had to be made in determining what comprised a decent standard of living and what a nation would be willing to pay.[71] Moreover since such decisions ultimately had to secure legislative approval, political considerations were never absent. Similar political and emotional factors help to explain Hoover's commitment to the protective principle. He never analytically demonstrated that "scientific" protectionism was the best means to reconcile the needs of the domestic economy with those of the international economy. Protectionism, however, not only accorded with Hoover's personal predilections, it also was politically expedient in the 1920s.[72]

Hoover's personal commitment to objective analysis was less than he realized; his own ability to discard political considerations was less than he supposed; his faith in voluntarism was greater than the situation warranted; and his pursuit of economic solutions to complex international questions was more inadequate than he presumed. The great issues of the day could not be solved by experts dealing exclusively with international economic and financial variables. In the modern industrial world, international economic issues were so closely intertwined with strategic and political factors that the latter could not be dismissed in dealing with the former. Thus, Hoover's great desire to economically integrate Weimar Germany into his cooperative capitalist system foundered on French apprehensions of what a revitalized, even though disarmed, Germany might portend for French security. Hoover's view of human behavior and international motivation presupposed that an economically satisfied and republican nation would be a cooperative partner in world affairs. But the French remained skeptical and Hoover was slow to placate their anxieties. In fact, French obstructionism infuriated him and bred a deep distrust. "During the whole period from 1918 to 1939," he subsequently wrote, "[France] was the stumbling block to every proposal for world advancement." Given this attitude (and the domestic political climate), he tried to keep the United States free of commitments to guarantee what he considered to be France's self-destructive concept of security.[73]

IV

The refusal to incur strategic commitments lest it embroil the United States in unforeseen political and military problems highlighted a vital element of Hoover's New Era approach to foreign policy. The maintenance of European stability and the extension of international trade, though immensely important to American self-interest, were not so vital as to necessitate strategic involvements and military guarantees. The United States, Hoover believed, was sufficiently self-contained to withstand upheaval and even revolution abroad, though naturally this would entail some difficult readjustments for the American economy. In fact, he found comfort in America's relative economic self-containment and claimed that, if necessary, this condition would enable the United States to sustain itself economically regardless of events elsewhere. In other words, according to Hoover, the domestic economy and the internal market remained the basic determinants of American well-being. This did not mean that events abroad were unimportant; it simply meant that they were not critical unless the nation's security was endangered. And in the 1920s Hoover saw no such threat.[74]

Thus, during the era of the Republican ascendancy Hoover sought to establish a balanced view of the interrelationships between domestic well-being and international stability. He desired to play a constructive role in European and world affairs without compromising domestic priorities as he defined them and without incurring dangerous commitments as he perceived them. Yet his efforts to establish a stable world order failed because of his overconfidence in the ability of business experts to deal with complex problems, because of his disregard of the political and strategic ramifications of international economic issues, because of his unfounded faith in the ability of the private sector to respond wisely and unselfishly to international questions, because of his oversensitivity to domestic political crosscurrents, because of his suspicion of foreign peoples and foreign systems, and because of his personal inability to reassess the wisdom of traditional Republican principles, like protectionism.

But despite all these shortcomings, Hoover's "New Era" approach to foreign policy deserves careful scrutiny and is entitled to sympathetic criticism. During the 1920s Hoover did seek to pursue a middle course between the extremes of irresponsible isolationism and dangerous overcommitment, policies that beleaguered American foreign relations in subsequent decades. While endeavoring to influence events abroad and make them conform to American interests and ideals, he remained wary of overestimating America's dependence on the international economy and skeptical of the benefits of strategic commitments when the nation's vital interests were not threatened. His efforts, although flawed, remain noteworthy because they underscore how difficult it is to balance American foreign interests with American overseas commitments and to reconcile domestic needs with international imperatives.

NOTES

1   See, for example, David Burner, *Herbert Hoover: A Public Life* (New York, 1979); Joan Hoff Wilson, *Herbert Hoover: Forgotten Progressive* (Boston, 1975); Craig Lloyd, *Aggressive Introvert: A Study of Herbert Hoover and Public Relations Management* (Columbus, Ohio, 1972); Martin L. Fausold and George T. Mazuzan, *The Hoover Presidency: A Reappraisal* (Albany, 1974); Robert H. Zieger, *Republicans and Labor, 1919-1929* (Lexington, 1969), especially pp. 61-70, 271ff.; Ellis W. Hawley, "Herbert Hoover, the Commerce Secretariat, and the Vision of an Associative State, 1921-1928," *Journal of American History,* 61 (June 1974), 116-40; Evan B. Metcalf, "Secretary Hoover and the Emergence of Macro-economic Management," *Business History Review,* 49 (Spring 1975), 60-80; Barry D. Karl, "Presidential Planning and Social Science Research: Mr. Hoover's Experts," *Perspectives in American History,* 3 (1969), 347-409; Carolyn Grin, "The Unemployment Conference of 1921: An Experiment in National Cooperative Planning," *Mid-America,* 55 (April 1973), 83-107; Albert U. Romasco, *The Poverty of Abundance: Hoover, the Nation, the Depression* (New York, 1965); Gary Dean Best, *The Politics of American Individualism: Herbert Hoover in Transition* (Westport, Conn., 1975); the essay by Ellis Hawley in J. Joseph Huthmacher and Warren I. Susman, eds., *Herbert Hoover and the Crisis of American Capitalism* (Cambridge, Mass., 1973), pp. 1-33; Robert H. Zieger, "Herbert Hoover: A Reinterpretation," *American Historical Review,* 81 (October 1976), 800-10.

2   Internationalists during the era of the First World War recognized the interrelationships between American well-being and world stability, but unlike post-World War II globalists they wanted to carefully circumscribe the nation's political commitments. See Warren F. Kuehl, *Seeking World Order: The United States and International Organization to 1920* (Nashville, 1969); also see Charles de Benedetti, "Alternative Strategies in the American Peace Movement in the 1920s," *American Studies,* 13 (Spring 1972), 69-71. Two excellent studies shedding considerable light on Hoover's approach to foreign policy in the 1920s are: Joseph Brandes, *Herbert Hoover and Economic Diplomacy: Department of Commerce Policy 1921-1928* (Pittsburgh, 1962); Joan Hoff Wilson, *American Business and Foreign Policy, 1920-1933* (Lexington, Ky., 1971). For a brief discussion of globalism and its implications, see William Taubman, ed., *Globalism and Its Critics: The American Foreign Policy Debate of the 1960s* (Lexington, Mass., 1973).

3   "Mr. Hoover's Inauguration Address to the American Institute of Mining and Metallurgical Engineers," February 17, 1920, copy in New York Public Library (NYPL); also see Herbert C. Hoover, *Addresses Delivered During the Visit of Herbert Hoover to Central and South America, November-December, 1928* (Washington, 1929), pp. 33, 36, 47; Herbert Clark Hoover, *The New Day: Campaign Speeches of Herbert Hoover* (Stanford, 1928), p. 11.

4   Hoover, *Addresses,* p. 58.

5   Herbert Hoover, "America's Next Step," World Peace Foundation *Pamphlets,* 6 (1923), 67-68.

6   Department of Commerce, *Fourteenth Annual Report of the Secretary of Commerce* (Washington, 1926), p. 34. (Hereinafter this source shall be cited as Department of Commerce, *Annual Report,* year, page.) Also see undated memorandum, "Hoover's Thoughts on Foreign Trade," [mid-1920s], Herbert Hoover Papers (Herbert Hoover Presidential Library, West Branch, Iowa), Commerce Section, Foreign Trade; Hoover, *New Day,* p. 98.

7 Hoover, *New Day,* pp. 64-65; also see, for example, *ibid.,* pp. 117-19; Herbert Hoover, "Backing up Business: The Larger Purpose of the Department of Commerce," *Review of Reviews,* 78 (July 1928), 278-79.

8 For the quotation, see Herbert Hoover, "Foreword," in Elisha M. Friedman, *America and the New Era* (New York, 1920), p. xxiv; also see "Mr. Hoover's Inauguration Address to the American Institute of Mining and Metallurgical Engineers," February 17, 1920, p. 8; Department of Commerce, *Annual Report,* 1922, pp. 30-32; Conference on Unemployment, *Report of the President's Conference on Unemployment* (Washington, 1921), pp. 28-30, 33-34, 158-59.

9 United States Interdepartmental Committee, "Agriculture," March 1927, Records of the Bureau of Foreign and Domestic Commerce (RG 151, National Archives), 600.2 (Geneva, Agriculture). For a good brief description of the work of the experts in the Department of Commerce, see Brandes, *Hoover and Economic Diplomacy,* pp. 3-22.

10 Department of Commerce, *Annual Report,* 1924, p. 10; Theodore Joslin, ed., *Hoover After Dinner: Addresses Delivered by Herbert Hoover* (New York, 1933), pp. 9-10; Conference on Unemployment, *Report,* p. 29; Herbert Hoover, *American Individualism* (Garden City, 1922), pp. 10-11.

11 For the quotations, see Joslin, *Hoover After Dinner,* pp. 10, 23; also see Hoover, *New Day,* p. 39; Hoover, "America's Next Step," 65-66.

12 For Hoover's attitudes, see, for example, Hoover, "America's Next Step," 64-65; "Mr. Hoover's Inauguration Address to the American Institute of Mining and Metallurgical Engineers," February 17, 1920, p. 8; Hoover to Benjamin Strong, August 30, 1921, Benjamin Strong Papers (Federal Reserve Bank of New York, New York City), 013.1 (Hoover); Hoover, *New Day,* pp. 39, 115.

13 For discussions bearing on the nature of the open door policy during this period, see, for example, Wilson, *American Business and Foreign Policy,* especially pp. 157-219; Carl Parrini, *Heir to Empire: United States Economic Diplomacy, 1916-1923* (Pittsburgh, 1969); Joseph S. Tulchin, *The Aftermath of War: World War I and U.S. Policy toward Latin America* (New York, 1971); Michael J. Hogan, *Informal Entente: The Private Structure of Cooperation in Anglo-American Economic Diplomacy, 1918-1928* (Columbia, Mo., 1977).

14 See, for example, Hoover, "Backing up Business," 280; Herbert Hoover, *The Memoirs of Herbert Hoover,* 3 vols. (New York, 1951-52), 2:13-14; Herbert Hoover, "Momentous Conference," *Journal of the American Bankers Association,* 13 (January 1921), 462-63; also see Everett G. Holt, "Foreign Government Price Fixing of our Import Raw Materials," in Department of Commerce, *Annual Report,* 1926, pp. 36-37.

15 Hoover, "Foreword," in Friedman, *America and the New Era,* p. 14; Joslin, *Hoover After Dinner,* p. 10.

16 Hoover, "America's Next Step," 61-67.

17 "Mr. Hoover's Address Before the Students of Stanford University," October 2, 1919, 3ff., copy in NYPL. As opposition to the League proliferated, Hoover qualified his view and supported the peace treaty with reservations. See Hoover, *Memoirs,* 2:10-13.

18 *Ibid.,* p. 36.

19 *Ibid.,* pp. 79ff.; also see, for example, Conference on Unemployment, *Report,* pp.,

174

THE "NEW ERA" AND AMERICAN FOREIGN POLICY, 1921-29

147-49, 158-59; for the primacy of European affairs, see Robert Neal Seidel, "Progressive Pan Americanism: Development and United States Policy Toward South America, 1906-1931," Ph.D. Diss. (Cornell U., 1973), 521, 600.

20 For Hoover's view, see Herbert Hoover and Hugh Gibson, *The Problems of Lasting Peace* (New York, 1942), pp. 213-14; for concern over the issue of currency instability, also see, for example, "Western Bankers Dinner and Conference at the White House," June 23, 1921, Warren Harding Papers, Ohio Historical Society (Columbus, Ohio), Box 88, File 57, Folder 1; Charles E. Mitchell, *Back to First Principles* (n.p., 1922), pp. 8, 16; Special Committee of the Chamber of Commerce, "European Problems Affecting American Business," *Nation's Business,* 9 (October 5, 1921), 2-3; House, Committee on Banking and Currency, *Exchange Stabilization* (Washington, 1921).

21 Hoover to Strong, August 30, 1921, Strong Papers, 013.1 (Hoover); Strong to Pierre Jay, August 29, 1921, *ibid.,* 320.115 (Jay).

22 A. C. Miller, "The Federal Reserve Policies, 1927-29," *American Economic Review,* 25 (September 1935), 447; for central bank cooperation, also see the excellent studies by L. V. Chandler, *Benjamin Strong: Central Banker* (Washington, 1958); Stephen V. O. Clarke, *Central Bank Cooperation, 1924-1931* (New York, 1967); Richard H. Meyer, *Banker's Diplomacy* (New York, 1970).

23 Evidence of the close contact between the Treasury Department and the Federal Reserve Bank of New York may be found in the letters and memoranda pertaining to Strong's European trips, 1925-29, Strong Papers, 1000.5-1000.9 (Strong's Trips); Winston-Strong Correspondence, Bureau of Accounts (RG 39, National Archives), Box 220; for Republican officials' support of Strong's efforts, also see United States Treasury Department, *Annual Report of the Secretary of the Treasury, 1928* (Washington, 1929), pp. 348-49; Howard H. Quint and Robert Ferrell, *The Talkative President; The Off-the-Record Press Conferences of Calvin Coolidge* (Amherst, Mass., 1964), p. 142; Chandler, *Strong,* pp. 247-58.

24 See Meyer, *Bankers' Diplomacy,* p. 8; for Strong's negotiations with central bankers, see, for example, the memoranda of his talks with the French in 1926, Strong Papers, 1000.7 (Strong's Trips, 1926).

25 Hoover's bitter criticisms of Federal Reserve policy are well known. See Hoover, *Memoirs,* 3:6-14. But also notice his recognition of the importance of Federal Reserve attempts to restore the gold standard. See Department of Commerce, *Annual Report,* 1925, pp. 35-37; *ibid.,* 1926, pp. 12-13, 50.

26 Robert H. Van Meter, "The United States and European Recovery, 1918-23: A Study of Public Policy and Private Finance," Ph.D. Diss. (U. of Wisconsin, 1971), 299.

27 *Ibid.,* 295-305; also see Hoover to Harding, January 4, 1922, Harding Papers, Box 5, File 3, Folder 2.

28 Hoover, "America's Next Step," 62-63.

29 Hoover to Harding, January 4, 1922, Harding Papers, Box 5, File 3, Folder 2; Julius Klein to Walter S. Tower, January 4, 1922, BFDC Records, 600.2 (Genoa Conference).

30 Financial leverage could be exerted by either restricting private American financial aid or refusing to reduce war debt payments. See, for example, Hoover to Harding, December 31, 1921, Harding Papers, Box 88, File 57, Folder 3; Hoover to Andrew

Mellon, January 6, 1923, Hoover Papers, Commerce Section, Foreign Debts; Hoover to Charles Evans Hughes, November 20, 1924, General Records of the Department of State (RG 59, National Archives), 851.51/499 (filed as 800.51/499).

31 Hoover to Harding, January 4, 1922, Harding Papers, Box 5, File 3, Folder 2; Klein to Tower, January 4, 1922, BFDC Records, 600.2 (Genoa Conference). For widespread business concern regarding the impact of reparations, see, for example, Special Committee of the Chamber of Commerce, "European Problems Affecting American Business," 3; Special Committee of the National Foreign Trade Council, "Report on European Conditions," in *Official Report of the Tenth National Foreign Trade Convention* (New York, 1923), pp. 15ff; Strong to James A. Logan, October 3, 1921, Federal Reserve Bank Papers (Federal Reserve Bank of New York), C797.

32 Hoover, *Memoirs,* 2:182; Alan G. Goldsmith, *Economic Problems of Western Europe* (n.p., 1923), pp. 1, 22; Charles Evans Hughes, *The Pathway of Peace* (New York, 1925), pp. 53–58, 108; undated memoranda (probably August 1922), by Roland Boyden, Leland Harrison Papers (Manuscript Division, Library of Congress), Box 2.

33 For the ties between the "experts," government officials, and American financiers, see the materials in R-6, 12, 14, 16, Owen D. Young Papers (Van Hornesville, New York); Alan Goldsmith—Christian Herter Correspondence, in Leonard P. Ayres Papers (Manuscript Division, Library of Congress), Box 4; diary entries, October-December 1923, William Phillips Papers (Houghton Library, Harvard University), Box 1A; Thomas W. Lamont Papers (Baker Library, Harvard University), Boxes 176, 177; also see Hughes, *Pathway of Peace,* pp. 108, 57–58; Charles G. Dawes, *A Journal of Preparations* (New York, 1939). For a superb account of American influence on the 1924 reparations settlement, see Stephen Schuker, *The End of French Predominance in Europe: The Financial Crisis of 1924 and the Adoption of the Dawes Plan* (Chapel Hill, 1976).

34 See the Goldsmith-Herter Correspondence in Ayres Papers, Box 4; also see Goldsmith and Herring to Hoover, April 12, 1924, BFDC Records, 3266 (Incoming Confidential Cables); Alanson Houghton to William Castle, April 6, 1924, William Castle Papers (Herbert Hoover Presidential Library, West Branch, Iowa), Box 4.

35 For the attitudes of Hoover and the Department of Commerce, see Department of Commerce, *Annual Report,* 1924, p. 7; Goldsmith to Ayres, August 19, 1924, Ayres Papers, Box 4; for Hoover's desire to cooperate with the Agent General for Reparations, see Hoover to S. Parker Gilbert, August 5, 1925, Hoover Papers, Commerce Section, Gilbert.

36 For Hoover's views on the war debts, see Hoover to Harding, January 4, 1922, Harding Papers, Box 5, File 3, Folder 2; Hoover to Mellon, January 6, 1923, Hoover Papers, Commerce Section, Foreign Debts; Hoover to John S. Hamilton, December 31, 1921, *ibid.;* for Hoover's Toledo speech, see *The Commercial and Financial Chronicle,* 115 (October 21, 1922), 1781ff. For the Republicans' initial desire to treat the war debts through the administrative branch of government, see Melvyn Leffler, "The Origins of Republican War Debt Policy, 1921–1923: A Case Study in the Applicability of the Open Door Interpretation," *Journal of American History,* 59 (December 1972), 591–92; Message of Harding to Congress, December 6, 1921, in Department of State, *Papers Relating to the Foreign Relations of the United States,* 2 vols. (Washington, 1936), 1:xxiii.

37 Hoover, drafts of letter to Joseph H. DeFrees, January, 1922, Hoover Papers, Commerce Section, Economic Recovery in Europe; Hoover to Mellon, January 6, 1923,

Hoover Papers, Commerce Section, Foreign Debts; Hoover to L. D. Coffman, April 27, 1926, *ibid.*

38   Hoover to Adolph Ochs, May 31, 1926, *ibid.*

39   Lamont to Dwight Morrow, October 29, 1925, Dwight Morrow Papers (Amherst College Library, Amherst, Mass.), Lamont File; also see Grosvenor Jones to Harold Phelps Stokes, January 4, 1926, Hoover Papers, Commerce Section, Foreign Debts; Hoover to Young, September 18, 1925, Young Papers, I-13.

40   Hoover to Harding, January 4, 1922, Harding Papers, Box 5, File 3, Folder 2; Memorandum, February 4, 1923, Hoover Papers, Commerce Section, Hughes; Hoover, "The French Debt," September 30, 1925, Hoover Papers, Commerce Section, Debts—France.

41   For the quotations, see Hoover to Hughes, April 29, 1922, General Records of the Department of State, 800.51/316; Herbert Hoover, *The Future of our Foreign Trade* (Washington, 1925), p. 13; also see Hoover, *Memoirs,* 2:85-91. For the government's definition of a "productive" loan, see Treasury Department, *Annual Report,* 1926, p. 5. Initially, Hoover also had hoped to tie American loans to American exports, but the complaints of bankers compelled a reassessment of this practice. See Gilbert to Strong, May 21, 1921, Strong Papers, 012.5 (Gilbert); Eliot Wadsworth to Fred Dearing, September 24, 1921, General Records of the Department of State, 811.51/3016.

42   For Hoover's opposition to government loans, see Hoover, "Momentous Conference," 462-63; Hoover, *Memoirs,* 2:13-14.

43   See Hoover to Hughes, December 13, 1921, December 30, 1921, April 29, 1922, General Records of the Department of State, 811.51/3043, 811.51/3106, 800.51/316.

44   In addition to the references cited in footnotes 41 and 43, also see Investment Bankers Association of America, *Proceedings of the Eleventh Annual Convention* (Chicago, 1922), p. 173; Hoover to Harding, December 31, 1921, Hoover Papers, Commerce Section, Foreign Loans; Goldsmith to W. C. Huntington, March 22, 1922, BFDC Records, 640 (French Loans); Hoover to Hughes, November 20, 1924, General Records of the Department of State, 851.51/499 (filed as 800.51/499). For secondary accounts of Republican loan policy, see, for example, Herbert Feis, *The Diplomacy of the Dollar* (Baltimore, 1950); Wilson, *American Business,* pp. 101-23; Tulchin, *Aftermath of War,* pp. 175-205.

45   See the excellent account by Brandes, *Hoover and Economic Diplomacy,* pp. 63-147.

46   *Commercial and Financial Chronicle,* 124 (May 7, 1927), 2687-88; for Hoover's attitudes on loans to German municipalities in particular, see the materials in Hoover Papers, Commerce Section; Foreign Loans—Germany; BFDC Records, 640 (Germany —Foreign Loans).

47   For opposition to Hoover's efforts to apply financial leverage on an extensive scale, see, for example, Harrison to Frank Kellogg, January 28, 1927, General Records of the Department of State, 800.51/558; J. T. Marriner to Castle, June 21, 1927, *ibid.,* 800.51/566; Castle to Houghton, January 7, 1926, Castle Papers, Box 2; *Commercial and Financial Chronicle,* 124 (May 7, 1927), 2687-88; Morrow to Lamont and Dean Jay, July 8, 1927, Morrow Papers, Lamont File; Brandes, *Hoover and Economic Diplomacy,* pp. 151-213.

48   See Hoover's foreword to "The Balance of International Payments of the United

States in 1922," *Trade Information Bulletin,* No. 144 (Washington, 1923), 2; also see the subsequent studies put out annually by the BFDC entitled, "The Balance of International Payments of the United States in 1923 [1924, 1925, . . .]," *Trade Information Bulletins,* Nos. 215, 340, 399, 503, 552, 625, 698 (Washington, 1923-29); also see the annual statistical presentation and examination of American foreign trade in Department of Commerce, *Commerce Yearbook* (Washington, 1921-29).

49   Hoover, *New Day,* pp. 129-40; Department of Commerce, *Annual Report,* 1922, pp. 17-20; Hoover to Kellogg, July 28, 1926, Hoover Papers, Commerce Section, Foreign Debts; Ray Hall, "The United States Balance of Payments for 1927 and 1928," *Annalist,* 34 (August 16, 1929), 302, 310; Ray Hall, "French-American Balance of Payments in 1928: Our 'Unfavorable' Position," *ibid.,* 34 (November 1929), 908.

50   See, for example, Hoover, *Future of Our Foreign Trade,* pp. 11-12; undated memorandum, "Hoover's Thoughts on Foreign Trade," [mid-1920s], Hoover Papers, Commerce Section, Foreign Trade; Department of Commerce, *Annual Report,* 1922, pp. 18-20; "Foreign Trade of the United States in 1929," *Trade Information Bulletin,* No. 684, 1-5; G. B. Roorbach, "Capacity of World Markets to Absorb Europe's Surplus Products and to Afford Employment to Expanding Population," *Proceedings of the Academy of Political Science* (January 1928), 77-96; F. W. Taussig, "Tariff Bill and our Friends Abroad," *Foreign Affairs,* 8 (October 1929), 9-10.

51   Department of Commerce, *Annual Report,* 1922, pp. 17-20; Hoover, *New Day,* pp. 35-40; Hoover to Oswald Knauth, December 23, 1922, Hoover Papers, Commerce Section, Tariff—1923-1925; Memorandum on the Probable Effect of the New Tariff on Our Import Trade, unsigned, undated, *ibid.;* J. Honn to Louis Domeratzky, September 28, 1922, *ibid.;* Henry Chalmers to Hoover, December 29, 1925, *ibid.*

52   For Hoover's support of the protective principle, see, for example, Hoover, *New Day,* pp. 128ff.; for his views on the application of the protective principle and the setting of tariff rates, see Hoover, *Memoirs,* 2:292-99; "The Beginnings of the Flexible Provisions of the Tariff Law," p. 11, Box 296, Hoover Papers, Presidential Subject Files, Tariff Commission—Flexible; Ogden Mills to Hoover, April 23, 1930, *ibid.;* Hoover to Harding, March 16, 1923, Hoover Papers, Commerce Section, Tariff; Memorandum, unsigned, undated [March 1923, by Hoover?], *ibid.;* Henry Stimson to Felix Frankfurter, February 5, 1930, Felix Frankfurter Papers (Manuscript Division, Library of Congress), Box 103.

53   Culbertson to Hoover, April 5, 1923, October 11, 1924, Box 294, "Tariff Commission—Dennis, Alfred," OF, HHCD; Homer Hoch to Hoover, May 7, 1923; *ibid.;* also see Culbertson to Morrow, September 10, 1921, "Culbertson," Morrow Papers; J. Richard Snyder, "Coolidge, Costigan, and the Tariff Commission," *Mid-America,* 50 (April 1968), 131-48.

54   Hoover, *Addresses,* p. 32.

55   For Hoover's complacence, see Hoover to Charles Hebberd, November 24, 1925, Hoover Papers, Commerce Section, Economic Situation in Europe; for a fairminded evaluation by a former associate, see Joseph S. Davis, "Herbert Hoover, 1874-1964: Another Appraisal," *South Atlantic Quarterly,* 68 (Summer 1969), 295-318. Even while Hoover's reputation was at its peak, the *New Republic* began questioning his expertise. See, for example, "The Role of the Expert," *New Republic,* 56 (November 14, 1928), 340-41; also see George Soule, "Herbert Hoover, the Practical Man," *ibid.,* 53 (December 28, 1927), 160-62.

56   Young to Hoover, January 25, 1926, Young Papers, I-73; Gilbert to Garrard

178   *THE "NEW ERA" AND AMERICAN FOREIGN POLICY, 1921–29*

Winston, October 16, 1925, Strong Papers, 1012.1 (Gilbert); Winston to Strong, July 16, 1926, *ibid.,* 012.6 (Winston); Memorandum, by Strong, May 27, 1928, *ibid.,* 1000.9 (Strong's Trips).

57   Department of Commerce, *Annual Report,* 1927, pp. xix–xx.

58   For Hoover's views and actions regarding raw materials monopolies, see "Backing up Business," 280; Brandes, *Hoover and Economic Diplomacy,* pp. 63–147.

59   See *infra,* pp. 32–34.

60   Department of Commerce, *Annual Report,* 1927, pp. xx.

61   Walter T. Layton, "Europe's Role in World Trade," *Proceedings of the Academy of Political Science,* 12 (January 1928), 161–62; Taussig, "Tariff Bill," 11–12; H. Hallam Hipwell, "Trade Rivalries in Argentina," *Foreign Affairs,* 8 (October 1929), 150–54.

62   For Hoover's discussion of the tariff during the 1928 campaign, see Hoover, *New Day,* pp. 24–25, 70, 101–02, 128ff.; for a defense of the tariff which reveals Hoover's parochial nationalism, see "Draft," no date [1925], no signature [Hoover], Hoover Papers, Commerce Section, Foreign Loans—Great Britain; for criticism of Hoover, see "The Menace of Tariff Revision," *New Republic,* 56 (September 5, 1928), 60–62; "Role of the Expert," 340–42; Davis, "Hoover," 64–65. For an interesting analysis of the impact of American protectionism, which substantiates some of Hoover's assumptions, see M. E. Falkus, "U.S. Economic Policy and the 'Dollar Gap' of the 1920's," *Economic History Review,* 24 (November 1971), 599–623.

63   Winston to Morrow, July 8, 1926, Morrow Papers, Winston File; Memorandum, by Martin Egan, October 5, 1925, *ibid.,* Lamont File; Richard Olney to Winston, October 22, 1925, Records of the Bureau of Accounts, Box 220 (unmarked folder); diary entry, November 7, 1925, volume 11, Charles E. Hamlin Papers (Manuscript Division, Library of Congress); also see Hoover's personal account of his negotiations with the Caillaux Mission in Hoover Papers, Commerce Section, Debts—France.

64   See the materials in Strong Papers, 1000.9 (Strong's Trips, 1928); Strong to Gilbert, March 3, 27, 1928, *ibid.,* 1012.2 (Gilbert); Gilbert to Morrow, May 16, 1927, Morrow Papers, Gilbert File; Russell Leffingwell to Lamont, July 20, 1927, Lamont Papers, 103–12; Young to Basil Miles, January 9, 1928, Young Papers, R-30.

65   See Memorandum on War Debt Settlement [1927], Hoover Papers, Commerce Section, Foreign Debts; Hoover, *New Day,* p. 138.

66   For example, with the coming of the depression American tourist expenditures overseas rapidly diminished. Yet this had been an invisible import that Hoover often had referred to as providing the debtors with the capacity to pay war debts.

67   For the Hoover administration's attitude toward the negotiations leading to the Young Plan, see Department of State, *Foreign Relations,* 1929, 2:1029–83; Memorandum of Conversation between Mills and George Harrison, May 8, 1929, George L. Harrison Papers (copies deposited at the Federal Reserve Bank of New York, New York City), 2013.1; diary entry, August 28, 1930, volume 10, Stimson Diaries, Henry L. Stimson Papers (Sterling Library, Yale University).

68   For the experts' disillusionment with Hoover, see especially diary entries, April 10, 17, 1929, May 17, 18, 1929, "Notes on the Young Plan," by Stuart Crocker, Young Papers. Hoover's antipathy to Old World power politics is evident throughout his of-

ficial career. See, for example, the latter chapters of volume one of his *Memoirs* which were written during the 1920s. Hoover, *Memoirs,* 1:275-482; Davis, "Hoover," 299-301.

69   For Hoover's attitude regarding unproductive loans, see Hoover to secretary of commerce, January 9, 1932, Hoover Papers, Presidential Subject Files, Foreign Affairs—Financial Correspondence; Grosvenor Jones to Robert Lamont, July 13, 1929, *ibid.* For the vast amount of information on American loans to Germany, see materials in Hoover Papers, Commerce Section, Foreign Loans—Germany; BFDC Records, 640 (Germany); Bureau of Accounts Records, Box 85; General Records of the Department of State, 800.51/507½, 509½, 520, 558, 560, 561.

70   The difficulty of regulating the outflow of American capital was most evident in the government's futile effort to prevent loans to France so long as the French refused to ratify the debt agreement. See Jones to Hoover, February 17, 1927, Hoover Papers, Commerce Section, Foreign Loans—France; "The State Department and Foreign Loans," *The Index* (February 1928), pp. 6-7. For the difficulty of determining what constituted a "productive" loan, see, for example, A. N. Young, "The Loan Policy of the Department of State," *Far Eastern Review,* 24 (March 1928), 102.

71   Treasury Department, *Annual Report,* 1926, p. 213. For the balancing of "subjective" and "objective" factors bearing on the debt issue, see Leffler, "The Origins of Republican War Debt Policy," 599-601. For the balancing of similar factors bearing on the reparations question, see especially the Goldsmith-Herter Correspondence, Ayres Papers, Box 4.

72   For attitudes toward protectionism in the 1920s, see Frank W. Fetter, "Congressional Tariff Policy," *American Economic Review,* 23 (September 1933), 413-27; also see William R. Allen, "Issues in Congressional Tariff Debate," *Southern Economic Journal,* 20 (April 1954), 340-55.

73   For Hoover's attitudes, see, for example, Hoover and Gibson, *Problems of Lasting Peace,* p. 143; Hoover, *Memoirs,* 2:181-82; Hoover to Harding, January 4, 1922, Harding Papers, Box 5, File 3, Folder 2. The French contended that in defining the armed strength of a nation the industrial capacity of that nation had to be considered as well as its human and financial resources. See, for example, Department of State, *Foreign Relations,* 1927, 1:164.

74   For Hoover's views on the relative economic self-containment of the United States and its advantages, see, for example, "Drafts," by Hoover, January, 1922, Hoover Papers, Commerce Section; Herbert Hoover, "A Year of Cooperation," *Nation's Business,* 10 (June 5, 1922), 13; Herbert Hoover, "The Question of Stability is a Great Human Problem," *Journal of the American Bankers Association,* 23 (October 1930), 257; also see Department of Commerce, *Commerce Yearbook,* 1924, pp. 460, 514-16; *ibid.,* 1928, 92ff; John Richard Meredith Wilson, "Herbert Hoover and the Armed Forces: A Study of Presidential Attitudes and Policy," Ph.D. Diss. (Northwestern U., 1971), 7-10.

SUMMARY OF COMMENTARY BY DISCUSSANTS AND CONFEREES

Discussion of the paper began with a formal commentary by Professor William Julian of Central College. It offered, he thought, a persuasive reinterpretation of Hooverian diplomacy, and he proposed not to challenge its central arguments but to comment on them. For Hoover, he noted, foreign policy and domestic policy were complementary aspects of a larger whole, one constituting an extension of the other. At work was a mind-boggling vision of Weberian rationalization, a kind of business pacifism that embraced globalist goals and sought to achieve what the Wilsonians had failed to achieve at Versailles, yet eschewed military tools and traditional forms of political action. This was a vision, Julian thought, that has endured, not one that was transitional in nature. But anything approaching a successful implementation of it required a particular kind of political order that failed to develop in the 1920s. Those assuming the role of experts failed to establish the kind of consensus, authority, and legitimacy that was envisioned, and other nations, especially France and Japan, refused to accept the legitimacy of America's rationalizers and cooperate in the ways envisioned.

In a second commentary, Professor Joseph Brandes of William Paterson College commended Leffler for his mastery of source materials and new interpretations and for his success in bringing new perspectives to bear on the diplomacy of the 1920s. Like Julian, however, Brandes noted that success for Hoover's initiatives depended upon the development of a particular kind of political order, one that had little chance of developing in the world of the 1920s. And even if the world had been more rational, he thought, Leffler was correct in pointing to conceptual flaws and contradictions in the Hoover approach, especially in regard to the tariff, voluntaristic action, juridic mechanisms, and open door principles. In addition, Brandes pointed to some gaps in the paper. It had not, for example, dealt with Hoover's actions in regard to branch factories abroad, with the distinctions he drew between Americans and foreigners, with the tension between Hoover the ideologue and Hoover the practical administrator, or with what Hoover's goal of an enlarged but circumscribed government meant in terms of specific activities. Finally, Brandes noted and commented on the kind of documentation being used by Hoover scholars. There was a question here, he thought, as to how much of the public relations output could be taken seriously and how much was a mask for other goals and motives.

Following the commentaries, much of the discussion revolved around Hoover's vacillation between economic nationalism and an expansionism geared to expanded international trade. Responding to comments and questions from Robert Zieger, both Leffler and Joan

Hoff Wilson noted the swing of the Hoover Administration toward an internationalist orientation in 1931 and 1932. But this, Leffler argued, became most noticeable after the possibilities for domestic action were exhausted. Prior to that time Hoover worked to expand international trade. But he also viewed various forms of protectionism as contributing to growth, progress, and national well-being; and when trade expansion could not be achieved without sacrificing national protection, he was inclined to forego it and concentrate on expanding the domestic market. The globalists of a later period, Leffler added, were inclined to make the other choice.

A second topic that came in for considerable discussion was the failure of Hoover's efforts to steer American lending abroad into "reproductive" channels. In response to questions from Thomas Thalken and Robert Wood, Leffler elaborated upon this aspect of American diplomacy, noting particularly the high interest rates that were attracting American capital to Europe, Hoover's realization that much of the money was being wasted, and the refusal of leading American bankers to forego short-term profits and cooperate in controlling the capital flow. The episode, Leffler thought, illustrated both a misplaced faith in private enlightenment and Hoover's inability to change the established priorities of those making Federal Reserve policy.

Finally, an extended discussion was touched off by George Carey's comments concerning the seminars in general. As a conservative, he noted, he had long admired Hoover and had been inclined to resist the efforts of liberals to claim him as one of their own. But having learned about his numerous failures and about the gap between Hoover's goals and his accomplishments, he was inclined to think that maybe the liberals could have him. In response, a number of speakers defended Hoover. If he had failed, it was noted, he had also attempted much more than most of his contemporaries, had wrestled with problems for which his critics had no solutions either, had addressed himself to the issues that have mattered in twentieth-century America, and had, as Robert Murray put it, dominated the making of presidential policy for twelve years. Historians, Murray added, speak of an Age of Roosevelt yet rarely of a Roosevelt policy. But for the period from 1921 to 1933, they do recognize and write about Hoover policies, and these appear not just in one area but in many. Few matters of importance escaped Hoover's attention. Yet no one individual outshone him in any of these many areas. As Murray saw it, moreover, success and failure were relative. No system could be expected to solve all problems; and the one that Hoover was associated with, he thought, could take some of the credit for a generation of peace and for eight years of economic growth and rising real wages.

Comments supporting particular aspects of Murray's position also came from Robert Zieger, Martin Fausold, and Peri Arnold. In addition, Alan Seltzer and others noted the academic biases affecting evaluations of Hoover, especially those toward debunking almost all public figures and toward discounting public statements of a philosophical or idealistic bent.

Herbert Hoover with assistant secretaries William MacCracken (left) and Walter Drake (right). The photograph was taken in Hoover's office in 1926. *Courtesy United Press International.*

Herbert Hoover and his bureau chiefs following his nomination for the presidency, June 15, 1928. The man on Hoover's right is Julius Klein. *Courtesy Herbert Hoover Presidential Library, West Branch, Iowa.*

Joseph Brandes

Product Diplomacy: Herbert Hoover's Anti-Monopoly Campaign at Home and Abroad

Editor's Introductory Note

Joseph Brandes, currently professor of history at the William Paterson College of New Jersey, was an early student of Hoover's economic diplomacy and a pioneer in seeking to understand the mixture of nationalism and internationalism that Hoover espoused. His *Herbert Hoover and Economic Diplomacy,* published in 1962, was both a perceptive study of Hooverian ideology and a detailed examination of how this ideology was applied in the programs of the Bureau of Foreign and Domestic Commerce. As such, the book became both a stimulus to new inquiry and a key work in an emerging revisionist scholarship, with which Brandes has maintained contact and to which he has continued to contribute. He is also an authority on American Jewish history and the author of *Immigrants to Freedom* (1971).

In the paper published here, Brandes traces and analyzes Hoover's actions against foreign economic combinations and especially against the British rubber cartel that threatened America's expanding automobile industry. There are numerous parallels, he notes, between this situation and the raw material and fuel crises of recent years, parallels that make the subject more interesting and more relevant than it was once thought to be. And having pointed these out, he examines not only the development and nature of the threat but also Hoover's perceptions of it, the ideology and political factors shaping his responses, his arguments during the debate over American protectionism, and the impact of his campaigns on foreign and domestic behavior. Hoover, he concludes, was more than a politician responding to pressures from industrial groups. His concerns were with protecting an economy geared to mass production and consumption, an economy that was conceived of as the key to progress and harmony, both at home and abroad. And while his prescriptions for doing this called for market restoration, they also recognized the limitations and weaknesses of this remedy and would supplement it with constructive forms of trade control and cooperative action. Within the prescriptions were tensions and contradictions that Hoover never fully resolved.

Here as elsewhere, Brandes joins with those who have seen Hoover as a practical idealist yet have denied that the ideals to which he subscribed were those of laissez-faire capitalism. Although he attacked the rubber cartel and similar institutions as leading inevitably to irrational and exploitive forms of market control, he supported other forms of national protection and cooperative action as being rational and progressive. And while these rational and progressive forms tended to be those in which Americans were engaged, thus lending credence to charges that Hooverism was little more than the pursuit of national advantage, there were also areas in which he granted significant roles to foreign governments and transnational organizations. Of these Brandes tells us relatively little. But they have been explored in other recent scholarship. And taken in conjunction with this, Brandes's work seems to point to an engineering ideal of harmony through rational structures and relationships as being more important than the ideals of unfettered competition or national power.

Product Diplomacy:
Herbert Hoover's Anti-Monopoly Campaign
at Home and Abroad

Though history may not repeat itself, there are some interesting echoes in the 1970s of the struggle against foreign combinations of raw materials in the 1920s. As secretary of commerce, Herbert Hoover fought the cartel-like price-fixing of rubber, potash, sisal, and even coffee. Then, as now, the world's most affluent and advanced industrial nation represented the political economy of continued expansion. Real growth was the key to stability and social progress at home, to power abroad, and growth was seen as depending to some extent on access to and competitive markets in key raw materials.

Conditioned by a heritage of limitless resources and productive ingenuity, Americans tended to assume a mastery of their own fate (especially in the 1920s). They seemed unwilling to face the nation's growing dependence on various foreign supplies and on an effective functioning of the international economy. Yet, some policy makers did perceive dangers that would become an overriding national concern by the mid-1970s.

It was a crisis long in the making, traceable to America's mass production industries. In the 1920s, the automobile industry in particular seemed threatened by foreign restrictions of the rubber supply and sharply rising rubber prices. Then, as now with oil or bauxite or a score of other commodities, a wide range of "solutions" was offered —including measures to achieve national self-sufficiency and to retaliate in kind. Anti-foreign attitudes also rose to the fore, as pressures were brought to bear against the officially-sponsored cartels and this issue became commingled with such other economic foreign policy issues as inter-allied war debts. Naively, perhaps, then as now, Americans sought to ascertain which of their erstwhile allies could still qualify as their friends.

During the Republican ascendancy of the 1920s, the grand marshal of economic policy at home as abroad was Herbert Hoover, a competent and willing leader in the anti-cartel struggle. Among his more moderate weapons was a strikingly contemporaneous public relations campaign for conservation, featuring such slogans as "Economize on Rubber" and "Help Hoover Against the English Rubber Trust," and accompanied by the patriotic appeal of "1776–1925."[1] In addition, he was able to bring a wide range of other weapons to bear in the spheres of public and intergovernmental pressure.

Indeed, many of the issues and responses of the 1920s are echoed within the raw materials crises (not oil alone) of the 1970s, as if reflecting a kind of repetitive aspect of industrial America's political economy. In an approach not unlike Hoover's, a senior fellow of the Brookings Institution advises that "only unity among consumers can effectively counter unity among producers." Without a revision of international trade rules, he warns, the problem could become just as acute for raw materials dominated by "several other commodity cartels," including copper, bauxite, and coffee.[2] Brazil's "coffee cartel" (Hoover's old nemesis, the Coffee Institute) also announced steep price increases for 1974, labeling its decision an "A-Bomb."[3]

As always, it seems, public policy has had to consider diverse economic interest groups, not to mention the ever-elusive concept of the national interest encompassing the American consumer. Yet, the clashing pressures have always been complex. In the coffee trade, for example, the concerns of roasters were not identical with those of the distributors, and among the consumers of rubber from British Malaya were such politically influential manufacturers as Goodyear, Goodrich, and U.S. Rubber as well as their ultimate customers for tires or hot water bags. Behind the Big Three of rubber manufacturing, moreover, were such Wall Street firms as Dillon, Read and Kuhn, Loeb, and Company, involved with foreign investments. Consequently, financial considerations cutting across international boundaries clashed with the notion of safeguarding America from the foreign monopolies' grip.

Assessing the "morals" of "multinational" oil corporations, Leonard Silk inquired recently whether they could ever be expected to pursue other goals than short-term profit maximization, or display greater obedience now to the demands of the United States than to those of Saudi Arabia.[4] Ironically, federal policies encouraging foreign investment, justified for decades on the grounds of national security, culminated in Senator Henry M. Jackson's charges of "corporate disloyalty" against the Arabian American Oil Company. It had refused to supply U.S. military forces during the Arab-Israeli War of 1973. In this light, Hoover's early insistence (1922) that "America should have at least a quarter interest in this [oil] business [as] a matter of national pride . . ." seems a bit quaint. He was appealing at the time for the broadest possible participation by American firms in the Mesopotamian oil fields and, as he frequently did, was offering advice "from the point of view of American commercial interests."[5]

Perennially, it seems, Americans have disagreed among themselves on issues of private profit and governmental intervention, production quotas and import controls, tax and tariff policies, corporate and social responsibilities, enforcement of anti-trust laws, divestiture, and even nationalization. A mingling of populist and progressive impulses, with a dose of *petit bourgeois,* gave rise periodically to skepticism directed against domestic as well as international big business. Congressional investigations and pressure for more vigilant scrutiny by the Justice Department or regulatory agencies have been the outcome. In this vein were the past complaints of some farm-state congressmen, in the course of 1926 hearings, that profiteering by tire manufacturers had gone far beyond the actual price increases of crude rubber. New York's fiery Fiorello H. La Guardia, as well as southern and western congressmen, remained unconvinced that governmental efforts to combat raw materials cartels would benefit anyone except the large corporations. And American industry's defensive efforts— encouraged by Hoover—to create a rubber buying pool were condemned by others as violating the anti-trust laws.[6]

In a somewhat parallel mood perhaps, Senator Frank Church of Idaho, chairman of the Subcommittee on Multinational Corporations early in 1974, found that "Wall Street lawyers were sent to the Middle East . . ." and had worked out an "arrangement . . . to abruptly reduce the taxes paid by the companies to the United States Treasury while dramatically increasing the tax revenues accruing to the oil producing governments." Others have noted the interlocking directorates among the oil companies, including a number of investment bankers serving on the boards of two or more oil companies, as cause for potential actions by the Justice Department, Federal Trade Commission, and the Securities and Exchange Commission.[7] Above all, perhaps, these charges of Clayton Act violation have been intended to mobilize public reproach, always a potent weapon in a democratic society. In brief, echoes of the 1920s persisted into the economic foreign policy debates of the later era.

Hoover's Attack on Foreign Combinations: the 1920s Ideology

The Hoover policies were based on an ideological amalgam of nineteenth-century classical economics with the needs of twentieth-century business in the United States. A "free" economy was revered by Hoover as the democratic force on which depended the continued progress of all the American people. Not merely the advancement of entrepreneurial interests or material progress, but all the things which made America great stemmed from the competitive business tradition modified by changing circumstances.

In practice, the application of these principles was shaped by the fact that Hoover preferred a pragmatic approach to specific issues. On the one hand, for example, he fought bitterly for free international access to raw materials, especially those the United States did not possess. Relying on nineteenth-century theories of free trade and "comparative advantage," he assailed the resort to "monopoly" control of such products as rubber, coffee, potash, and others. International amity was threatened, Hoover asserted, by foreign combinations to restrict prices and production. On the other hand, he defended American tariff protectionism as essential to continued national prosperity, minimizing the opposition aroused at home and abroad by the Republican trade policies. And American prosperity, he believed, was the cornerstone upon which world-wide recovery and prosperity must rest.

In combating foreign "monopolies," Hoover appealed to American national feeling and kept himself in the forefront as the champion of American economic rights abroad. Against such foreign interests, he mobilized a counter-offensive which in some respects exerted greater pressure than the offending "monopolies." The Commerce Department, for example, effectively blocked loans to the Brazilian coffee interests and to the Franco-German potash cartel, and British rubber interests were threatened with a well-financed American buying pool.

Efficient service to private American interests became the keynote of the Commerce Department's widespread operations. Yet Hoover had accepted the cabinet position in Harding's administration partly because of a desire to put into practice his own economic and social principles. His experience as relief administrator in Europe had convinced him more firmly than before that the ways of "American individualism" were superior to any other system, that unlike some of European capitalism, private enterprise in the United States fostered opportunity for all individuals and was thus an expression of equality and "social justice." Belief in these traditional American ideals was the truly "liberal" approach, Hoover maintained, although he was himself attacked often by self-styled progressive and internationalist groups.

It would be misleading to imply that Hoover's concept of the voluntary partnership between government and business was intended to serve the interests of business alone. The Commerce Department was no passive partner sacrificing its own initiative either to Wall Street or Main Street. Thus, in spite of the opposition of many investment houses, Hoover promoted a program of governmental supervision over foreign lending so that the diplomatic and economic interests of America would be given due consideration. Hoover insisted on adequate loan standards, as a governmental responsibility, to prevent "unproductive" uses and eventual loss to American investors or consumers.

Surely, as concluded by Peri Arnold, Hoover was "no simple *laissez-faire* ideologue."[8] Hoover attempted to coordinate governmental actions with private economic interests in the name of the public good. He was well aware of the instabilities and losses resulting from the business cycle, the striving for profit through economies of scale and technological efficiency. Competition was hardly synonymous with productivity. Moreover, he believed, American individualism was uniquely tempered by the necessary cooperativeness of the frontier heritage and its social concerns. By contrast with the still-festering problems of Europe, the actual accomplishments of American society represented "the one great moral reserve in the world today."[9]

These virtues could be extended by a judicious partnership of free enterprise "voluntarism" with the benevolent supervision of the state. "Regulations to prevent domination and unfair trade practices, yet preserving rightful initiative, are in keeping with our social foundations," Hoover maintained.[10] When the Department of Commerce responded to the needs of American business, whether surveying alternate sources of crude rubber or finding export markets for the finished product, it was going beyond mere service to a limited constituency or clientele. It was, as Hoover saw it, serving the nation by providing aid to its "most creative and beneficial element,"[11] especially when the latter was threatened from abroad.

Thus, the effects of artificially high rubber prices were painted by Hoover on a broad canvas. Not only were domestic distributors and manufacturers hurt by fluctuating inventory values, but the cartel's actions caused an "arousal of national feeling" and even a determination by the whole "consuming world to fight militantly for its existence." We of the wealthy United States "could take care of ourselves," Hoover proclaimed aggressively, "we have it within our powers to retaliate." And a strong national response had become necessary because the normal "higgling of merchants [was] lifted to the plane of international relations, with all its spawn of criticism and hate." The international monopolies of raw materials ran counter to the cherished "belief that economic progress must depend upon the driving force of competition."

Their interference with the "inalienable right" of buyers to bargain with sellers threatened the basis of international commerce and well-being, "for no single nation can dissociate its prosperity from the prosperity and good will of all of them." None could boast the right to monopolize a product which other nations required "for their standards of living and comfort," especially when prices were raised "far beyond [a] reasonable profit" because "no voice at all" was granted to consumers. As such restrictions spread and were backed by governmental patronage or direct legislation, they could "only lead to mutual disaster."[12]

With his first-hand knowledge of world affairs, Hoover knew how distant were the ideals of economic equilibrium and cooperation in the aftermath of World War I. His wartime commander-in-chief, President Wilson, saw little cause for optimism after peace was achieved. "It is evident to me that we are on the eve of a commercial war of the worst sort," he warned in 1920, "and I am afraid that Great Britain will prove capable of as great commercial savagery as Germany has displayed for so many years in her competitive methods."[13]

Friction had begun during the war when the British, controlling three-fourths of the world's plantation supply in their southeast Asian colonies, had listed crude rubber as contraband. American manufacturers had been "greatly exercised over [the] embargoes." And foreshadowing the tensions of the 1920s, Secretary of State William Jennings Bryan had threatened: "If American manufacturers are not to obtain necessary supplies, prices of American goods which [Britain] may desire will be greatly increased, if, indeed the exportations from this country be not ultimately prevented."[14] It was a case of nationalism and neutral rights on the part of the Great Commoner, and an issue that had been painstakingly resolved through American reassurances that the finished product would not reach Britain's foes.

With the war over and wartime controls largely scrapped, Hoover saw a "world rapidly gaining stability." But he still feared the snowballing effect of new restrictions abroad leading to protectionist pleas at home "every time some industry fell into trouble." Fortunately, the United States had not yet followed the example set by foreign combinations. Even the farm relief bills being considered in Congress were characterized by a basic generosity. They offered "the benevolent aspect of proposing to fix a higher price to our home consumers than to foreigners and to thus bless the foreigner with cheaper food."[15] But "we" would have to protect our interests, and the British and other sponsors of price-fixing combinations should realize that their actions were threatening those competitive commitments which were the key to economic progress.

As the world's major agricultural exporting nation, America could not be counted upon for unlimited generosity or patience in the face of provocation. On the other hand, Britain was a foremost importer of foodstuffs and raw materials, Hoover liked to note, vulnerable to the threat of an American *cotton* producers' combination, for example. Although distasteful ideologically, retaliation might nonetheless be required "from a national point of view." This was a reality which the British government should be urged to consider in a "comprehensive" manner, recognizing that "they" might suffer more than the United States from the same "currents which they have been to some degree responsible for putting in motion."

In short, Hoover hoped that the British Government could be persuaded diplomatically to desist from the harmful effects of price fixing on "the whole fabric of international commerce and of wholesome international relations . . . [even] world welfare. . . ."[16] Such was Hoover's explicit advice to Secretary of State Kellogg, to be transmitted through our ambassador in London, Alanson B. Houghton, toward the end of 1925. But Britain did not yield.

Nor were Hoover's ideas without detractors at home. His opposition to loan flotation on behalf of the accused cartels inspired a *Wall Street Journal* plea "begging him not to overburden himself." Could not the nation count on a capable secretary of the treasury, Andrew Mellon, and his equally effective colleague, Frank Kellogg, to conduct economic foreign policy? "Mr. Hoover's Helpfulness" in aborting a $40,000,000 flotation for the German Potash Syndicate—"something of a monopoly in its way"—was a disappointment to Lee Higginson & Co. and to other financiers. The journal claimed that potash was used mainly in cotton and truck farming, but little in the major wheat and corn belts where substitutes were available.

Moreover, Hoover might "wisely let the Brazilian coffee industry alone," and discontinue his persistent tie-in between foreign pricing policies and access to American financial markets. The combinations were able to obtain their loans in London, anyway. Worse still was Hoover's use of loan restrictions as "a club for the collection of foreign debts." Generally, the journal found, Wall Street might need "Washington's advice but not Washington's control." "Mr. Hoover is not really necessary in such councils," concluded its New Year's editorial of 1926.

Hoover did not shrink from such blunt challenges. In a press release marked specifically for the western farm papers, the secretary of commerce relished the role of America's progressive conscience, speaking out against Wall Street opportunism. When the time of reckoning came for "the American banking community," Hoover predicted, "the commissions which might be collected on floating such loans would be no compensation." There would be a "justifiable criticism . . . from the American potash and coffee consumers when [they] become aware that American capital was being placed at the disposal of these agencies through which prices were held against our own people and which if located upon our own soil would be a violation of our laws."[17]

In an official memorandum, Hoover acknowledged the availability of European funding for the Brazilian coffee valorization program. It only confirmed his view of the occasionally irresponsible Europeans willing to "enter into a gamble to hold the price of coffee." Still, "it was better that it be done by some outsider than done by American bankers against the interests of the American public." If the government was responsible for the welfare of farmers requiring potash, at least equal care was demanded by the "numerical importance of the coffee consumer." It was, he said "wholly impossible for the American Government to be either directly or indirectly a party to further conspiracies against the American consumer," and hence imperative that loans to Sao Paulo or similar foreign combinations be disapproved.[18]

While Hoover's acceptance of classical economics included at least a limited recognition of comparative advantage in international trade, it did not extend to the totally free flow of capital across national boundaries. The national interest, defined as the greatest good for the nation's greatest numbers, sometimes required that the "invisible hand" of the world's market places be superseded. Millions of jobs, after all, were tied to the continued prosperity of the American automobile industry, now threatened by British rubber restrictions. And because of this, the federal government was justified in launching an intensive search for alternate sources. Whether plantations "under American control" in the Philippines, or encouragement to Firestone's mammoth projects in Liberia, or synthetic production at home, there was a need for engineering developments that the "invisible hand" had not brought forth.

"It may be that Mr. Hoover has an exaggerated idea of government help," was the significant plaint of some of his opponents.[19] At times, his hard line on loans and the "sensational speeches" of his anti-monopoly allies in Congress (such as House Majority Leader John Q. Tilson) caused diplomatic repercussions in Latin America as well. Even the *Times* of Argentina was cited as predicting a "come-back" of British economic influence because Hoover "interfered so very definitely in the matter of lending money to the Brazilians." Insensitive to "South American dignity," he had failed to seek the tactful screen of a bland rejection by Wall Street intermediaries, preferring a blunt statement of official policy.[20]

Hoover's disclaimer was a model of statesmanlike rectitude:

> No one wishes to maintain the good will of foreign nations more than I do, but I would be serving the American people badly if I did not bespeak their interest as consumers against the monstrous imposition which has been imposed upon them in many directions. Furthermore, unless the growth of foreign monopolies directed against consuming countries can be halted, we shall all be confronted with an era of international friction such as we have never hitherto conceived.[21]

Further, in a typical display of national confidence, Hoover warned that the United States was "strong enough" to take the lead in combating foreign monopolies. The diplomatic pressures of those "few" governments fostering such restrictions would be more than outweighed by the gratitude of fifty-odd consuming nations. And in separate advisory letters to Kellogg, he urged continuing counter-pressures against Britain to "shift their policy," not only on rubber but also on the financing of potash and coffee restrictions. Through such financing, he concluded, the "British become parties to further impositions upon our consumers."[22]

Classic ideals of economic growth mingled with consumer protection and moral indignation. In a little over a year, from the Spring of 1924 to Summer 1925, coffee prices rose from thirteen to thirty cents a pound through artificial restrictions, a condition condemned by Hoover for "mulcting the American people at the rate of $200,000,000 annually." With profits of 65% and higher, the managers of the Brazilian valorization scheme—"nothing but a group of speculators"— grew fearful of declining consumption. For American resistance ultimately proved effective, creating unmanageable surpluses. Having realized the "folly of their program," the Brazilians vainly sought loans to prevent "general disaster." They could not have these, Hoover maintained, nor "any contract entered into for restraint of trade and plunder of the American people."

Only if direct participation were granted to "American consumers . . . a strong hand in the control of the valorization scheme itself," could a loan to Sao Paulo be considered. And it would be much better if there were a complete abandonment of such foreign combination schemes. If allowed to fail, their collapse "might be one of the best lessons the world has had that the American people cannot be perpetually held up."[23]

As if to amend Harding's classic statement, Hoover pronounced that "it is the business of the Administration to give such protection to the American consumer as it can" in the face of foreign conspiracies, even if Wall Street preferred to finance them.[24] To a degree, this was consistent with his definition of American individualism as the motor for profitable efficiency but also as a "constant militant check upon capital becoming a thing to be feared."[25] Government-supported cartels stifled consumption as well as competition. Consequently, through 1928, Hoover continued a wary opposition to funding for Brazil's Coffee Institute, refinancing proposals included.[26]

By 1928, Hoover and Julius Klein, his hard-working director of the Bureau of Foreign and Domestic Commerce, had managed to mobilize the American industry into a defensive National Coffee Council. The latter could eventually advise "Candidate Hoover" that having "become the dread of Brazilian Coffee Interests" he might well relent in his new role as presidential nominee and assure Latin Americans that no hostility was intended except for the monopoly's "excessive and artificially maintained prices."[27] Eventually, of course, Hoover would tour Latin America and seek to establish a more cordial relationship.

The Struggle Over Rubber

Fence mending would also be required for the relationship between the United States and Britain. For here the growing dependence of the United States on rubber imports, the efforts of British plantation owners and their political allies to control the supply and price of rubber, and Hoover's attacks on this British cartel all worked to create much ill feeling.

The plantation rubber industry's growth was a twentieth-century phenomenon paralleling the dynamic American automobile industry which it supplied. Rubber production, concentrated in Britain's Asian colonies, was subject to the uncertainties of colonial investment and fluctuating markets. World War I caused further trading instabilities, and wartime price inflation had then yielded to sharp declines during the depression of 1920–21. Plantation interests suffered, as did the American manufacturers caught with high-priced inventories. For the latter, including Goodyear, U.S. Rubber, and Goodrich, the strains of depression brought closer dependence on such investment banking houses as Morgan and Dillon, Read. Only the Firestone Company was able to avoid a degree of control by financiers.

Faced with surpluses and further price declines—from a high of over sixty cents a pound in 1918 to twenty-eight cents by October 1921 —the British Rubber Growers' Association appealed for governmental aid. Winston Churchill, secretary of state for the colonies, appointed a special committee consisting mainly of growers and headed by Sir James Stevenson (who was also chairman of the influential Committee for Demobilization and Reconstruction). With rubber down to twelve and a half cents by August 1922, and Dutch growers refusing cooperation, the British decided to go it alone with a plan of production quotas to maintain prices. They were frankly suspicious of American proposals for cooperation between growers and consumers or for a joint investment program leading to greater profitability, some even fearing a "plot to bankrupt our rubber producing concerns so that the people in America could have bought up the whole lot."[28]

The British were not impressed, apparently, with appeals on behalf of business and consumers or with other American "free trade" shibboleths when these were accompanied by protectionist tariffs. Confronted with a war debt obligation to Washington of about $4.6 billions, many Englishmen (including Winston Churchill as the new chancellor of the exchequer) could see one means of repayment in higher prices for British rubber. Moreover, it was "impossible," in Churchill's words, for the government "to witness the financial ruin of the rubber-producing colonies."[29]

Subsequently, the British legislation formalized as the Stevenson Act was denounced by Secretary of Commerce Hoover for placing a "super-charge upon the American consumer of from $625 to $675 millions per annum." Later, looking back on the 1920s through the medium of his *Memoirs,* Hoover upbraided Winston Churchill for the part he played, when, as secretary of state for the colonies, he initiated this "worst example" of foreign price controls. The Stevenson Act, Hoover recalled, "forced up" rubber prices from a "highly profitable" 20 cents per pound (in 1922) to a $1.21 by 1925, "and the extra dollar was mulcting the United States at the rate of $900,000,000 per annum." [The damage estimate apparently had grown with the passage of time.][30]

Under the terms of the Stevenson Act or "Plan," which was enforced by colonial legislation in British Malaya and Ceylon, the actual production of each rubber plantation for the year ending October 31, 1920, was fixed as the "standard output." When the Plan went into effect, in November 1922, rubber exports were limited to only 60% of "standard." If a planter chose to ship 65% of his "standard output," the usual duty of one penny per pound was raised to four pence on the entire shipment, not merely on the excess. Beyond 65% of "standard," each 5% increase added a penny's tax to the total shipment. In a none-too-successful attempt to adjust the Plan to changing market conditions, a cumbersome system was set up whereby the permitted percentage of "standard" production could be raised or lowered.[31] In practice, this lack of elasticity contributed to charges of greedy profiteering and exploitation of consumers.

In tackling the problem, Hoover and the Department of Commerce did not await an initiative from the industry. They led rather than followed. Thus, when the "Big Three" in control of the Rubber Association of America were persuaded by a growers' delegation to accept the Stevenson Plan on a trial basis in 1923—after all, "stabilization" might benefit both protagonists—Hoover was skeptical. He doubted that British governmental supervision could provide a sufficiently flexible supply at "fair" prices, bluntly warning the delegation of American intentions to survey alternative sources.

By contrast with the conciliatory efforts of U.S. Rubber Company Director John W. Davis, former ambassador to Britain, and of the Morgan interests, Hoover encouraged an independent search for new sources at both the governmental and private levels. Specifically, Harvey Firestone's determinations for a "head-on attack" against the British rubber controls found an ever-responsive ally in the Department of Commerce.[32]

Congressional adherents of Department of Commerce policy were influential, providing budgetary increases at a time when other governmental funding was slashed. Included among them were such Anglophobes as Senator Medill McCormick, chairman of the Foreign Relations Committee, and a man strongly supportive of achieving economic independence from "British colonial restrictions . . . stifling American consumers." By March 1923, Congress had responded to Hoover's calls for a "National Defense against this price control" with a half-million-dollar appropriation to finance both a world-wide search for alternative sources and rubber-producing experiments within the Western Hemisphere. In addition, the Commerce Department received a mandate to ascertain "whether these controls were being used to the detriment of the American consumer."[33] If necessary, it was also indicated, the Webb-Pomerene Act could be amended so as to permit import buying pools that could reinforce the demand side of the equation.

The ensuing survey explored investment opportunities and generated debates over the virtues of growing rubber in the Philippines— under the American flag—as compared to new Latin American plantations. Firestone's ambitions in Liberia were also encouraged. There, it was thought, ample lands and cheap labor would facilitate an American development to rival those of European possessions. Before the Rubber Survey ended, Department of Commerce agents had been sent to the tropical wilderness of Central America, the Philippines, Ecuador, and the bargaining tables of London and The Hague.

Though less dramatic and less publicized than the exploratory expeditions, the Commerce Department's negotiations with the Netherlands government and the Dutch growers may have been a more influential factor in weakening the British controls. In spite of official British pleas for cooperation with their restriction scheme, the Dutch producers remained outside the system, and their decision to compete made the Stevenson Plan less effective.

In February 1923, Hoover discussed with the Netherlands minister in Washington (A. C. de Graeff) "the apprehensions of American capital" concerning the possibility that Holland might join forces with the British rubber controllers. This possibility was subsequently denied by an official telegram from The Hague, transmitted to Hoover in the expectation that it would (according to de Graeff) "remove the apprehension which till now seems to have withheld American capital from investing on a larger scale in rubber plantations in . . . the Netherlands East Indies." Replying for Hoover, Dr. Klein agreed that this could be expected and expressed the Department's gratification.[34]

Until the end of 1924, the campaign continued to appear as more of a governmental crusade than a project of the Rubber Association of America. Except for the Firestone Company, the major manufacturers were wary of the risks involved in plantation rubber and of the joint financial ventures being proposed to reduce such risks. Even with price increases to twenty-four cents a pound, the industry preferred to place its faith in the "free" forces of international trade and finance, an attitude encouraged by the bankers' Anglophilism. Within limits, moreover, they expected to pass the higher costs along to the consumer. On March 6, 1924, Hoover again urged the legalization of a buying pool, using as his vehicle a well-publicized letter to Senator Arthur Capper of Kansas. But this proved premature. Although the senator presented the proposal, it failed to win sufficient backing.

In his letter Hoover argued that "if by an extension of the Webb Pomerene Act . . . our consumers were allowed to set up common purchasing agencies for these imported raw materials where there is a positive combination in control, I am confident that our people could hold their own." Pooled buying he continued, would be particularly effective in an industry where there were so few primary purchasers of raw materials.[35] Nor did he give up on efforts to secure it. From 1925 through 1927, as prices rose, the needs of a booming economy became more acute, and changes took place in the rubber companies' boards of directors; Hoover's campaign gained new momentum, and in 1928 Congress would debate the Newton Bill to legalize an American buying pool. Ironically, by this time, its opponents could claim that other measures had already broken the back of the British combination.

Slaying the Dragon of Foreign Monopoly

In the spring of 1925, rubber prices reached seventy cents per pound, and during that summer they climbed to $1.10. Under these circumstances, Hoover and the Department of Commerce found it much easier to awaken the militancy of the Rubber Association of America. Clearly, the British growers had not delivered on their promise to maintain adequate supplies within a reasonable price range. It was a situation that required the fuller mobilization of both the Commerce and State departments.

On one front, Hoover expressed "gratification" with the Firestone Company's aid in the department's world-wide Crude Rubber Survey. There would, he pledged, be further "cooperation between the Department and [Firestone's] representatives," including those charged with the vast Liberian investments.[36] On another, Hoover sympathized with the concerns expressed by Senator Walter Edge of New Jersey. The latter had received "timely and logical" reports from the Department of Commerce, and he wondered now whether the price-gouging planters might "make more money than is necessary almost for the discharge of the British debt." Even though this could be the case, he felt, "some of our own interests seem to be protecting them," and there was merit, he thought, in retaliating with higher American cotton prices through a special tax on exports to Britain.[37] Otherwise, Senator Edge feared, New Jersey's tire manufacturers would face extinction.

If there was any advantage to the high prices, Hoover noted publicly, it consisted of an inducement to greater domestic self-sufficiency through "chemical reclamation." Previous estimates that 20% of American supplies might be derived from this source were now doubled, this coming at a press conference that followed a meeting with industry leaders. Until this potential could be realized, however, the great concern was with inadequate releases of rubber, in violation of "assurances by Lord Stevenson."[38] An industrial delegation also met with Secretary of State Kellogg, who gave them a "sympathetic but naturally indefinite" reply to their request for pressure on London. Apparently, no such action would be taken without due guidance from Commerce.[39]

Higher prices also gave new life to proposals for an American buying pool. Again, in August 1925, Hoover urged Congress to review the limitations of the Sherman Anti-Trust Act placing "our people" at a disadvantage on the world's market places. Overseas buyers, he noted, enjoyed the protection of our antimonopoly laws, and on top of this we prevented "combinations of our consumers . . . to protect themselves against combinations of foreign producers."[40] Nor was Hoover happy about journalistic reports linking the discomforts of the American consumer with the necessary repayment of British war debts, as if one justified the other.

In the public relations field, the Commerce Department's Editorial Division recognized that "sky-rocketing" prices made rubber "one of the hottest new subjects."[41] The result was a continuing flood of press releases, departmental surveys, reports, and exhortations, as well as the secretary's usual monthly meetings with the editors of trade papers. Opinion leaders such as publishers and bankers were cautioned, however, against presuming that American firms were profiting "by this [foreign] manipulation." Such price rises had almost bankrupted the industry in the depression of 1920. He also counselled patience. To those who pressed for quick retaliation, he pointed out the "difficulty of inaugurating international trade wars . . . involving many thousands of innocent exporters and others." Admittedly, the situation was so grave that "nothing can stop the demand for reprisals." But he "earnestly hoped that such a national boycott could be avoided."[42]

On December 10, 1925, as rubber prices peaked at over $1.20 per pound, the press received another major policy statement in the form of another letter to Senator Capper. "It is inherent in all unregulated monopolies everywhere," Hoover wrote, "that they can never be content with reasonable returns but must sooner or later undertake extortion." The British controls of East Indies rubber were "a sufficient illustration of where these things carry." While denying approval of "trade reprisals," Hoover advocated an urgent list of "wholly defensive" measures. Among these were the "discouraging" of loans to such combinations, voluntary conservation measures, the development of alternate sources and of substitutes, and cooperative "bidding" on the buyers's side.[43]

The glare of publicity was to some degree essential and inevitable. Yet, it brought curious political overtones at home and abroad. The foreign combinations being opposed were, after all, primarily those administered by British authorities, and the *Journal of Commerce,* with its own set of economic biases, tended to be critical editorially. Hoover, it charged, had begun a "War on British Rubber Trade Restriction." Ironically, the images appearing there were almost diametrically opposed to the label of "British sympathizer" that the Hearst press kept trying to pin on Hoover. For a time, at least, the Hearst chain preferred to ignore some of the campaign against British rubber controls rather than change its views, and this it continued to do even as P. J. Croghan of Commerce's Editorial Division accumulated a file of anti-Hoover protests from British newspapers.[44]

Indeed, diplomatic officials were hard put to keep up with their reports on the anti-Hoover and anti-American material in the British press. From Belfast, for example, Consul Henry P. Starrett reported widespread hostility on the "rubber question," an hostility, he felt, that was exacerbated by American attitudes on tariff protection and the payment of inter-allied war debts. As the Belfast *Northern Whig* (December 24, 1925) put it, "Great Britain, Brazil, and other powers are simply retaliating now . . . on account of the nonsensical, outrageous and damnable rates of the Fordney-McCumber Tariff Law." The "composite view," Starrett concluded, "wears an ugly aspect."[45]

The embassy in London also collected clippings of "ill natured comment" aroused by what the *Outlook* called Hoover's "diatribe" against the Stevenson Plan. The latter, according to this periodical, had saved the rubber industry and even increased the world's production. Consequently, Hoover's "assumption of moral superiority" was unjustified, especially in view of American tariff policies and attempts by the United States to raise prices on cotton, copper, corn, and the products of "infant industries." Nor was the United States acting unselfishly when, having almost achieved a corner on gold, it undertook "energetic measures" against the export of American capital. The kind of "laissez-faire which Mr. Hoover advocates," added the *New Leader,* "can only mean . . . the triumph of the Trust."[46]

Even the staid London *Times,* quoted by the United States embassy in "strictly confidential" dispatches, considered the attack on British rubber controls to be "inaccurate, unwise, and calculated to arouse ill feeling on the part of Americans imperfectly familiar with the facts." Its editors feared that "Hoover's laments may . . . serve to check a world-wide movement for the amicable adjustment of difficulties between the nations by mutual concession and agreement."[47]

In addition, the embassy anxiously informed the State Department that Prime Minister Stanley Baldwin (Conservative) intended to make political capital out of the American threats to retaliate with controls on cotton and wheat. Baldwin, it was feared, would use these threats to obtain government subsidies for the expansion of cotton and wheat resources within the empire, thus decreasing the need for American supplies. Left unsettled, the Stevenson Plan controversy could lead to a full-scale trade war and autarchic national policies.[48]

Other segments of the British press concentrated on invidious estimates of American wealth, coupled with personal attacks on Secretary Hoover. The *Manchester Guardian* expounded on the prosperity of the typical American motorist and the high profits of the tire manufacturers. It concluded that "Mr. Hoover . . . has been making himself a little ridiculous" in fighting the Stevenson Plan at a time when American "monopolies" operated as they pleased. In support of its contention, the newspaper quoted Congressman Loring M. Black's (D., N.Y.) statement that it made no sense "to legislate for the British when we cannot legislate for ourselves."[49]

The London *Daily Telegraph* also advised Hoover to look to the American rubber manufacturers if he honestly wished to find those who "fleeced" the American motorist. In spite of their wealth, continued the editorial, American companies unwilling to assume the risks of developing plantation rubber were now finding fault with the justifiable profits of British capital. Nor was it logical for Hoover to charge the Stevenson Plan with monopoly when Harvey S. Firestone possessed the resources to start his own 100,000-acre rubber-growing project in Liberia.[50]

In a similar lead editorial titled "Hooverism," the *Yorkshire Post* censured the Department of Commerce for having replaced "the Anglo-American sentimental attachment" of the war years with a crude debtor-creditor relationship. Attacking the Hoover letters to

Senator Capper, the *Post* concluded bitterly that "in the United States abuse of Great Britain is always a good political move."[51]

Understandably, such sentiments were amplified in the *Rangoon Gazette,* a journal described by Consul Charles J. Pisar (Burma) as closely connected with the Colonial Office. The *Gazette* saw in "Mr. Hoover . . . one of those political economists who would like [to see his country] . . . prosperous while all others are either poverty stricken or struggling with second rate conditions." Its editorial, captioned "America versus Europe," predicted a combination of aggrieved European debtors and raw material producers united in "an economic Pact of Locarno directed against America."[52]

Eventually, a British protest delegation descended upon the State Department, consisting of Envoy Extra-ordinary and Minister Plenipotentiary Sir Henry G. Chilton (in Washington through the years of the Stevenson Plan crisis, 1924–28) and Sir John Broderick, commercial counselor of the British Embassy. The two Englishmen demanded that the American Government should "either permit them to put their own views forward [to the American public] or . . . stop the Department of Commerce from making its attacks on the policies of the British Government." They declared it "inconceivable" for a corresponding official of the British Board of Trade ever to make similar accusations in public against the official trade policies of another government.[53]

An exchange of confidential telegrams between Kellogg and Ambassador Alanson B. Houghton in London shed light on the diplomatic problems raised by the Stevenson Plan. In July 1925, after "consulting fully with Rutherford, Vice President of [the] Goodyear Company," Houghton conferred with Foreign Secretary Sir Austen Chamberlain regarding the gravity of the rubber situation. He warned Chamberlain that the United States was fully prepared to encourage the use of rubber substitutes, and to seek independent sources of supply.[54]

If American manufacturers were forced out of business because of high rubber prices, with consequent unemployment in the United States, Houghton continued, the "effect on public opinion at home would be unfavorable, and [would] tend to bring up our position on free exports." There was no telling then what counter-measures might be considered by an aroused Congress.[55] All this was a rather thinly veiled threat of retaliatory American controls on cotton and wheat, which probably did not surprise Chamberlain. Previously, on several occasions, Hoover and the congressional investigators of raw material "monopolies" had commented bluntly on the availability of this weapon and pointedly reminded the British that the value of their exports to the United States had increased by 74% between 1913 and 1925.[56]

Houghton finally explained his lack of success with the Foreign Ministry by declaring that "relief can be obtained" only through a broad settlement of differences "on general grounds of high policy."[57] Kellogg's telegraphed response repeated the demands of the Rubber Association of America, which had urged "further representations to the British Government" with insistence "that the restriction plan should be entirely suspended November first [1925]." This also coincided with "Secretary Hoover's views." But as Kellogg saw it, the virulence of the American anti-Stevenson campaign "might make it more difficult for the British Government to modify its policy," especially if the news of State Department pressure on the British were "to leak out into the press."[58]

Confronted with American pressures, the British held out the prospect of increased standard production allowances as well as the release of an additional 6,000 tons by early 1926. Sir Austen Chamberlain, foreign secretary, personally assured Ambassador Houghton that "His Majesty's Government regret that they cannot go further than this." They were, he said, sympathetic to the complaints of American consumers. But meager financial reserves, labor problems, and high risks had put British producers in a difficult position. And American manufacturers, he thought, were partly at fault. They had operated as speculators and failed to build up adequate inventories. The embassy viewed Chamberlain's response as a "great concession," and Hoover, after receiving the relevant position papers from Acting Secretary of State Joseph E. Grew, acknowledged the British action as "helpful." He doubted, however, that an early and substantial increase in production was feasible.[59]

Hoover's goal was not concessions, even if they resulted in substantially greater supplies. It was elimination of the Stevenson Plan with its official restrictions and future uncertainties. "The whole question of governmental control of prices," he noted, "fills me with grave misgivings for the future of world relations."[60] His attitude was in tune with his vision of a dynamic international community derived from equal access to resources, markets, and investments. Under a kind of world-wide Open Door, American business could flourish.

Yet significantly, he was far less ready to attack U.S. advantages in Latin America than to complain about "closed doors" in the Far East or Middle East.[61]

Criticizing the Stevenson Plan's use of an average-price concept which incorporated the fluctuations of many years, the Department of Commerce persisted in its complaint that "the just price mentioned by the British Government . . . is just 35% of that now being charged us." America was thus being overcharged far beyond the theoretical free market equilibrium price. In the past American manufacturers who had accumulated rubber inventories had suffered serious losses. They had been "tricked" and "held up by price manipulation." And if the peak prices declined again as a result of the new concessions, the American manufacturer would have to slash his own prices and "write off great losses upon his inventories."[62]

In the fall of 1925 the Rubber Association warned Kellogg and Hoover that the promised release of additional supplies was being delayed through "circumstances probably not understood by the British Foreign Office." The result was an "increased measure of danger confronting a great American industry," which necessitated further pressures in London.[63] Kellogg's response was to consult Hoover on "the taking of formal action by the Government of the United States." Initially, he was told to hold off until the situation in regard to rubber shipments became clearer. But as prices continued to rise, Hoover not only counseled Kellogg to "be perfectly firm" but also renewed his campaign to deny American credit to foreign combinations. Legislation might be passed, he suggested, under which uncooperative bankers could be charged with complicity to violate the Sherman Anti-Trust Act.[64]

Subsequently, the investment firm of Dillon, Read and the Big Three rubber manufacturers undertook their own negotiations with London seeking to replace the Stevenson Plan with a new syndicate controlled by Wall Street. Churchill, as chancellor of the exchequer, seemed intrigued by the proposal and by its potential for easing Britain's balance-of-payments problem. But the plan was quashed by Washington. In an "urgent and confidential" message, Kellogg reiterated Hoover's principles: "This Government cannot countenance any plan to fix the price of rubber or any other commodity. Furthermore, participation by American citizens would certainly be a violation of the spirit if not the letter of our anti-trust laws." If consummated, such a scheme would threaten "the whole fabric of international commerce and even of wholesome international relations." It would justifiably earn the opprobrium of all responsible world powers. And as one of these powers, the American government had "a primary duty to discourage international combinations . . . from becoming interlocked with international finance." It seemed as if the Clayton Act were writ large for the world's acceptance!

Seemingly contrite, Sir Austen Chamberlain disclaimed a knowledge of American law and provided assurances of even greater allowable rubber exports, up to 100% of standard production, by February 1, 1926. The British foreign secretary regarded this "maximum measure of relief" as equivalent to virtually suspended controls, with a likelihood that the Stevenson Plan itself would be subject to substantial "modification" in line with American interests.

Houghton, however, remained suspicious, especially in view of the continuing high prices and of Churchill's "very clever" maneuvers with the American financial delegation. And, indeed, on the intrinsic issue of governmental controls, Churchill informed Sir Esme Howard (ambassador to Washington) that His Majesty's Government was hardly "in a position to enforce upon the colonies concerned [Malaya and Ceylon] the abolition of control."[66] Thus the diplomatic struggle continued to build.

The next initiative came from Harvey Firestone, who, bolder than the Big Three of the Rubber Association, now proclaimed bellicosely that although "we are trapped by a maneuver for British imperial advantage . . . we can minimize the immediate cost to America." This could be done "by meeting an invading nationalism with a defending nationalsim,"[67] one that would have as its goal an independent American control of rubber sources. Although Secretary of State Charles Evans Hughes had once warned Firestone that the age of gunboat diplomacy was over, he now moved, with the aid of Hoover and Kellogg to acquire "extensive control" over the administration of Liberia, including (by the end of 1926) a lease for up to 1,000,000 acres of rubber plantation land.[68]

Suspecting that the larger, well-financed American manufacturers sought to preserve the Stevenson Plan as a means of protecting their own high-priced stockpiles, Firestone requested Hoover to affirm his stand for outright abolition. And unconcerned "that a sudden drop would cause the large manufacturers tremendous losses," he insisted that "stable prices can only be reached by the unrestricted workings of the law of supply and demand." In any case, the supply of reclaimed rubber was expected to double to 200,000 tons in 1926.[69]

Hoover's friendly response emphasized that he was still "unalterably opposed" to any kind of arrangement with London's restriction authorities. In turn, Firestone praised Hoover's anti-monopoly campaign for the downward pressure it had created on prices. Even as the exchange took place, Hoover continued to alert the public to the alarming prospects for the coming year. At present prices, the 900,000,000 tons of needed rubber would cost the nation $666,000,000 more than it would if sold at what the price-fixing body itself had declared to be a "fair" price.[70]

Hoover, though, must have doubted that such predictions would come to pass. On the one hand now, he received confirmation that British exports from Ceylon and Malaya would, indeed, rise to 100% of standard production by the promised date of February 1, 1926. On the other, he was encouraged by new prospects for American rubber manufacturers "collectively establishing and financing some organization to stimulate production through providing capital, guaranteeing future prices, establishing purchasing and collecting agencies [etc.]." In Brazil especially, inquiries were made regarding assurances against export duties, abstention from joining governments which restricted free production, and other attitudes toward large-scale American rubber development. And before the end of 1925, Hoover had received affirmative responses from Rio de Janeiro, including a promise that combinations would be eschewed as "wholly injurious to Brazilian interests."[71]

Summation

Throughout 1925 Hoover had marshaled his forces against foreign combinations, and by early 1926 he was scoring a number of successes. The House Committee on Interstate and Foreign Commerce endorsed his wide-ranging program for independent rubber sources, recommending governmental aid to obtain such concessions. Conservation measures, the use of reclaimed rubber, and relentless pressures against the Stevenson Plan also had their effects. By May, rubber prices were down to fifty cents a pound and continuing to decline.

The battle against scarce and high-priced rubber had apparently been won. Yet throughout, Hoover's concerns had been far more fundamental. He was striving somehow to transfer to a world level the values which he considered uniquely American. These were not necessarily reflected in the policies of all big businesses. For the initiative and efficiency which Hoover so much admired were found more often in enterprises of medium magnitude. These were still striving for growth, still competitive, not yet the giants secure in their control of entire industries, not yet above requiring productive governmental aid. Beyond business, however, Hoover proclaimed also a concern for the countless Americans whose jobs and living standards he saw intertwined with its economic fortunes.

It was good politics, of course, to urge an Open Door policy on behalf of American business and for the protection of American consumers. This was especially true in view of America's postwar nationalism and the further disillusionment with Europe. Such a policy embraced the mood of the era, and it was far from isolationist.

Yet what Hoover was attempting can also be seen as an extension of the peculiar relationship between the emergence of the United States as a world power and its progressive reform movement. Thus, Hoover spoke out fervently on behalf of jobs for American workers and safeguards for consumers, as well as opposing wasteful loans to military dictatorships. The personality of Theodore Roosevelt epitomized this paradox of the big stick abroad and benevolent public policy at home —a contradiction wrapped within the elusive and changing concepts of national interest. In the 1920s, Hoover opposed demands that the government of the Philippines modify its immigration and land policies in favor of plantation development, while at the same time he backed Firestone in Liberia. The former, he feared, verged on the stifling of economic opportunity through official bureaucratic restrictions and monopolistic advantages to larger firms.

Among the forces shaping Hoover's ideology there was, inevitably, the impact of that latter-day progressive and wartime chief, Woodrow Wilson. A strong sense of morality, a faith in the Puritan ethic and in the unique values of America, a commitment to democratic government as a means of implementing such ideals—these were undoubtedly crystallized by the experience of volunteer public service in World War I and beyond.

Individualism and group cooperation could blend, as they had in the idealized image of the frontier. In an age of revolution and social upheaval, such as the postwar world, the goals of material advancement seemed as urgent as ever. In the 1920s, when American economic policy was shaped so much by Hoover, perhaps the nation's Department of Commerce sought even to adapt that old frontier shibboleth of "internal improvements" to the newer world-wide opportunities and frontiers transcending national lines. Through trade channels, at least, American values as well as American products would be exported abroad.

New opportunities could be developed best, in Hoover's view, by channeling the efficient individualism of American enterprise into the international economy. While governments could advise, inform, and provide safeguards for the free play of market forces, they could not displace them without risk to economic progress itself. Thus, the government-sponsored combinations controlling vital foreign resources were viewed as major impediments to be overcome if America's dynamic capitalism was to serve the nation and the cause of world progress.

NOTES

1 *New York Times,* December 27, 1925.

2 C. Fred Bergsten, "Some Vital Commodities Are Subject to 'Resource Diplomacy,' " *New York Times,* Sunday, January 27, 1974; Eric Sevareid's T.V. editorial, "The Era of Product Diplomacy," February 20, 1974.

3 "Brazil Is Raising Prices of Coffee," *New York Times,* December 24, 1973; for Brazil's governmental Coffee Institute in the 1920 struggle, see Joseph Brandes, *Herbert Hoover and Economic Diplomacy: Department of Commerce Policy, 1921–1928* (Pittsburgh, 1962), pp. 133, 137, passim (available in reprint edition, Westport, Conn., 1975: Greenwood Press).

4 Leonard Silk, "Multinational Morals," *New York Times,* March 5, 1974.

5 "Aramco Concedes Denying Oil To U.S. Military Since October," *ibid.,* January 26, 1974; Hughes to Hoover, "Confidential," August 17, 1922; Hoover to Hughes, August 19, 1922, Herbert Hoover Papers (Herbert Hoover Presidential Library, West Branch, Iowa), Commerce Section, Hughes.

6 United States Congress, House, Committee on Interstate and Foreign Commerce, *Hearings on Crude Rubber, Coffee, Etc.,* 69 Cong., 1 Sess. (Washington, 1926), 55–56, 273; La Guardia and others, in *Congressional Record,* 70 Cong., 1 Sess. (April 5, 1928), 5971, 5983–84, 5996.

7 Senator Church hearings, *New York Times,* January 31, 1974; "25 on Boards of Oil Companies Scrutinized in Antitrust Inquiry," *ibid.,* March 12, 1974.

8 Peri Ethan Arnold, "Herbert Hoover and the Department of Commerce: A Study of Ideology and Policy," Ph.D. Diss. (U. of Chicago, 1972), 22.

9 Herbert Hoover to Woodrow Wilson, in Hoover, *Memoirs,* 3 vols. (New York, 1951–52), 1:457.

10 Herbert Hoover, *American Individualism* (Garden City, 1922), p. 55.

11 Arnold, "Hoover and Commerce," 81.

12 Herbert Hoover, "Foreign Combinations Now Fixing Prices of Raw Materials Imported Into the United States" (Washington, 1925), pp. 3–4, 6, 8–9, 11.

13 Woodrow Wilson to Undersecretary of State Franklin L. Polk, March 4, 1920 (Polk Mss, Yale University Library), in John A. De Novo, "The Movement for an Aggressive American Oil Policy Abroad, 1918-1920," *American Historical Review,* 61 (July 1956), 858-59; Frank R. Chalk, "The United States and the International Struggle for Rubber, 1914-1941," Ph.D. Diss. (U. of Wisconsin, 1970), 33.

14 Bryan to Ambassador Walter Hines Page, November 12, December 2, 1914, in *Munitions Industry, Report on Existing Legislation,* 74 Cong., 2 Sess., Senate Report No. 944, Part 5 (1935), 99-100, cited in Chalk, "Struggle for Rubber," 11-12.

15 Hoover, October 31, 1925, in *Munitions Industry, Report,* cited in Chalk, "Struggle for Rubber."

16 Hoover to Kellogg, letter and memorandum, November 28, 1925, Hoover Papers, Commerce Section, Secretary of State Kellogg.

17 "Mr. Hoover's Helpfulness," *Wall Street Journal,* January 1, 1926, and "Statement by Secretary Hoover Regarding Foreign Monopolies," January 4, 1926, Hoover Papers, Commerce Section, Foreign Comb., Misc.

18 Hoover Memorandum, August 25, 1925, Hoover Papers, Commerce Section, Foreign Loans.

19 *Wall Street Journal,* January 1, 1926.

20 *The Times of Argentina,* November 16, 1925, article enclosed by H. F. McCreery of Hard & Rand Inc., December 22, 1925, Hoover Papers, Commerce Section, Foreign Loans, Sao Paulo. For additional background on Hoover's anti-monopoly stand, as well as a fresh, comprehensive, scholarly treatment of related themes, see Joan Hoff Wilson's, *American Business & Foreign Policy, 1920-1933* (Lexington, 1971), esp. 171-75.

21 Hoover to McCreery, January 5, 1926, Hoover Papers, Commerce Section, Foreign Loans, Sao Paulo.

22 Hoover to Kellogg, November 28, 1925, Hoover Papers, Commerce Section, Secretary of State Kellogg.

23 Hoover memorandum, August 25, 1925, Hoover Papers, Commerce Section, Foreign Loans.

24 *Ibid.*

25 Hoover, *American Individualism,* p. 38.

26 Hoover to Charles Evans Hughes, February 8, 1928, Hoover Papers, Commerce Section, Foreign Loans.

27 Berent Friele, National Coffee Council (U.S.), to Julius Klein, June 25, 1928; Klein to Friele, July 6, 1928, Bureau of Foreign and Domestic Commerce Records (National Archives, RG 151), 640 (Brazil).

28 James H. Thomas speech to Parliament, July 27, 1925, *Parliamentary Debates,* 187:104, quoted in Chalk, "Struggle for Rubber," 31.

29 Churchill, quoted in Howard and Ralph Wolf, *Rubber: A Story of Glory and Greed* (New York, 1936), pp. 220-21.

30 *Fourteenth Annual Report of the Secretary of Commerce,* 39; Hoover, *Memoirs,* 2:82.

31   A factual report on the operations of the Stevenson Plan was presented by Representative Walter H. Newton (Minnesota) during the congressional debate on his bill to legalize American pools for the purchase of rubber and other raw materials. *Congressional Record,* 70 Cong., 1 Sess. (April 5, 1928), 5974–80.

32   Chalk, "Struggle for Rubber," 44–45, 52, 62; Brandes, *Hoover,* chapter 4, "Rubber in the Political Economy of Britain and America."

33   U.S. Congress, House of Representatives, Committee on Appropriations, *Third Deficiency Appropriations Bill, 1923,* 67 Cong., 4 Sess. (Washington, 1923), p. 496; also the later *Preliminary Report on Crude Rubber, Coffee, Etc.,* of the House Committee on Interstate and Foreign Commerce, 69 Cong., 1 Sess. (Washington, 1926), p. 1, passim.

34   A. C. de Graeff to Hoover, February 12, 1923; Julius Klein to de Graeff, February 21, 1923, BFDC Records, 254 (Dutch East Indies); see also Ervin Hexner, *International Cartels* (Chapel Hill, 1945), p. 285, and Wolf, *Rubber,* p. 231.

35   Hoover to Capper, March 6, 1924, quoted fully in Charles R. Whittlesey, *Government Control of Crude Rubber* (Princeton, 1931), Appendix D, p. 216. Hoover's letter was distributed through the major Department of Commerce offices to numerous newspapers; see Chalk, "Struggle for Rubber," 67, 291.

36   Hoover to Mark Felber, Firestone Tire & Rubber Co., March 18, 1925, Hoover Papers, Commerce Section, Foreign Comb.—Rubber.

37   Walter E. Edge to Hoover, May 27, 1925; Hoover to Edge, May 28, 1925, Hoover Papers, Commerce Section, Foreign Comb.—Rubber.

38   Statement by Secretary Hoover at Press Conference, June 2, 1925; A. L. Viles, General Manager, The Rubber Association of America, to E. G. Holt, Acting Chief, Rubber Division, "For the information of the Secretary," June 4, 5, 1925, Hoover Papers, Commerce Section, Foreign Comb.—Rubber.

39   P. L. Palmerton, Chief, Rubber Division, to Harold Phelps Stokes, Secretary's Office, July 18, 1925, Hoover Papers, Commerce Section, Foreign Comb.—Rubber.

40   Hoover to Representative Clarence Mac Gregor (New York), August 5, 1925, with enclosures, Hoover Papers, Commerce Section, Foreign Comb.—Rubber.

41   See, for example, P. J. Croghan, Editorial Division, August 6, 1925, Hoover Papers, Commerce Section, Foreign Comb.—Rubber.

42   Hoover to Justus Collins, Kanawha Banking & Trust, Charleston, W. Va., September 19, 1925, and copy of memorandum, Hoover Papers, Commerce Section, Foreign Comb.—Rubber.

43   Hoover to Capper, December 10, 1925 (released for morning papers December 15, 1925), Hoover Papers, Commerce Section, Foreign Combinations: Statements of H. H.

44   Croghan to Stokes, May 26, 1925; *Journal of Commerce,* editorial, May 25, 1925; London's *Morning Post* editorials as cited in the *New York Times,* December 27, 1925, all in Hoover Papers, Commerce Section, Foreign Comb.—Rubber.

45   Henry P. Starrett (U.S. Consul, Belfast), January 4, 1926, State Department Records (National Archives, RG 59), 841.6176/69.

46   *The Outlook* (London), November 7, 1925, the *New Leader* (London), November

6, 1925, and other clippings contained in the reports of Ray Atherton (first secretary, U.S. Embassy, London), November 13, 1925, State Dept. Records, 841.6176/37.

47   U.S. Embassy (London) to the State Department, "Strictly Confidential" Dispatch #681, January 6, 1926, State Dept. Records, 841.6176/67, including editorial from the London *Times,* January 5, 1926.

48   *Ibid.*

49   U.S. Embassy (London) to the State Department, January 21, 1926, State Dept. Records, 841.6176/72, including editorials from the *Manchester Guardian,* January 12, 1926, and the *Daily Telegraph,* January 9, 1926.

50   *Ibid.*

51   *Yorkshire Post,* January 6, 1926, quoted by Stillman W. Eels (U.S. Consul, Leeds), January 6, 1926, State Dept. Records, 841.6176/68.

52   Clippings from the *Rangoon Gazette,* dispatch of Consul Charles J. Pisar (Burma), February 1, 1926, State Dept. Records, 841.6176/77.

53   Memorandum by William R. Castle, assistant secretary of state, November 3, 1926, State Dept. Records, 841.6176/123.

54   Houghton to Kellogg, July 23, 1925, State Dept. Records, 841.6176/6.

55   *Ibid.*

56   *Preliminary Report,* 5. Part of this increase was the result of an intensified demand for rubber in the United States, and inflated prices.

57   Houghton to Kellogg, July 23, 1925, State Dept. Records, 841.6176/6.

58   *Ibid.;* Kellogg to Houghton, July 27, and October 10, 1925, State Dept. Records, 841.6176/26, 27.

59   Aide-Memoire, U.S. Embassy, London, July 22; Chamberlain to Houghton, August 15; F. A. Sterling, counselor of embassy, to the secretary of state, August 17, 18; Grew to Hoover, September 8; Hoover to the secretary of state, September 14, 1925, all in Hoover Papers, Commerce Section, Foreign Comb.—Correspondence, Sec'y of State.

60   Hoover to Kellogg, September 25, 1925, Hoover Papers, Commerce Section, Foreign Comb.—Correspondence, Sec'y of State.

61   For a definition of the Open Door, see Joan Hoff Wilson's insightful discussion in *American Business,* p. 9, passim.

62   Department of Commerce, "Memorandum On Dispatches From The American Embassy In London Relative To The Rubber Situation," with Hoover letter to Kellogg, September 25, 1925, Hoover Papers, Commerce Section, Foreign Comb.—Correspondence, Sec'y of State.

63   Viles letter and memorandum to Kellogg, October 7, 1925, Hoover Papers, Commerce Section, Foreign Comb.—Correspondence, Sec'y of State.

64   Kellogg to Hoover, October 10; Hoover to Kellogg, October 13, November 13, 1925, all in *ibid.*

65   Houghton to Kellogg, November 25, Kellogg to Houghton, December 1, with covering letter to Hoover, December 2, 1925, all in *ibid.*

66   Houghton to Kellogg, December 4, with Kellogg's covering letter to Hoover, December 4; Chamberlain to Howard, December 3, 1925, all in *ibid.*

67   Firestone, quoted in James C. Lawrence, *The World's Struggle With Rubber* (New York, 1931), p. 46.

68   Chalk, "Struggle for Rubber," 89–90; see also 95–97, 132–34, 146–47, passim.

69   Firestone to Hoover, "Confidential," December 12, Hoover to Firestone, December 14, confirming a personal conference, Firestone to Hoover, December 16, 1925, Hoover Papers, Commerce Section, Foreign Comb.—Rubber.

70   Harold Phelps Stokes, assistant to Mr. Hoover, To the Editor of the *New York Times,* December 31, 1925, including passage from letter to Senator Capper, Hoover Papers, Commerce Section, Foreign Comb.—Rubber.

71   Kellogg to Hoover, December 23, incl. reports from Houghton, Hoover to Kellogg, December 17, incl. wording of instructions to embassy in Rio de Janeiro; Leland Harrison, assistant secretary of state, to Hoover, December 24, 1925, Hoover Papers, Commerce Section, Foreign Comb.—Rubber.

Summary Of Commentary By Discussants And Conferees

Discussion of the paper began with formal commentaries by Professor Ellis W. Hawley of the University of Iowa and Professor Joan Hoff Wilson, who was at the time affiliated with California State University, Sacramento. Both commentators were impressed with the parallels that Brandes had drawn between the situation of the 1920s and that of recent years, and both praised the way in which he had reconstructed and documented the rubber controversy. Each, however, raised questions about the paper's conceptual framework, noting, in particular, its tendency to slight the managerial and cooperative ideals with which Hoover was associated elsewhere and therefore to make him more of an anti-monopolist and free trader than he actually was. The anti-monopoly campaigns, Hawley suggested, are better understood as a rationalizer's attack on managerial malpractice than as drives to create the world envisioned in classical economics. Had they been more successful, they might well have been followed by campaigns to build new managerial institutions. But given the structural peculiarities of the rubber industry and the power of those being attacked, they failed to develop much beyond efforts to displace the malpractitioners through appeals to nationalist and competitive ideals. Wilson also thought that Hoover's use of free trade, anti-monopoly, and consumerist rhetoric could not be taken as reflective of his real goals and intentions. But unlike Hawley, she was inclined to see Hoover and his associates as practitioners of a diplomatic "realism" that used whatever was expedient and feasible to advance national interests. Elaborating upon this point later, she suggested that New Era diplomats, Hoover included, were disposed to build American monopolies where they could, to share markets where they had to, and to accept competition where it was unavoidable.

In addition, the commentators made several other points. Hawley agreed with Brandes that Hoover's programs envisioned a coordinated amalgam of public and private activities; but he did not see this as justifying the label of "neo-mercantilist." Wilson was more inclined than Brandes to see both the rubber and coffee campaigns as failures. And in both commentaries, there were questions raised about divisions within the American business community, about the different courses taken by rubber and oil diplomacy, and about the relationship of the events described to such matters as political ambition, European stability, and Latin American development.

The subsequent discussion from the floor began with a series of remarks by Michael Hogan, author of *Informal Entente: The Private Structure of Cooperation in Anglo-American Economic Diplomacy, 1918–1928*. In these Hogan argued that there was an Open Door ideology at work in the American diplomacy of the 1920s. The latter was not neo-mercantilist in the sense of accepting trade warfare as the normal state. Nor could it all be reduced to mere expediency, as Wilson seemed to be suggesting. But the Open Door conception of the period was no longer identical with the free trade conception of classical economics. It had been redefined to recognize the need for managerial coordination and investment safeguards, and in a number of areas its proponents seemed willing to settle for a kind of Anglo-American partnership institutionalized at both the governmental and private levels. That such institutions failed to develop in rubber, Hogan thought, was due partly to the resentment aroused by Hoover's charges and partly to the uncompromising positions taken on American tariffs and the workings of the Stevenson Plan.

Given an opportunity to respond, Professor Brandes then made several points. The British, he suspected, entered partnerships where they felt compelled to, and not because policy was being made by the cooperative-minded. In oil such a partnership had seemed preferable to continued conflict. But in rubber, which was grown chiefly within the

British Empire, they were much more resistant to calls for open doors or shared development. He also suspected that the neo-mercantilist label as applied to American policy had some justification, at least in effect if not in intention. Hoover and his supporters, after all, had worked to enhance the nation's favorable balance of trade, keep gold within the country, and restrict outward investment flows; and they had persisted in this despite the criticism of economic internationalists and the warnings of international financiers. Finally, Brandes suspected that the commentators were seeking a degree of consistency in Hoover that did not exist. Like other politicians, he could at times embrace contradictory lines of policy and simply ignore or paper over the inconsistencies in his economic and social thought.

As the session drew to a close, several other items were also brought into the discussion. There were comments, both from the floor and from the panel, concerning how foreign cartels threatened not only American living standards but groups interested in foreign investment opportunities. There were observations, especially from Melvyn Leffler, concerning Hoover's perceptions of a future in which America was likely to become increasingly dependent on raw material imports and would therefore have to become more of an exporting nation. There was further discussion of how Hoover's political ambitions may have led him to assume the role of monopoly fighter, especially in the period from 1926 to 1928. And in response to questions from Francis O'Brien, there was some speculation about the relationship between Hoover and Louis Brandeis and what this may have contributed to Hoover's anti-monopoly stance. On this, Neil Basen volunteered the information that the two men had drunk sherry together and discussed public issues. But neither he nor others had any knowledge of specific influences.

GEORGE W. CAREY

Herbert Hoover's Concept of Individualism Revisited

EDITOR'S INTRODUCTORY NOTE

George W. Carey, currently professor of government at Georgetown University and editor of *The Political Science Reviewer,* has published extensively in the fields of political theory and American political history. His essays have appeared in scholarly and political journals. He is the co-author, with Willmoore Kendall, of *The Basic Symbols of the American Political Tradition* (1970); and he is the editor, again with Kendall, of *Liberalism Versus Conservatism* (1966). In addition, he has edited *A Second Federalist* (1967) and *The Post-Behavioral Era* (1972). His scholarship has focused particularly on the tensions between conservative values and popular democracy.

In the paper published here, Professor Carey analyzes the political and social thought of Herbert Hoover and concludes that it should be seen as neo-traditional rather than modern or liberal. Like other recent reinterpreters of Hoover, he disassociates the author of *American Individualism* from those theorists who developed the tenets and assumptions of modern liberalism. Hoover, he argues, did not postulate a state of nature or see government as arising from a social contract. He did not view political philosophy as having no legitimate concern with transcendent moral values. Nor did he equate individual freedom with the absence of regulation and social control. His teachings were therefore fundamentally different from those of such "moderns" as Machiavelli, Hobbes, Locke, Rousseau, and Mill. Yet unlike most of those who have reinterpreted Hoover, Carey does not emphasize the Great Engineer's quest for a planning society in which disciplined associations draw upon scientific expertise to resolve social problems and create the social context for a fuller individualism. He is more impressed with the organicist, transcendental, and pluralist elements in

Hoover's thought, and especially with Hoover's view that ordered liberty, to be achieved through restraining the individual and the economic group as well as the state, would kindle the spiritual awakening needed for true enlightenment and progress. Such tenets, Carey maintains, place Hoover's thought outside modernist modes and within a conservative stream that has rejected contractualism, concerned itself with political virtue, and sought to strengthen the transmitters of virtuous traditions.

In the Hoover that he has uncovered, Carey is inclined to see a man whose teachings should have been heeded and whose wisdom still has relevance for those engaged in political life. He begins, however, by noting that Hoover was not a systematic theorist, and in the latter portions of his paper he examines two questions about which Hoover failed to think very deeply or comprehensively. One was the matter of equal opportunity, an expansive concept that could be used to justify more and more controls and ever larger exercises in social readjustment. The other was the problem of how to sustain a virtuous tradition in a society where its primary transmitters—the family, the school, and the church—were being undermined by bureaucratic growth and ethical relativism.

Critics may disagree with some of Carey's judgments, especially, as the discussion following the paper indicated, with his views concerning the virtue and relevance of Hooverian political ideals. In addition, one wonders whether Hoover's thought can be equated with what is found in *The Challenge to Liberty* and certain portions of *American Individualism*. Did it not also include the engineering, managerial, and technocratic ideas that pervaded Hoover's post-World War I writings and many of his statements as secretary of commerce? Was he not involved in devising organizational substitutes for the intermediate institutions that had previously sustained virtuous traditions? And could not these efforts be regarded as a form of the social planning and bureaucratization that he later criticized?

Herbert Hoover's Concept of Individualism Revisited

At the outset we must frankly acknowledge that Herbert Hoover was by no means a *systematic* political theorist. Proof of this is to be found in his major writings concerning individual liberty and freedom, writings which by common consent among scholars emphasized his more general views of the state, society, and individual and also give us insight into the rationale for his decisions and behavior as a public servant.[1] We think it fair to say that to this very day Herbert Hoover is pictured by the vast majority of historians and political scientists as the self-made man, a believer in rugged individualism,[2] attributes which, so his critics are wont to maintain, served to incapacitate him from effectively handling the severe economic crises of the early thirties.[3]

Such characterizations of Hoover, we submit, tend to divert our attention from his teachings, teachings which merit our careful examination today perhaps more so than at any other time in our nation's history. More important, from the theoretical point of view, Hoover's conceptions of individualism and freedom, however incomplete they may be, represent a positive and unique contribution to our thinking about the perennial problems associated with the proper relationship between the state and individual. To put this otherwise, there is in Hoover's writings a distinctive approach to these problems which serves to set him apart from previous theorists who have preoccupied themselves with like matters.

To show this, four major sections comprise this paper:

(a) How and in what ways have modern conceptions of individualism developed? What seem to be the predominant themes of the "moderns" in the development of their theories regarding the individual and the state?

(b) What seem to be the major thrusts or themes of Hoover's theory of individual liberty? How and in what ways do these contrast with or expand upon those of the moderns?

(c) What are some of the perplexing problems associated with Hoover's theory? What elements of the broader theory seem vague or ill-defined?

(d) Where do we stand today relative to Hoover's teachings and injunctions? Have we abandoned the major tenets of his philosophy? If so, to what extent? What does the future seem to hold in terms of the direction our society is likely to take?

Finally, by way of a postscript, an effort is made to indicate the relevancy and saliency of Hoover's thought.

I

At least two basic questions seem pertinent to our discussion of the so-called "moderns." First, who are the moderns and why are they labeled such? Second, what conceivable purpose can be served in examining certain salient aspects of their theories? Specifically, what insights can such an undertaking provide that are relevant to Hoover's notions of individualism?

A complete answer to the first question would take us well beyond the scope of our topic. We can say, however, that moderns are called such because their approaches to the study of the state and individual represent a break with traditional approaches utilized by, among others, Socrates, Plato, and Aristotle. To quote the late Leo Strauss:

> It was possible to speak of the classical solution to the problem of political philosophy because there is a fundamental and at the same time specific agreement among all classical political philosophers: the goal of political life is virtue, and the order most conducive to virtue is the aristocratic republic, or else the mixed regime. But in modern times, we find a great variety of fundamentally different political philosophies. Nevertheless, all modern political philosophies belong together because they have a fundamental principle in common. This principle can best be stated negatively: rejection of the classical scheme as unrealistic.[4]

We will have occasion to deal with some of the ramifications of this difference later.

While there is some dispute about who deserves the title of "father" of the modern school of thought, most serious students accord it to Machiavelli. Again, to quote Professor Strauss:

> The founder of modern political philosophy is Machiavelli. He tried to effect, and he did effect, a break with the whole tradition of political philosophy. He compared his achievement to that of men like Columbus. He claimed to have discovered a new moral continent. His claim is well founded; his political teaching is 'wholly new.' The only question is whether the new continent is fit for human habitation.[5]

We must also note in this connection, for reasons we will spell out later, that there is a philosophical linkage between Machiavelli's teachings and approach, principally those found in *The Prince,* and the social contract theorists of the presumed "age of enlightenment." These, of course, include Hobbes, Locke, and Rousseau. To this list, we must add the most modern of moderns, John Stuart Mill, whose approach to individualism and freedom as set forth in his *On Liberty* represents an interesting variation of modernistic themes and has in a relatively short period of time become something of a "bible" for modern liberals.[6]

We can treat of our second question, the relevance of the moderns to Hoover's theory of individualism, simply by noting that the belief is widely held that the roots of American liberty and individualism are to be found in the writings of the moderns, particularly in John Locke's *Second Treatise of Civil Government.* For instance, Louis Hartz writes:

> In America one not only found a society sufficiently fluid to give a touch of meaning to the individualist norms of Locke, but also found letter-perfect replicas of the very images he used. There was a frontier that was a veritable state of nature. There were agreements, such as the Mayflower Compact, that were veritable social contracts. There were new communities springing up *in vacuis locis,* clear evidence that men were using their Lockian right of emigration, which Jefferson soberly appealed to as 'universal' in his defense of colonial land claims in 1774. A purist could argue, of course, that even these phenomena were not enough to make a reality out of the presocial men that liberalism dreamed of in theory. But surely they came as close to doing so as anything history has ever seen. Locke and Rousseau themselves could not help lapsing into the empirical mood when they looked across the Atlantic. 'Thus, in the beginning,' Locke once wrote, 'all the world was America. . . .'[7]

To this one might add that the words of the second paragraph of our Declaration of Independence, which proclaim that among our unalienable rights are "life, liberty, and the pursuit of happiness," bear more than a cousinly relationship to the Lockean ends of civil society, "life, liberty, and property." Yet, one can maintain that the theories of Hobbes and Rousseau also played dominant roles in shaping both our institutions and prevailing notions relative to the individual's role in our society.[8] Whatever the case may be, the theories of the moderns which we shall briefly examine form a fitting background for our analysis of Hoover's theory of individualism. They will form a backdrop against which we can more fully perceive the originality of Hoover's theories. Certainly we will be in a better position to comprehend both the philosophical bases of his approach and how it differs from those which are widely accepted today.

We will begin our survey of the moderns with Machiavelli because he marks out, however vaguely, the path which later moderns followed in one fashion or another. We must, at the outset, realize that Machiavelli's teachings are subtle and complex. For instance, after reading *The Prince* for the first time, one is apt to conclude that Machiavelli's chief concern or purpose is to inform the prince (in this case Lorenzo the Magnificent, although theoretically it could be any prince) of the means and techniques by which sovereign control can be retained and expanded. The following chapter headings would certainly indicate that this is his primary purpose: "The Way to Govern Cities or Dominions that, Previous to Being Occupied, Lived under Their Own Laws"; "Of New Dominions Which Have Been Acquired by One's Own Arms and Ability"; "Of New Dominions Acquired by the Power of Others or by Fortune"; or "How a Prince Must Act in Order to Gain Reputation." Thus, a standard interpretation of *The Prince* is that it is a practical political manual in the broadest sense of the word "political." What is more—as many standard interpretations would have it—the evil side of Machiavelli's teachings (and they are replete throughout the book)[9] should in large measure be "forgiven" or at least understood in light of Machiavelli's strong sense of nationalism and his fervent desire for a unified Italy.

However, when we read Machiavelli more closely, we see what can be termed a "double theoretical bifurcation." Chapter XV of *The Prince* provides us with a picture of one bifurcation. We quote:

> It now remains to be seen what are the methods and rule for a prince as regards his subjects and friends. As I know that many have written of this, I fear that my writing about it may be deemed presumptuous, differing as I do, especially in this matter, from the opinions of others. But my intention being to write something of use to those who understand, it appears to me more proper to go to the real truth of the matter than to its imagination; and many have imagined republics and principalities which have never been or known to exist in reality; for how we live is so far removed from how we ought to live, that he who abandons what is done for what ought to be done, will rather learn to bring about his own ruin than his preservation.[10]

This passage is more than a "put down" of the traditional political theorists.[11] We are told in no uncertain terms that it is fruitless and harmful to inquire into life as it ought to be. Rather, we should observe and study life as it is.[12] And the clear implication of this is that man is to be viewed as an "object" or "atom" apart from any concern with transcendent moral values, higher aspirations, or his place in the transcendent order of being. Exorcised from political theory or philosophy is the contemplation of the "whole" man; that is, a being concerned with his relationship to and place in a transcendent order. That portion exorcised (for the sake of convenience, we shall hereafter call it X) pertains to "inner" knowledge and consequently is not observable or measurable nor, is it within Machiavelli's framework, particularly useful. What is important is the observable behavior of man and the full intellectual grasp of those techniques by which individuals can be manipulated.

The second bifurcation is less important than the first and flows directly from it. Machiavelli's antipathy toward the Church, Christianity, and religion in general is clearly revealed at various points in *The Prince*. Obviously this is quite in keeping with his first bifurcation. But his approach here presages the conflict which is to come concerning the legitimate powers or domain of church and state. Moreover, Machiavelli's secularism is to become a trademark of the social contract theorists.

While there are differences between the social contract theories with which we are concerned, their similarities are more striking and important. Having followed Machiavelli's lead of eliminating X, contract theorists were, so it would appear, faced with the problem of finding a substitute. Why so? Simply because, among other things, most thoughtful citizens presumably living in a civil society are apt to ask a series of questions which can only be answered within the framework of a systematic theory. The questions could be: What is the extent of my obligation to the state? What is the obligation of the state to me? What are my freedoms within the state? On what basis or foundation does the state exercise control over me? What are the ends or purposes of the state? The answers to these and like questions provided by the social contract theorists are (a) the terms of the social contract; and (b) the nature of man as determined by his outward or external behavior in the *state of nature.*

These two "answers" are highly interrelated through a process which is evident in all of the social contract theories under consideration here. For Hobbes the state of nature was in actuality a war of all against all; a condition in which to use the well known phrase, life was "solitary, poor, nasty, brutish, and short." Self-preservation (protection against *violent* death) provides the reason why each individual signs a social contract, thereby leaving the state of nature, and gives to the sovereign those powers which are necessary for this end. In Hobbes's case these powers vested in the sovereign are far reaching.[13] We cannot say that Locke, for all the kind words we hear about him, was much different. As John Courtney Murray puts it:

> The first impulse of the law of nature, which is that of self-preservation, is, says Hobbes, that of 'getting themselves out of the miserable condition of

Warre.' Locke puts it more politely: 'Thus mankind, notwithstanding all
the privileges of the state of Nature, being but in an ill condition while they
remain in it, are quickly driven into society.'[14]

The major difference between Locke and Hobbes is that Locke
through the very same process lists preservation of property (i.e., unlimited accumulation of wealth) as another obligation thrust upon the
sovereign (i.e., majority) through the social contract. Rights other
than life, liberty, and property are promulgated by the majority
through the enactment of positive law.

To be sure, Rousseau entertains doubts about this whole process.
However, he still postulates a social contract.

> I assume, for the sake of argument, that a point was reached in the
> history of mankind when the obstacles to continuing in a state of Nature
> were stronger than the forces which each individual could employ to the
> end of continuing in it. The original state of Nature, therefore, could no
> longer endure, and the human race would have perished had it not changed
> its manner of existence.[15]

And Rousseau continues:

> Such a concentration of powers can be brought about only as the conse-
> quence of an agreement reached between individuals. But the self-preserva-
> tion of each single man derives primarily from his own strength and from
> his own freedom. How, then, can he limit these without, at the same time,
> doing himself an injury and neglecting that care which it is his duty to de-
> vote to his own concerns? . . .
> Some form of association must be found as a result of which the whole
> strength of the community will be enlisted for the protection of the person
> and property of each constituent member, in such a way that each, when
> united to his fellows, renders obedience to his own will, and remains as free
> as he was before. That is the basic problem of which the Social Contract
> provides the solution.[16]

For Rousseau it was the mythical "general will" which emerged as the
true sovereign within the state as a result of the contract. Each individual having surrendered all his rights would, along with all other individuals who have done likewise, collectively possess sovereignty. Of
course, one of the prescriptions in Rousseau's theory is that each individual must think of the general interest and good of the society in
the exercise of sovereign power; he should not allow partial or self-
interest to mold his thoughts, a stipulation noticeably absent in
Locke's theory.[17]

Enough has been said to show that the social contract theorists replaced X by simple *postulation*. That is, by postulating the conditions of the individual in the state of nature they were able to derive a contract which specified the goals of government and the state, the status of the individual within the state, and the obligations of the individual and state to each other. For this reason, these theories have both static and secular characteristics which place them quite apart from most traditional theory which was intimately concerned with questions such as: What is the good state? What are the constituents of justice? What are the duties and obligations of the good citizen? What are the legitimate sources of authority both within and without the state?

And what of John Stuart Mill? His work *On Liberty* is widely heralded as the finest we have in defense of individual liberty. Certainly the very objective of the book reveals Mill's concern with this matter.

> The object of this Essay is to assert one very simple principle, as entitled to govern *absolutely* the dealings of society with the individual in the way of compulsion and control, whether the means used be physical force in the form of legal penalties, or the moral coercion of public opinion. That principle is, that the *sole end* for which mankind are warranted, individually or collectively, in interfering with the liberty of action of any of their number, is self-protection. That the only purpose for which power can be rightfully exercised over any member of a *civilised community,* against his will, is to prevent harm to others. His own good, either physical or moral, is not a sufficient warrant. He cannot rightfully be compelled to do or forbear because it will be better for him to do so, because it will make him happier, because, in the opinion of others, to do so would be wise, or even right. These are good reasons for remonstrating with him, or reasoning with him, or persuading him, or entreating him, but not for compelling him, or visiting him with any evil in case he do otherwise. To justify that, the conduct from which it is desired to deter him must be calculated to produce evil to someone else. The only part of the conduct of any one, for which he is amenable to society, is that which concerns others. In the part which merely concerns himself, his independence is, of right, absolute. Over himself, over his own body and mind, the individual is sovereign.[18]

The remainder of the book is an amplification and refinement of this theme. Though Mill seems to have difficulty in differentiating between "self-regarding" and "other-regarding" acts, there can be no question about the thrust of his teachings for he allowed such an extremely wide latitude for individual freedom that he may properly be called the "father" of what is fashionably termed the "open society."[19] This, no doubt, accounts for his popularity among civil libertarians today.

We should note three facts concerning Mill's *On Liberty*. First, the work is by no means as broad and encompassing as those we have surveyed above. For instance, Mill is not interested in the origin of the state, though at one point he expressly states that he does not believe in the social contract.[20] Second, the work reveals Mill's animosity toward traditional political theory largely on grounds that traditional theories called for a constriction of individual liberty well beyond those specified by Mill. And third, throughout the work we see the belief expressed that in civilized countries, particularly England, sovereignty was passing on to the people or a majority thereof so that the problem of controlling abuses of power had to be dealt with inside a different framework than had previously been utilized.

> Like other tyrannies, the tyranny of the majority was at first, and is still vulgarly, held in dread, chiefly as operating through the acts of the public authorities. But reflecting persons perceived that when society is itself the tyrant—society collectively over the separate individuals who compose it— its means of tyrannising are not restricted to the acts which it may do by the hand of its political functionaries.[21]

Mill supports his prescriptions regarding individual freedom without X. This should come as no surprise. For X he seems to substitute a basic principle of utilitarianism; namely, if his teachings are followed, the well-being, good, and happiness of the society will be maximized. Thus, the endless questioning and challenging of prevailing and accepted truth will eventually have these beneficial effects. But since liberty of the individual seems to be an end within itself, divorced from all transcendent standards, we must take Mill's assertions as a matter of faith.

II

Nothing can be clearer from Hoover's major writing on individualism and liberty than that he did not share the rationalistic, nominalistic, and individualistic approach utilized by the social contract theorists. For reasons we have partially touched upon this is somewhat surprising. In recent decades public discourse and debate have increasingly assumed a posture that is, to say the least, fully consonant with the social contract mode of thinking. One might go so far as to say that the predominant view of individualism and freedom is a derivative of the social contract formulation. We hear more and more about "individual rights" in a context wherein we are led to assume that such rights inhere in the individual prior to the formation of government. Moreover, government is sharply criticized for not advancing or protecting these inherent individual rights. In both the political and economic spheres the rights contended for also seem to flow from a desire to promote a far greater degree of equality among citizens than presently exists. For this reason alone, the sheer number of rights asserted has multiplied dramatically extending far beyond those originally set forth by the leading contract theorists.[22]

Perhaps, however, this current trend is not really current at all. To state this otherwise, it could be that the predominant American conception of individualism has always been cast in terms of individual rights. Our finest scholars, as we have mentioned, are wont to remind us of the philosophical contributions made by social contract theorists to our American heritage. We do, indeed, have a contract (i.e., Constitution) and we have acknowledged rights in our Bill of Rights. Beyond this, our "great" presidents, Jefferson, Jackson, Lincoln, Wilson, Roosevelts I and II, were all men who were presumably devoted to the expansion and realization of individual rights.[23]

But if this is so, then Hoover's theory of individualism is the more remarkable because of its radical departure from this tradition. We can see this by contrasting key elements of Hoover's theory with those of the contractualists. We shall do this point by point.

(1) Hoover does not postulate a state of nature. This is not to say that he makes no observations about the nature of man. His observations, however, are not postulations but derived from his experience within the confines of an on-going social and political system. His appraisal can properly be termed a "mixed" one.

> If we examine the characteristics of human nature and human behavior we find they are most born in man and change but slowly. Without attempting to determine relative importance, we find that they comprise certain hereditary instincts and certain acquired desires.
>
> There are selfish instincts and impulses of self-preservation, acquisitiveness, curiosity, rivalry, ambition, desire for self-expression, for adulation, for power.
>
> There are the altruistic instincts of courage, love and fealty to the family and to the country; of pity, of kindness and generosity; of love of liberty and of justice; the desire to work and construct, for expression of creative faculties; the impulse to serve the community and nation; and with these also hope, faith, and the mystical yearnings for spiritual things.[24]

Hoover also maintains that these characteristics of human nature must be acknowledged in "any workable philosophy or framework of government,"[25] if the betterment of the community is to be achieved. Presumably these characteristics of human nature are to be found in one degree or another. They are also modified "by education, by moral and spiritual training, by the vast fund of human experience which we pass on with increments to each succeeding generation."[26] "A free society," Hoover continues, "maintains as many potential centers of enterprise, leadership, and intellectual and spiritual progress as there are individuals."[27] And though he recognizes that the day will probably never come when all individuals are imbued with the characteristics of altruism, the mark of a free society is to allow and encourage the development of these characteristics. Yet, a free society cannot, at least for an unforeseen time, ignore the human characteristics of self-interest "as a motive force to leadership and to production. . . ."[28] To do so would signify the death of society.

(2) Hoover's theories regarding individualism are predicated upon an organic conception of society. In this respect, it differs from contractual theories in at least two respects. First, society for Hoover, as it was for the traditionalists, is a "given." This, of course, explains why Hoover had no need to postulate a state of nature. And, though Hoover does not expressly state that he proceeds throughout from an organic premise, it seems quite evident that he would not quarrel with John C. Calhoun's position on this matter:

> . . . I assume as an incontestable fact that man is so constituted as to be a social being. His inclinations and wants, physical and moral irresistibly impel him to associate with his kind; and he has, accordingly, never been found, in any age or country, in any state other than the social. In no other, indeed, could he exist, and in no other—were it possible for him to exist— could he attain to a full development of his moral and intellectual faculties or raise himself, in the scale of being, much above the level of the brute creation.[29]

Second, because Hoover does accept the organic conception of the state, he is concerned with partial and voluntary units and organizations within the state. In keeping with the organic theory he writes:

> The unit of American life is the family and the home. Through it vibrates every hope of the future. It is the economic unit as well as the moral and spiritual unit. But it is more than this. It is the beginning of self-government. It is the throne of our highest ideals. It is the center of the spiritual energy of our people.[30]

But his prime concern is with the economic sector of society where he felt the greatest threat to individual freedom resided. Of individualism he writes:

> Our Government's greatest troubles and failures are in the economic field. Forty years ago the contact of the individual with the Government had its largest expression in the sheriff or policeman, and in debates over political equality. In those happy days the Government offered but small interference with the economic life of the citizen. But with the vast development of industry and the train of regulating functions of the national and municipal government that followed from it; with the recent vast increase in taxation due to the war;—the Government has become through its relations to economic life the most potent force for maintenance or destruction of our American individualism.[31]

Despite his concentration on the economic aspects of society, Hoover acknowledges that "all our social and economic and governmental gears are deeply enmeshed."[32] Certainly this implies a pluralistic view of society which introduces dimensions ignored or neglected by contract theorists, namely, the role of interrelated intermediate institutions which stand between the state and individual.

(3) Hoover did not view all men as equal in the same sense of the social contract theorists. This again is the product of his organic conception of the state and represents a departure from what seems to be the modern prevailing view of equality.

> We in America have had too much experience of life to fool ourselves into pretending that all men are equal in ability, in character, in intelligence, in ambition. That was part of the clap-trap of the French Revolution. We have grown to understand that all we can hope to assure to the individual through government is liberty, justice, intellectual welfare, equality of opportunity, and stimulation to service.[33]

And such an understanding is essential for the continued vibrance and progress of the social and economic order.

> Our social, economic, and intellectual progress is almost solely dependent upon the creative minds of those individuals with imaginative and administrative intelligence who create or who carry discoveries to widespread application. No race possesses more than a small percentage of these minds in a single generation. But little thought has ever been given to our racial dependency upon them. . . . They must be free to rise from the mass; they must be given the attraction of premiums to effort.[34]

The emergence of this leadership will, Hoover reasons, benefit the whole because the accomplishments of the more gifted will eventually "trickle down" to those of lesser talents, imagination, and ability.

(4) Hoover believed that individualism could only thrive in a system of "ordered liberty." This is a recurrent theme in his major works. The word "ordered" assumes significance because it clearly implies a recognition of rules and restraints on individuals, associations, and government, if the kind of individualism which Hoover seeks is to be realized.

What are these rules and restraints? Many of them are formal and represent or reflect the basic ideals of the American conception of liberty as handed down to us from the past. They are, so to speak, the outgrowth of our tradition. Our Bill of Rights and its major provisions embody part of our ordered liberty. Referring to the authors of the Bill of Rights, Hoover states:

> They introduced in the first amendments a concrete definition of the guarantees of liberty for the individual by declaring among other things that there should be no governmental or any other interference in the freedom of worship, of speech, of the press, of peaceable assembly, of petition, no invasion of the security of their persons, houses, papers, and effects against unreasonable searches and seizures, and then only by warrant of law.
> They insisted that a person accused of crime should have the right of speedy and public trial by an impartial jury; that he should be informed of the charge; that he should have the right to call witnesses and be assisted by counsel; that he should not be compelled in any criminal case to bear witness against himself; that he should not be deprived of life, liberty or property without due process of law, and that private property should not be taken for public use without just compensation.[35]

The post-Civil War amendments and the extension of the franchise to women made it quite clear that "our system is built not only upon declared rights and securities but upon an equality of these rights to all."[36]

At the level of governmental processes and structure, our forefathers saw fit to provide that "the law should spring from the expressed will of the majority."[37] The independence of the legislative, executive, and judicial branches, along with the checks and balances between state and national authority, were intended to provide that ours would be a "government of laws and not of men."[38] And the amendment process is such as to insure that our basic liberties and form of government can only be altered after due delay and deliberation on the part of the people.

But such specifications for their observance depend upon the prudence and virtue of the people.

> Our American System has ever recognized that borders between liberty and license, between free speech and slander, order and disorder, enterprise and exploitation, private interest and public interest are difficult to define. But the domain of liberty can be defined by virtue, reason, by the common will, and by law. It cannot be defined by arbitrary power.[39]

The essence of ordered liberty "is justice, self-restraint, obligation to fellow-men. Its practice is a sensitive adjustment of conflicting rights and interests through a spirit of decency and cooperation in human relationships, reinforced by governmental restraints, to the end that men may enjoy equal protection."[40]

Clearly Hoover's teachings regarding liberty differ from those of Mill. The most obvious is that Hoover, operating as he is within the organic conception of the state, seems concerned about constraining the individual through acknowledged rules and processes endemic to the American experience. Put otherwise, maximization of liberty, in Hoover's system, is a complicated enterprise calling for restraint, cooperation, and prudence among all components of the society. To be sure, a high premium is placed on the value of liberty because it is a necessary condition or means to the cultivation and refinement of the altruistic character of individuals. This, by itself, separates Hoover's theory from Mill's, for Hoover, as we shall see, did hold to transcendent values. As Hoover put the matter, "True Liberalism seeks all *legitimate* freedom first in the confident belief that without such freedom the pursuit of other blessings is in vain."[41]

(5) Unwarranted concentration of power is, Hoover holds, a danger to liberty and the ideal of individualism. This is true in both the political and economic spheres. If, for example, there is undue economic concentration through monopolistic practices, the opportunity for individuals to fulfill their just aspirations is hampered.

> The entrance of the Government [in controlling the economy] began strongly three decades ago, when our industrial organization began to move powerfully in the direction of consolidation of enterprise. We found in the course of this development that equality of opportunity and its corollary, individual initiative, was being throttled by the concentration of con-

trol of industry and service, and thus an economic domination of groups builded over the nation. At this time, particularly, we were threatened with a form of autocracy of economic power. Our mass of regulation of public utilities and our legislation against restraint of trade is the monument to our intent to preserve an equality of opportunity. This regulation is itself proof that we have gone a long way toward the abandonment of the 'capitalism' of Adam Smith.[42]

There is at least an equal fear exhibited by Hoover that government may likewise stifle the forces of individual initiative. He has no kind words to say about communism, fascism, nazism, or regimentation which he perceives to be philosophies antagonistic to the very ideals of American individualism. Typical of his appraisal of these alternative philosophies are the following remarks about socialism:

True American Liberalism utterly denies the whole creed of Socialism. The disguised or open objective of Socialism is equality in income, wages or economic rewards. The tenet of equality in true Liberalism is a tenet of equality in birth, equality before the law, and equality of opportunity as distinguished from equality of reward for services. True Liberalism insists that to equalize rewards and possession of material things robs the individual of free imagination, inventiveness, risk, adventure, and individual attainment, development of personality, and independence from a monotony that would sentence the soul to imprisonment. It denies the Socialist contention that men will be more free when compelled to work under, and to work for, only one employer—the government.[43]

All other competing systems he sees in this same light. But he goes beyond this to assert that such systems rest upon regimentation wherein the rulers set priorities independent of any popular control or check. Speaking again of socialism he pictures dire consequences for political democracy.

The Socialists claim they would maintain democratic institutions and all other freedoms except economic freedom. Democratic institutions would not last long. Producing economic equality by regimenting of the whole population into government employees scarcely assures the election of an independent legislative body or any other independent official. Nor can such administration be conducted during the existence of legislative bodies, with all their inevitable interference, with all their necessary sectionalism, party criticism, and their perennial pull and haul for advancement of individual constituents. Legislative bodies cannot exist if they delegate their authority to any dictator, but without such delegation every member of these bodies in such a scene is impelled by the interest of his constituents constantly to seek privilege and to interfere in the administering of economic agencies.

For Socialism to maintain its hold against those who still aspire to liberty every guaranty of freedom—free speech, free press, assembly or a free legislative body, a free judiciary—ultimately must be suppressed. In order to give Socialism a fighting chance the whole structure of our government —constitution, courts, legislative and executive arms—must be merged under despotism."

And this again he sees as the inevitable result in following through with any of the competing philosophies.

Clearly Hoover wrote *The Challenge to Liberty* in response to Roosevelt's early New Deal policies. He saw in them a distinct movement in this country toward regimentation largely in the economic sphere. Hoover details why he feels New Deal policies have led to "Regimented Industry and Commerce," "Government in Competitive Business," "Regimented Agriculture," "Managed Currency and Credit," and "Managed Foreign Trade." All of this he contends has led to a vast bureaucracy whose principal function is to issue orders and directives which dictate what individuals and groups must do. And accompanying this has been a two-fold concentration of power, namely, the national government expanding its sphere of authority at the expense of the states coupled with a dramatic shift of power to the executive branch.

> The whole process of Regimentation with its enormous extension of authority and its centralization in the Federal Government grievously undermines the State jurisdiction over its citizens; State responsibility, and in the end State's Rights. It thereby undermines one of the primary safeguards of Liberty."

The very growth of the national bureaucracy, Hoover argues, carries with it dangers to political freedom.

> Bureaucracy has already developed a vast ramifying propaganda subtly designed to control thought and opinion. The constant use of the radio, the platform, and the press, by device of exposition, news and attack with one point of view, becomes a powerful force in transforming the nation's mentality and in destroying its independent judgment. Bureaucracy's instinctive defense to criticism is to color the information and news with its objectives rather than presenting a cold analysis of results. It goes further in resentment to criticism and attempts to meet it with denunciation. We witness this vituperative impatience from those who believe they are serving the

common good. Critics are smeared by personal attack upon character and motives, not answered by sober argument.[46]

What is more, the trust and cooperation among subsidiary groups necessary for the maintenance of individualism and ordered liberty breaks down as each group competes for favors from the bureaucracy.

(6) The proper role of government in Hoover's theory is that of regulation and control in order to expand the opportunities for individual achievement. Such control and regulation is imperative for a healthy society.

> The continuous adjustment of our society to new forces introduced by advancing science, the unending battle against economic domination, all require constant reform and amendment of our laws if we are to preserve liberty. The growing recognition of public responsibility in the advancement of general welfare requires new commitments of government.[47]

How can regulation or control increase individual liberty and what is the difference between regulation and regimentation? To answer these questions, Hoover recurs to the "traffic control" metaphor.

> In the early days of road traffic we secured a respect for liberties of others by standards of decency and courtesy in conduct between neighbors. But with the crowding of highways and streets we have invented Stop and Go signals which apply to everybody alike, in order to maintain the same ordered Liberty. But traffic signals are not a sacrifice of Liberty, they are the preservation of it. Under them each citizen moves more swiftly to his own individual purpose and attainment. That is a far different thing from the corner policeman being given the right to determine whether the citizen's mission warrants his passing and whether he is competent to execute it, and then telling him which way he should go, whether he likes it or not.[48]

The principal questions which must be asked or answered in each case where the government delves into economic matters are "Does this act safeguard an equality of opportunity? Does it maintain the initiative of our people?"[49]

(7) Hoover's individualism is distinctly an American individualism. He is quite emphatic on this point and throughout his works even shows a disdain for the varieties of European individualism. Our individualism is unique among the nations of the world and, as Hoover takes great pains to point out, has produced a degree of well-being that cannot be matched by any other nation on earth.

What, in sum, is his American creed of individualism? We quote it here because it summarizes so much of what we have said above.

> Our individualism differs from all others because it embraces these great ideals: *that while we build our society upon the attainment of the individual, we shall safeguard to every individual an equality of opportunity to take that position in the community to which his intelligence, character, ability, and ambition entitle him; that we keep the social solution free from frozen strata of classes; that we shall stimulate effort of each individual to achievement; that through an enlarging sense of responsibility and understanding we shall assist him to this attainment; while he in turn must stand up to the emery wheel of competition.* [50]

American individualism, is, then, almost synonymous with equality of opportunity within the confines of ordered liberty.

One is entitled to ask: Is not Hoover's philosophy of individualism simply a variation of modernistic theories? After all, he does promise us primarily materialistic rewards. How can one really differentiate between Mill's promises which are to be achieved through encouragement of a relatively extreme form of individualism and those of Hoover which are to be achieved through adherence to equality of opportunity? Is not Hoover, in fact, far more materialistic than Mill and far less concerned about the intellectual development and progress of society and the individual? In sum, cannot Hoover justly be accused of operating within the confines of modern political theory? Has not he, too, abandoned X or transcendent values in his theory?

In our view, Hoover is best regarded as a neo-traditionalist. We say this for the following reasons:

First, Hoover believed that his form of individualism would serve to kindle "the divine spark of the human soul. . . ." This "kindling" process is, as other passages reveal, a matter of faith.

> For centuries, the human race believed that divine inspiration rested in a few. The result was blind faith in religious hierarchies, the Divine Right of Kings. The world has been disillusioned of this belief that divinity rests in any special group or class whether it be through a creed, a tyranny of kings or of proletariat. Our individualism insists upon the divine in each human being. It rests upon the firm faith that the divine spark can be awakened in every heart. [51]

> Progress will march if we hold an abiding faith in . . . the divine touch in the individual. [52]

This faith rests upon certain assumptions: namely, that there is a divine spark in each individual (or, at least, the vast majority); that the best way, indeed the only sure way, to kindle it is through the individual for this will provide a sounder religious foundation for society; and that the kindling of this spirit will produce a high degree of consensus concerning the content and appropriate application of higher values. Whether these assumptions are sound (and there is reason to believe that they are) is beyond our inquiry. However we can say that Hoover held them or something very much akin to them.

Second, Hoover explicitly states that the American tradition embodies values above and beyond those of materialism. In this vein, he writes:

> The first concern of the American System is for spiritual health and growth of men. It does not accept that the end and object of civilization or the pursuit of happiness lies in being well-fed or growing fat. It denies the economic concept of history, or that blind materialism can long engage the loyalties of mankind. Its faith is that the divine spark, the ideals, the conscience, the courage, the patriotism, the heroism, and the humanism of men make human destiny. It holds that freedom is a prize to be sought for itself, for from it come the infinite satisfactions of the spirit, far more important than all the goods and gadgets of life.[53]

> But those are utterly wrong who say that individualism has as its only end the acquisition and preservation of private property—the selfish snatching and hoarding of the common product. Our American individualism is only in part an economic creed. It aims to provide opportunity for self-expression, not merely economically, but spiritually as well.[54]

And, third, as intimated above, the very vigor and health of American society depends upon the degree to which the character of altruism can be developed and enlarged by the divine spark. This is the transcendent concern, for if our people do not retain and cultivate those virtues which spring from the spiritual force, our institutions and legalisms (e.g., the Constitution, the Bill of Rights, political equality, federalism, etc.) will be but slender reeds in protecting us against regimentation and tyranny.

III

We took caution at the outset to say that Hoover was not a systematic political theorist, in the sense the word "systematic" is normally used. Certainly his major works, while conveying a message and revealing the thrust of his thinking about individualism, freedom and state, are not sufficiently comprehensive to answer troublesome questions for one bent upon restoring the kind and degree of individualism which Hoover felt to be endemic to the American character and tradition. We do not, we repeat, fault his works for these shortcomings for they were clearly written for other purposes and certainly not intended to be thorough political treatises. We cannot help but note, however, that there are at least two major areas *integral* to his thinking which call for more intensive examination than he provides. They are, as we see it, (a) the matter of equal opportunity, and (b) the retention and cultivation of the level of virtue and morality necessary for the preservation and advancement of "rugged" individualism. It is to these matters we now turn.

(a) Equality of opportunity, as we have taken pains to point out, is the cornerstone of Hoover's creed. And we think it fair to say, when most individuals are pressed to define or give substance to the ideal of equality, they will frequently respond that the essence of equality is equality of opportunity much in the same sense set forth by Hoover. We may surmise that one of the reasons for this is that most individuals do perceive many inequalities within society as well as between individuals; inequalities, moreover, that either cannot or should not be eliminated. Examples of this abound. Should not the virtuoso violin player receive more recognition and greater reward than the run-of-the-mill player? Should not superior athletes receive greater compensation than those who are of simply average abilities? Few, if any, would argue that measures should be taken to equalize the reward *or* the abilities of individuals in cases such as these (e.g., proclaim that only two strikes have to be called on Hank Aaron before he is declared "out"). The point is that we perceive inequalities which we feel are justified so that most are unwilling to subscribe to any theory of equality which holds that there should be a "levelling" of reward or ability. Clearly one way to skirt this dilemma is to translate or differentiate the symbol or value of equality (as, for example, found in the Declaration of Independence) to mean equality of opportunity. Such a translation at first glance seemingly avoids the pitfalls associated with equality conceived of as sameness. We can say, for instance, that those with equal ability should receive the same rewards. And more: the system theoretically should be such that individuals with the same ability have an equal opportunity to achieve the same rewards.

Having said so much we are led to one of the great controversies in modern political thought; a controversy, moreover, which lies at the base of many of our contemporary political conflicts concerning the direction of our social and political policies, as well as the allocation of governmental resources. The central question is: How far should we go (presumably through the agencies of government) in providing that the ideal of equality of opportunity is completely realized?

We can illustrate quite simply the nature of this concern by again using a hypothetical example. Suppose, for the sake of argument, that *a* and *b* possess the same inherent ability to play the violin. But suppose further that *a* is born to a poor family, while *b* is born to a wealthy family. In such a case, it might well be that *a*'s family will not be able to buy *a* a violin, much less pay for the lessons to develop fully his innate talents. The opposite of this might well be true with regard to *b*. So it is that from the moment of birth we are confronted with an inequality which would probably produce inequality of opportunity. The question that arises in these and analogous cases is: What steps can or should the government or society take to remove this source of inequality?

But there are other cases not so hypothetical. For the past two decades concern has been exhibited concerning the variance in the quality of primary and secondary education largely on the grounds that those who graduate from the better schools have an enormous head start in life.[55] As we know, this matter is complicated by racial frictions which exist within the society. Further, we do know that the family environment seems to have a significant influence upon the kind and degree of opportunity which will open up for a person in later life. And, so too do such factors as sex and family size.

We seek here only to stress that a multitude of factors and variables can and do affect the degree of equality of opportunity which does exist in any given society and for any given individual. Aware of this, certain schools of thought, principally the Utopian Socialists, formulated societies designed to remove many of the sources of inequality to insure as far as possible that each individual would have the same opportunity as another. The proposals they set forth for this end included elimination of the family structure, uniformity of education, rotation in the occupations, abolition of all inheritance, and equality of reward.

As much as we might find such "reforms" repulsive, a cogent case can be made that they are necessary if we are to maximize equality of opportunity. What we see at once, however, is that we are sacrificing individualism, liberty, and deeply ingrained ways of life. We see, in short, that the formula of equality of opportunity is an expansive one that does not avoid many of the difficulties associated with social readjustments designed to produce simple equality between individuals. What is more, we find ourselves having to weigh competing and incompatible values in determining how far to maximize equality of opportunity. As noted previously, this is the essence of much of our political debate since the 1930s. It certainly was such in the context that Hoover wrote his *The Challenge to Liberty*.

Hoover's seeming lack of concern about what his plea for equality of opportunity might conceivably entail is noteworthy. We may surmise that he felt the essence of equality of opportunity resided in impartiality in both the private and public spheres regarding who is to move ahead at certain junctures much as, to return to his metaphor, the traffic light does at intersections. In this he seems to assume that all qualified individuals are queued awaiting the green light. But there are those who would be wary of such a formulation and ask: Who made it to the intersection and who did not?[56] Are there not qualified people who through no fault of their own have been left by the wayside? Should we not try to create social conditions such that these people be given the opportunity to make the intersection? Roosevelt II must have had these and like considerations in mind when in his 1944 State of the Union Message he proclaimed:

> We have come to a clear realization of the fact true individual freedom cannot exist without economic security and independence. . . .
> In our day these economic truths have become accepted as self-evident. We have accepted, so to speak, a second Bill of Rights under which a new basis of security and posterity can be established for all—regardless of station, race, or creed.
> Among these are:
> The right to a useful and remunerative job in the industries, or shops or farms or mines of the Nation;
> The right to earn enough to provide adequate food and clothing and recreation;
> The right of every farmer to raise and sell his products at a return which will give him and his family a decent living;
> The right of every businessman, large and small, to trade in an atmosphere of freedom from unfair competition and domination by monopolies at home or abroad;
> The right of every family to a decent home;
> The right to adequate medical care and the opportunity to achieve and enjoy good health;
> The right to adequate protection from the economic fears of old age,

sickness, accident, and unemployment.
The right to a good education.
All of these rights spell security.[57]

Certainly Hoover would not deny these objectives. The core of his disagreement with Roosevelt would relate to the means by which they are
to be realized. This leads us to our second area of concern.

(b) The spirit of American individualism, Hoover contends, has
provided this nation with a material abundance unsurpassed by any
other modern nation. It has done so through the efforts of individuals
largely in the private sector operating with a minimal amount of governmental regulation. In brief, the spirit of American individualism
could be counted on to provide both for the good life and an inspired
spiritual atmosphere in which a great premium would be placed on enlightened self-interest and altruistic values. But the creed of American
individualism, as Hoover perceived it, was under attack by governmental programs which called for regimentation. Worse still, because
of the economic conditions which prevailed in the country many people were ready to turn their backs upon this creed and look to the national government for solution of the economic and social problems
confronting the nation.

In light of this, several questions would seem to require fuller ex-
ploration than Hoover provides regarding the preservation, restoration, and advancement of the creed. What accounts for the fact that
the creed was so readily abandoned? Why is it today that so many,
possibly a majority, do not and will not accept the tenets of American
individualism and seek further regimentation and control by the national government? What can be done to restore the creed? How, in
sum, is it possible to inculcate in the American people a morality appropriate to the restoration and maintenance of the spirit of American
individualism?

Hoover, in this connection, does realize the importance of education and the family in the process of transmitting the creed. Through
such institutions, he persistently maintains, individuals will learn to
curb their destructive impulses and, on the positive side, develop a
keener sense of healthy and enlightened self-interest. We are left to
wonder, however, whether these institutions had in fact served to reinforce and transmit the spirit of American individualism to the extent
Hoover believed. Certainly, one would hardly expect such an abrupt

change in basic American attitudes had the creed been as strong as Hoover suggests. Our best guess is that our traditional conception of individualism and its intrinsic worth was ready to be "taken." More precisely, the erosion of our tradition and its basic tenets had already taken place in the private sector (e.g., the education system, community associations, philanthropic institutions, the family, and the like) in which Hoover places so much faith for both transmitting the tradition and meeting the needs of society through cooperative interaction.[58] But be that as it may, the repulsion of challenges to it (regimentation, socialism, etc.) can only be effectuated if the sources of the transmission of the tradition are, for one reason or another, of a mind to do so. This is to say, that while Hoover may have been wrong with respect to the extent that the family and educational institutions would reinforce (and for good reason) the morality appropriate for the perpetuation of the American creed, he was right in placing emphasis upon these institutions for the perpetuation of this morality.

A crucial question relevant to this emerges when we consider our present state of affairs. Certainly no one can deny that the tenets of American individualism enunciated by Hoover have been severely compromised. But, we ask, how can the values which Hoover espoused be restored? Are they vanishing, if not lost forever? Again, consonant with Hoover's teachings, we would have to say that the process of restoration and invigoration would have to take place through the primary institutions of transmission which Hoover recognized.[59] Yet all objective evidence would indicate that today the family structure is probably in greater disarray than at any other time in our history, and that our educational institutions in the main are content to teach a curious form of ethical relativism and would hardly be a receptive vehicle of any creed that challenged the core values of collectivism or relativism.[60] And, in light of this, one can ask: Is there any hope at all?

Hoover is to be excused for not dwelling on these matters. He was not programmatic in the sense that his political adversaries turned out to be. It could well be that he did not perceive the narcotic effects of the welfare state wherein a dependency upon the central government would slowly evolve to, it would seem, a point of no return. And this interpretation is bolstered by Hoover's obvious concern to allow for the natural processes of a virtuous society to overcome the difficulties which confront it.

IV

Where do we stand today with respect to Hoover's teachings and injunctions?

The answer to this question must necessarily be incomplete and judgmental. In addition, it is a foregone conclusion that any appraisal will evoke partisan passions. Nevertheless, there are major trends and developments which bear upon the question.

Let us begin with one of the more obvious, namely, the enormous growth of the national government over the last four decades in terms of both size and power. Since 1930, for instance, the number of civilian employees working for the national government (and this excludes civilians working in the defense establishment) has grown at a rate three times that of the population. While the size of the bureaucracy has remained relatively stable in the last decade, its initial upsurge in growth began during the New Deal years and its continued growth after this period is primarily attributable to the extension or expansion of New Deal programs.

The consequences of this growth are manifold and do bear upon questions of concern in light of our notions of responsible and responsive democratic government. Indeed, how responsive is our government to the people? How and in what ways does the national government inhibit the liberty of the people unnecessarily? What powers for the manipulation of the 'popular will' does our government possess?

Again, there can be no definite answer to these and like questions. We can say, however, that because this growth has been relatively rapid and "topsy-turvy," lines of jurisdiction and authority between departments and agencies are often blurred and ill-defined.[61] Indeed, the organizational structure of any one major department at the national level is so highly complex that relatively few individuals know all the "ins and outs." Those familiar with the operations of a congressman's office know that one of the, if not *the*, major function(s) of a congressman or his staff is to direct the concerned but baffled constituent to the governmental agency or subdivision thereof which can handle his problems or provide the necessary information relevant to his concerns. In sum, citizens are increasingly turning to the national government for solutions to their problems and increasingly they are finding it more and more difficult to find out where to go. Similar difficulties arise in trying to fix responsibility within the bureaucratic apparatus.

On top of this, the movement since the mid-1930s has been toward further concentration of powers at the national level. We need not concern ourselves with the precise reasons for this other than to note that since the famous "switch in time that saved nine," we have witnessed a shell game of sorts. The Court allows Congress to exercise enormous powers, Congress in turn delegates to the president the power to exercise the powers which it has been given, and the president then delegates these powers to the agencies of a growing bureaucracy. At the same time, while powers are centralized at the national level through this process, they are also diffused at the national level because of the growing bureaucracy which nobody seems to comprehend fully. And to add to the confusion we have seen the growth of independent regulatory and judicial commissions—the FCC, FTC, ICC, NLRB, FPC, and so on. However confusing all of this may seem when it comes to the daily operations of the federal government, few would deny that the presidency has been the principal benefactor of this process of centralization. The evidence of this is overwhelming and undeniable in our judgment.[62]

That we have moved toward centralization along the very lines that Hoover feared seems, as we have just said, undeniable. Whether this has had the effects Hoover anticipated is still another question which merits our attention. At one level there have been many, prior to our most contemporary controversies, who have warned of imminent dangers. About a decade ago Amaury De Riencourt wrote:

> Throughout the first year of his rule, Roosevelt concentrated an increasing amount of power in his hands, overriding the reluctance of the disgruntled Congress. Administrative agencies assumed a degree of power and independence that left the legislative branch with very little influence on the dizzy course of events. Final decisions rested with a President who handled his huge power with increasing assurance as time went on. Roosevelt was not carrying out a constitutional revolution, as his enemies asserted, but was merely leading America back to the one and only path along which her history had been proceeding: the path toward growing executive power. It was not a fresh start but the fulfillment of a profound trend whose origin lay deep in the past.
>
> All those who deplored the trend, who lamented the waning of the former 'rugged individualism,' were belated romanticists who refused to move with the times. The spirit of the Roman *panem et circenses* was slowly pervading the atmosphere, without destroying the willingness to work but weakening the former self-reliance of pioneering days.
>
> The mainstay of American freedom—freedom *from* authority—began to give way now that a large majority of the people were willing to barter freedom for security.[63]

Still another important question remains: What are the capabilities of the national government in effectuating wide scale social and economic changes? The question is as pertinent today as it was when Hoover wrote, for the fact is that the people are turning to the national government for the solution to a wide variety of intricate problems. Indeed, the rhetoric of our most prominent politicians encourages such behavior.

Roger A. Freeman addressed himself to this question. His comments are worth extensive quotation.

> The growth of the modern service state in the United States during the third quarter of the twentieth century may in historical perspective well have been the most significant governmental development of its time. To its architects the coming of age of the welfare state—as it is more commonly called—is a matter of supreme pride and immense satisfaction. To its opponents it is the cause and make of the decline and the likely fall of a great nation which rejected its promise, forsook its destiny, and squandered its birthright. Future historians may see in retrospect whether the America of today and tomorrow is to be compared more closely to the Rome of the second century—the Golden Age of Antonines—or to the Rome of the fifth century—the time of the Goths, the Vandals and the Huns.
>
> The most visible manifestation of the new age, certainly the most amenable to measurement, is a vast expansion and intensification of public services in the broad field of social welfare, accompanied by a sharp incease in the size of public budgets and public payrolls. Dependence on government rather than on their own work output for the necessities of life and its amenities by a large number, and eventually a majority of its citizens is a distinctive mark of the welfare state, dating back to the days of *panem et circenses.*
>
> Everyone knows that federal spending has been soaring over the past few decades, far outpacing the growth rate of the nation's economy. Also, that the federal bureaucracy has dramatically expanded, at a much faster rate than the U.S. population or the civilian labor force. Everyone that is, who has *not* looked at the record.[44]

And what have been the results of this? "The least we might expect," Freeman writes, "is to have closer to the total 'to insure domestic tranquility, provide for the common defense, promote the general welfare . . . ,' to have sharply reduced crime and other social ills and lifted education to new heights." But he continues:

> . . . the evidence is to the contrary. Crime, delinquency, and most kinds of social ills, new and old, have been multiplying at a frightening rate, to a

point where Americans are less safe in their home, on the streets, in their pursuits than they have ever been—or as people in most other countries. Nor have there ever before been such anarchy-like conditions in the United States, mob violence, arson, looting, terror bombing, wanton destruction, assault and killing of law officers, as we have seen in recent years. The status and products of our education system do not reflect the fact that more than five times as much public money is now being allocated to it each year than was less than two decades ago. Instead of helping to achieve 'domestic tranquility,' educational institutions have become the breeding places, and often the cause, of civic strife and contempt of law. Schools and colleges rank lower now in the respect and affection of the American people than they have at any time.[65]

But the matter does not stop here. According to Freeman, and his case is documented to the hilt, aid to families of dependent children has increased, even granted the inflationary value of the dollar, by about 60% while the number of recipients of this aid program have quintupled since the program was initiated in 1952. Despite our efforts to aid the educationally disadvantaged children (within the last nine years to the extent of seven billion dollars), there has been a marked failure to produce any tangible results. And Freeman continues:

For more than three decades we have been trying to boost the price of farm products and to reduce farm production, at a cost to the public treasury which has now run well over $100 billion. Simultaneously, we worry over the high cost of food and the inadequacy of our food base for an 'exploding' population. . . .

We have over the past twenty-five years poured $143 billion into aid over the 100 foreign countries where in many cases it has reaped a harvest of thistles and venom while supporting self-destructive policies of the recipient governments. . . .

Grants to state and local governments have long been a popular device to promote and finance favored public services. But the multiplication of authorizations to well over five hundred in recent years has turned federal aid into an administrative nightmare which if continued longer will wind up in chaos. Plans to simplify intergovernmental aid by shifting some of the decisions to states and cities—through grant consolidations, fiscal grants, revenue sharing or tax credits—have so far been given the cold shoulder by members of Congress who feel that there is but little wisdom outside its own halls. . . .

Twenty-two years ago we started an urban renewal program which, at a huge expense, has since destroyed three times as many dwellings as it has completed, and has built mostly apartments which the former residents of the area cannot afford. It has been called a slum removal program because it has mainly shifted slums from one part of the city to another, sometimes spawned 'instant slums' to replace the old ones. The true welfare state enthusiasts blind themselves to the fact that slums are not decaying buildings but people.[66]

Freeman concludes:

> Never before has government in the United States claimed, held or exercised so many responsibilities for our personal affairs nor made so many decisions affecting most facets of our individual lives. The welfare state gave extravagant promises and assumed duties which, judging by the results, it is unable to discharge, leaving a trail of disappointment, bitterness, and polarization among major segments of the American people. Far from leading the country toward greater tranquility it has, by well-intentioned but ill-conceived actions, created, fueled, and fanned civic strife and upheaval which threaten to turn into anarchy.[67]

Freeman is not alone in recognizing the counter-productive effects of our national government in so many social-welfare areas, particularly those involving long range planning. But, over the years, in spite of these warnings, the movement toward more extensive programs of this kind has grown to enormous proportions and there seems no way to arrest the trend which, as we know, may ultimately have disastrous effects for not only the cultivation of individual responsibility but our entire economic structure as well. Welfare programs, government doles, and the like, as Roosevelt himself once observed, can eventually have a narcotic effect, and this certainly seems to be the case today. Along with this there has been a parallel movement in the fields of science and technology that reinforces the notion that our most perplexing social and economic problems can be solved through governmental planning. As some of our leading politicians have said, "If we can place a man on the Moon we can surely cure our urban ills."

In what ways are Hoover's theories regarding individualism and freedom relevant to our present state of affairs? We can see that he was not too far off the mark in predicting certain of the consequences of a big and paternalistic government. But we can ask how much different might matters be today if we had followed the injunctions set forth in his theories, particularly those dealing with individualism, freedom, and government? Here we can note but a few which are more or less obvious:

(1) There would probably be far less centralization than we have today. Primary reliance for the solution of social problems would rest

either in the private sector through the cooperation of relevant groups —trade associations, churches, schools, professional bodies, private research groups—or by the local and state governments. Problems would only be treated by the national government as a last resort and then only in cooperation with the subordinate units of government and the involved parties.

(2) From this would follow greater control and participation at the local level which would presumably allow for greater individual spontaneity and creativeness.

(3) Efforts would be made to achieve a greater cooperation between what are now antagonistic centers of power such as business, labor, and the government itself. As Hoover emphasized in his writings this cooperation during the earlier part of the century helped to account for the remarkable social and economic progress in the United States.

(4) There would exist a great hesitancy to endorse governmental programs which would discourage the individual from assuming his moral responsibilities to other individuals and to the community in which he lives. An attitude which is prevalent today towards those in need is "let the government take care of them." Certainly such a morality would be discouraged if Hoover's teachings were followed and cultivated.

(5) Avenues would be opened up for the spiritual and moral advancement of the individual through the numerous voluntary organizations in the United States. Certainly one of the chief functions of our political leadership would be to encourage and lend moral support to the activities of such organizations not for narrow partisan purposes but for the goal of advancing altruistic values.

(6) Government, particularly the national government, would move much more slowly and cautiously in the implementation of large scale social and economic programs. The immediate formulation and application of grand master plans to correct presumed or real social problems certainly would not be the order of the day.

We do not mean to imply that all would be sweetness and light if we had paid more attention to Hoover's philosophy. Moreover, it is clear that neither of our major political parties are about to abandon their ways and endorse effective measures that would turn back the clock so that we might have the opportunity to approximate more closely the ideals and goals envisioned by Hoover. At the same time, few can deny that there is today an increasing disenchantment with the path we have taken in the past forty years. And a good deal of this disenchantment is not related to materialistic concerns. On the contrary, it would seem that the growth of the centralized state wherein each individual and community are viewed as so many pawns on a chess board to be manipulated according to some master plan has produced deep frustrations. Individuals have increasingly lost their sense of purpose within the context of the community and likewise communities now are dependent on a centralized and impersonalized government whose organizations and procedures are akin to those depicted by Kafka.

Perhaps in the not too distant future "we the people" may well find the ways and means to return to that tradition outlined by Hoover. In pointing out the intricate and subtle relationship between the individual, community, and the state, by emphasizing the desirability and need for individuals to discover their place in the transcendent order, it followed the finest teachings of western civilization. At the very least, it poses alternatives which we would do well to ponder.

NOTES

1   Our principal focus throughout will be on two of Hoover's works which deal directly with the matter of the state and the individual: *American Individualism* (Garden City, 1922) and *The Challenge to Liberty* (Rockford, 1971; first published in 1934). We are well aware of the twelve-year gap between these two works, as well as the momentous events which occurred in the interim. For instance, *The Challenge to Liberty* is clearly an attack on major elements of Roosevelt's "New Deal" program. As we hope to show in our subsequent analysis, however, there is a constancy to Hoover's views concerning individualism revealed in these two works.

2   Hoover wrote in this connection: "While I can make no claim for having introduced the term 'rugged individualism,' I should be proud to have invented it. It has been used by American leaders for over a half-century in eulogy of those God-fearing men and women of honesty whose stamina and character and fearless assertion of rights led them to make their own way of life. Rugged individualism is indeed a distinguishing and enduring quality ever found among Americans." *The Challenge to Liberty,* pp. 54–55 (hereafter cited as *Liberty*).

3   On this point see Richard Hofstadter, *The American Political Tradition* (New York, 1956), chapter 11. See also Arthur A. Ekirch, Jr., *The Decline of American Liberalism* (New York, 1969). Writes Ekirch of Hoover: "Neither his rugged individualism nor the new business philosophy he had espoused as secretary of commerce appeared suited to the all-prevailing hard times. Deterred by individualistic leanings from calling for stronger government action to cope with the depression, and suspected in what economic measures he did recommend of favoring big business, he was doomed to failure. As one historian of American politics has well pointed out, Hoover, the 'victim of his faith in the power of capitalism to survive and prosper without gigantic governmental props . . . was the last presidential spokesman of the hallowed doctrines of laissez-faire liberalism, and his departure from Washington marked the decline of a

great tradition.' '' (Pp. 268–69.) This view of Hoover as the champion of laissez-faire liberalism has been challenged quite convincingly in more recent appraisals of Hoover's presidency and his prior public service. As Martin L. Fausold and George T. Mazuzan write in the "Introduction" to *The Hoover Presidency: A Reappraisal* (Albany, 1974): "He [Hoover] always opposed statism, yet he was not an advocate of laissez-faire, and he refused to abondon the notion that a proper blend of organized expertise, systematized associationalism, and enlightened individualism would provide the ideal blend of order and freedom." (P. 25.) Also in this volume see Ellis W. Hawley's "Herbert Hoover and American Corporatism, 1929–1933." See also the "Bibliographic Note" at the end of this volume, which points up the status of this ongoing debate.

4   Leo Strauss, *What Is Political Philosophy?* (Glencor, 1959), p. 40.

5   *Ibid.* See also Gerhart Niemeyer, "Humanism, Positivism, Immortality," *Political Science Reviewer,* 1:277–94.

6   It would certainly appear that Mill's views regarding individual liberty have had an enormous impact on certain Supreme Court justices (e.g., Douglas), the liberal mass media (e.g., *The Washington Post*), and liberal organizations such as the American Civil Liberties Union. Anyone familiar with our institutions of higher learning cannot help but note the pervasiveness of Mill's philosophy.

7   Louis Hartz, *The Liberal Tradition in America* (New York, 1955), pp. 60–61.

8   In this respect countless efforts have been made to show the Rousseauian spirit reflected by Thomas Paine and the Hobbesian influences represented by Alexander Hamilton.

9   "A man who wishes to make a profession of goodness in everything must necessarily come to grief among so many who are not good. Therefore it is necessary for a prince, who wishes to maintain himself, to learn how not to be good, and to use this knowledge and not use it according to the necessity of the case." *The Prince and the Discourses* (New York, 1950), p. 56.

10   *Ibid.*

11   Hobbes puts the matter more bluntly. "The natural philosophy of those schools [of the Grecians] was rather a dream than science, and set forth in senseless and insignificant language. . . . Their moral philosophy is but a description of their own passions. For the rule of manners, without civil government, is the law of nature; and in it, the law civil that determines what is *honest* and *dishonest,* what is *just* and *unjust,* and generally what is *good* and *evil.* Whereas they make the rules of *good* and *bad* by their own *liking* and *disliking;* by which means, in so great diversity of taste, there is nothing generally agreed on, but everyone does, as far as he dares, whatsoever seems good in his own eyes, to the subversion of commonwealth. Their *logic,* which should be the method of reasoning, is nothing else but captions of words and inventions how to puzzle such as should go about to pose them. To conclude, there is nothing so absurd that the old philosophers, as Cicero says (who was one of them), have not some of them maintained. And I believe that scarce anything can be more absurdly said in natural philosophy than that which now is called *Aristotle's Metaphysics;* nor more repugnant to government than much of that he has said in his *Politics;* nor more ignorantly than a great part of his *Ethics.*" Thomas Hobbes, *Leviathan* (New York, 1958), pp. 6–7.

12   See Niemeyer, "Humanism, Positivism, Immorality."

13   Among these powers are "the right of judicature and decision of controversy"; to

"judge what doctrines are fit to be taught them [the subjects]"; to "judge what is necessary for the peace and defense of his subjects"; "the right of making rules; whereby the subjects may every man know what is so his own, as no other subject can without injustice take it from him." Hobbes, *Leviathan,* chapter 18, book 2.

14   John Courtney Murray, *We Hold These Truths* (New York, 1960), p. 304.

15   Jean Jacques Rousseau, *The Social Contract* (new York, 1960), p. 179.

16   *Ibid.,* p. 180.

17   The revolutionary implications of Rousseau's theory are obvious. There is some debate about whether his theories contained the seeds for modern totalitarian thought and practice.

18   John Stuart Mill, *On Liberty* (New York, 1950), pp. 95–96.

19   Mill, as many have noted, does not face up to the question of how open a society can be and still remain open.

20   "Though society is not founded on a contract, and though no good purpose is answered by inventing a contract in order to deduce social obligations from it." Mill, *On Liberty*, pp. 176–77.

21   *Ibid.,* p. 89.

22   A complete list of "rights" that have been claimed in the last twenty years would be next to impossible. Among them would be the right to know, the right to learn, the right to leisure, the right to work, the right to die, the right to clean air, the right to read rapidly, the right to a guaranteed income, and so on.

23   That is, great presidents as judged by historians in our institutions of higher learning.

24   *Liberty,* pp. 25–26.

25   *Ibid.,* p. 25.

26   *Ibid.,* p. 26.

27   *Ibid.,* p. 27.

28   *Ibid.*

29   John C. Calhoun, *A Disquisition on Government* Indianapolis, 1953), p. 3.

30   *Liberty,* pp. 193–94.

31   *American Individualism,* pp. 51–52. (Hereafter cited as *Individualism.*)

32   *Liberty,* p. 40.

33   *Individualism,* p. 19.

34   *Ibid.,* pp. 22–23.

35   *Liberty,* pp. 19–20.

36   *Ibid.,* p. 20.

37   *Ibid.,* p. 21.

38   *Ibid.*

39   *Ibid.*, p. 24.

40   *Ibid.*, pp. 34-35.

41   *Ibid.*, p. 204. Emphasis added.

42   *Individualism*, pp. 52-53.

43   *Liberty*, pp. 57-58.

44   *Ibid.*, pp. 59-60.

45   *Ibid.*, p. 133.

46   *Ibid.*, pp. 135-36.

47   *Ibid.*, p. 145.

48   *Ibid.*, pp. 199-200.

49   *Individualism*, p. 55.

50   *Ibid.*, pp. 9-10. Emphasis in text.

51   *Ibid.*, p. 27.

52   *Ibid.*, p. 71.

53   *Liberty*, pp. 31-32.

54   *Individualism*, p. 37.

55   Almost every conceivable method has been tried by government to correct this situation—huge federal grants, integration, bussing, redrawing school district lines—but the situation seems to be getting worse.

56   The question, of course, arises whether there should be any such intersection at all.

57   *Congressional Record,* 78 Cong., 2 Sess., XC, Pt. 1, 55-57.

58   We note, for example, that Roosevelt already seemed to have a ready-made "brain trust" when he assumed office.

59   We should note that practically all political philosophers of past ages have recognized the importance of the education of the young in their theories.

60   Professor George C. S. Benson of Claremont College, who is engaged in an extensive study of ethical instruction in the family, church, and schools, has reached the conclusion that each of these institutions believes this training is provided by the other. As a consequence none of them is devoting serious attention to the whole matter of ethical training.

61   A condition we know Mr. Hoover was keenly concerned with in what are known as the Hoover Commission Reports.

62   Of course we are speaking here of concentration of powers in the government or public sector. To the extent that such a concentration has occurred in the private sector (education, corporations, unions, etc.) Hoover's principles are undermined.

63 Amaury De Riencourt, "Coming Caesars in America," in *Liberalism Versus Conservatism*, Willmoore Kendall and George W. Carey, eds. (Princeton, 1966), p. 247.

64 Roger A. Freeman, "The Wayward Welfare State," *Modern Age*, 15 (Fall 1971), 396.

65 *Ibid.*, p. 399.

66 *Ibid.*, p. 404.

67 *Ibid.*, p. 408.

SUMMARY OF COMMENTARY BY DISCUSSANTS AND CONFEREES

Discussion of the paper began with formal commentaries by Chancellor Joseph McCabe of Coe College, Professor Glenn Tinder of the University of Massachusetts at Boston, and Professor Robert Murray of Pennsylvania State University. Each commended Professor Carey for a thoughtful paper and for his awakening of the unappreciative to the depth, quality, and coherence of Hoover's political thought. Yet each also challenged portions of the paper and suggested other ways that the evidence might be read.

In the first commentary, Chancellor McCabe noted four aspects of the paper with which he disagreed. One was its failure to recognize that classical political philosophy had stressed order and security as well as virtue. A second was its claims for originality in Hoover's thought, claims that seemed to ignore how closely it resembled the organicism of Edmund Burke. A third was the assumption that Hoover's thought failed to change and develop over time, an assumption that ignored Hoover's own concerns about *American Individualism* being out of date. And a fourth was Carey's conclusion that Hoover had not thought deeply about ways of realizing his ideals. There was much here, McCabe suggested, that Carey had missed.

As second commentator, Professor Tinder expressed disappointment with the last few pages of the paper. He would readily agree, he said, that big government had not produced a just society. But Carey's attack on it simply ignored the extent to which the problems of modern societies required governmental responses. In addition, Tinder thought that Carey might have commented on what appeared to be other major deficiencies in Hoover's thought. Among these, so it would seem anyway, were his overly optimistic faith in human progress and perfectibility, his insufficient awareness of human evil or of the tragedy and mystery of the human condition, and his tendency to simplify transcendental ideas and ignore much of the intellectual debate over them.

In the third commentary, Professor Murray argued that Carey had not really located Hoover in any stream of traditionalist thought. He had merely cast out certain "moderns" that one might expect to find in Hoover's intellectual house. Also questioned was Carey's assumption about Hoover's intellectual consistency, and challenged in some detail were the assumptions permeating the latter portions of the paper. One could not assume, Murray insisted, that most Americans had favored reward differentials or that all the consequences of abandoning Hoover's teachings had been unfortunate. Nor could one ignore the roles of economic change, social modernization, and international conflict in producing pressures for bureaucratization, public services, and governmental action.

In a response to the commentaries and to initial questioning from the floor, Professor Carey made several points. Hoover's thinking, he noted, had paralleled and perhaps drawn upon the thinking of Edmund Burke. But it was still novel, he thought, to find an American individualist thinking along these lines. He also remained impressed with Hoover's perceptiveness, especially as to the consequences of imposing solutions from the top and taking actions injurious to community life and its cooperative impulses. And he continued to argue that Hoover's writings had initially described and then called for a return to virtuous national traditions. His major disappointment in studying Hoover, he declared again, was in finding so little concern with the means through which an appropriate morality could be cultivated and sustained.

In the discussion that followed, there were marked differences of opinion concerning the extent to which Hoover should be regarded as a serious political thinker. On one side were those who would dismiss *American Individualism* as little more than a collection of cliches and would recognize that Hoover, like most administrators and politicians, had embraced ideas as tools or weapons rather than as parts of a coherent philosophy. On the other side were those who insisted that he did have a coherent philosophy; that ideology did shape policy; and that if Hoover was not a major thinker, he was, in Alan Seltzer's words, an excellent second-rater. Seltzer urged further study of Hoover's thought, especially as it related to that of such figures as Abraham Lincoln and Theodore Roosevelt. And Robert Zieger urged that it be studied not in conjunction with Locke or Rousseau but as a thoughtful synthesis of various progressive ideologies.

Also coming into the discussion at various times were several other debates. One was touched off by Peri Arnold, who argued that the essence of Hooverism was corporative bureaucratization along Weberian lines, and that in reality public policy since 1932 represented a triumph of Hooverism rather than a rejection of it. A second revolved around differing assessments of the religious and engineering influences on Hoover's thought, with some attributing much to his Quaker background and others inclined to emphasize his internalization of a professional creed. A third had to do with the impulses making for big government. These were seen by some as coming more from organized interests and managerial elites than from popular action or a loss of popular morality. And a fourth centered on challenges to the view that decentralized government and voluntarist solutions were necessarily democratic and libertarian. In reality, Robert Zieger argued, they could serve as masks for industrial oppression and local tyrannies.

Finally, there were comments, particularly from Robert Wood, Thomas Thalken, and Joan Hoff Wilson, pointing up Hoover's belief that encroachments on economic liberty must inevitably lead to diminished political and civil liberty, his conviction that liberal institutions had to be saved outside of rather than through the state, and the care that he took to distinguish "rugged individualism" from the laissez-faire, dog-eat-dog, or wolfish variety. For him the term had connotations of responsible initiative and creative diversity that were ignored by those who seized upon it as an indication of unenlightened and reactionary thinking.

Index

Advisory Committee on the Census, 51
Agent General, 159
Agrarian radicalism, 146
Agricultural attaches, 119
Agricultural Conferences, 59
Agricultural Credits Act, 140(n. 12)
Agricultural Marketing Act, 136
Agricultural marketing cooperatives,
  57, 118-21, 125-26, 130-32, 135-36,
  145-46
Agriculture: and antitrust policy,
  131-32; organization of, 138(n. 3);
  politics of, 116-18, 120-37; prob-
  lems of, 56-57, 116, 118, 127, 136,
  152; and trade policy, 127, 132-34,
  137, 142(n. 32, 34)
Agriculture, Department of: and
  jurisdictional conflict, 22, 32, 57,
  119-22, 126-30, 140(n. 9); reorgani-
  zation of, 140(n. 9)
Alien Property Custodian, 36
Allen, Frederick L., 4
American Association for Labor
  Legislation, 39(n. 15), 58, 72(n. 65)
American Construction Council, 59,
  73(n. 73)
American Council of Agriculture,
  128-30
American Bankers Association, 117
American Farm Bureau Federation,
  117, 146
American Federation of Labor, 86-87,
  90-91, 96-99, 102, 194
American Individualism, 3
American Institute of Electrical
  Engineers, 51
American Relief Administration, 133
American System, 46-47, 65, 190-91,
  209-10, 236
Andrews, John, 72(n. 65)
Anglo-American partnerships, 215-16
Anti-collectivism, 46
Anti-monopoly tradition, 46
Anti-statism, 46
Antitrust laws, 49, 143(n. 45), 188-89,
  201, 206; and agriculture, 131-32;
  and associational activities, 52,
  16-62; Hoover's views on, 77-78.
  See also Foreign cartels
Arabian American Oil Co., 188

Armaments, limitation of, 153-54,
  157-58
Automobile industry, 187, 194
Aviation industry, 60

Babson, Roger, 74(n. 82)
Baldwin, Stanley, 203
Bank for International Settlements,
  168
Barnett, George, 99-100
Beard, Charles A., 1-2, 8
Benson, George C. S., 251(n. 60)
Bill of Rights, 230
Black, Loring M., 203
Blythe, Samuel, 36
Boone, Joel T., 36
Borah, William E., 19
Boulder Dam, 24
Brandegee, Frank B., 19
Brandeis, Louis, 216
Brandes, Joseph, scholarship of, 185
Brazil, rubber development in, 208
Brazilian coffee cartel, 187, 190,
  193-96
British rubber cartel, 185, 187, 190,
  196-208
British Rubber Growers Association,
  197
Broderick, Sir John, 204
Brody, David, 112
Brown, Walter, 129
Bryan, William Jennings, 192
Building codes, 55, 59
Bureau of Agricultural Economics,
  129, 140(n. 9)
Bureau of the Census, 22, 49, 62
Bureau of Crop Estimates, 140(n. 9)
Bureau of Customs Statistics, 22, 52
Bureau of Foreign and Domestic
  Commerce, 22-23, 49, 52-53, 60,
  133, 185, 196
Bureau of Labor Statistics, 22-23, 92
Bureau of Markets, 22-23, 57, 128-29,
  140(n. 9)
Bureau of Mines, 22, 56, 72(n. 59)
Bureau of Standards, 49, 51
Bureau of Unemployment, 26
Burke, Edmund, 252-53
Business Cycle Committee, 60
Business cycle control, 45, 152

Business Man's Conference on
Agriculture, 132–33
Business planning, 60–61
Buying pool, for rubber, 189–90,
199–202

Calhoun, John C., 228
Capacity-to-pay formula, 160, 164,
169
Capper, Arthur, 199, 201, 204
Capper-Volstead Act, 59, 140(n. 10)
Capper-Williams Bill, 120–21, 140
(n. 10)
Carey, George, scholarship of, 217
Central bank cooperation, 155–57
Chamberlain, Sir Arthur, 204–05, 207
Chamber of Commerce of the United
States, 51, 55, 117
Chilton, Sir Henry, 204
Ching, Cyrus, 97
Church, Frank, 189
Churchill, Winston, 197, 206–07
Clayton Act, 189, 207
Coffee, price of, 195
Coffee Institute. *See* Brazilian coffee
cartel
Coffee trade, 188, 196. *See also*
Brazilian coffee cartel
Coal industry: problems of, 55–56,
63–64; stabilization plan for, 63;
strikes in, 24, 33
Coal Stabilization Study, 59, 64
Collective bargaining, 85–86; Hoover's
endorsement of, 85–86, 90–91, 99
Colorado Fuel and Iron Co., 102
Colorado River Commission, 24, 33
Commerce Department of: advisory
agency for, 21, 49–50; and aid to
farmers, 134–35; and economic
stabilization, 48; expansion of, 22,
49–50, 52; and foreign loan controls,
162; information service of, 21, 23;
and jurisdictional conflict, 22–23,
32, 57, 119–22, 126–30, 140(n. 9);
and public relations, 201; services
of, 190–91; transformation of, 21–
24, 92; under Secretary Redfield, 68
(n.12)
Commercial attaches, 23, 33
Committee of Fourteen, 58
Committee on Civic and Emergency
Measures, 58, 63
Commodity divisions, 53

Community action programs, 55
Company unions, 80, 98–99
Conciliation Service, 92
Conference of Business Paper Editors,
51
Consensus history, 6
Conservation Division, 47
Construction, planning of, 54–55,
58–59
Cooke, Morris L., 88
Coolidge, Calvin, 36–37, 120–21, 130,
134–35; and Hoover, 37
Cooperative collectivism, 67–68(n. 11)
Cooperative competition, 46, 150
Cooperative marketing, 57, 59, 118–
21, 125–26, 130–31, 134–36, 145–46
Cooperative Marketing Act, 120
Corn-hog ratio, 141(n. 24)
Corporate pluralism, 66
Corporatism, in the United States,
117–18, 145
Cost-of-production principle, 164, 166
Cotton, as a retaliatory trade weapon,
192, 200, 203–05
Coxey, Jacob, 58
Croghan, P. J., 202
Crude Rubber Survey, 198–99, 200
Culbertson, William, 164
Currency stabilization, 155–59

Daugherty, Harry M., 19–20, 33,
35–36, 63, 66, 75(n. 90), 113
Davis, James J., 22, 25, 27–28, 33, 74
(n. 82), 113
Davis, John W., 198
Dawes, Charles G., 20
Dawes Plan, 159, 167
Decentralization, effects of, 254
De Graeff, A. C., 199
Denby, Edwin, 33
Dennison, Henry, 72(n. 65)
De Riencourt, Amaury, 243
Dillon, Read and Co., 188, 196, 206
Division of Building and Housing, 22,
24, 54–55, 59
Division of Simplified Practice, 59
Donithen, Hoke, 37
Durgin, William, 59

Economic Bill of Rights, 239–40
Economic growth: promotion of,
93–94; threats to, 186–87
Economic order, securing of, 47, 78

Economic recovery, in 1922, 64-65
Economic self-government, 2-3
Economic stabilization, 43-66
Editorial Division, 201-02
Edge, Walter, 62, 200
Edge Act, 71(n. 49)
Edge bills, 62
Eddy, Arthur J., 77
Electrical power industry, 60
Emergency Agricultural Credits Acts, 56-57
Emergency Tariff Act, 142(n. 32)
Employee representation, 82-87, 95-104
Engineers and reform, 88-89
Equality of opportunity: concept of, 237-40; problems of, 238-39
Equalization fee, 121, 123, 126
Executive reorganization, 41, 140(n. 9)
Export promotion, 53, 56-57, 119, 122, 134, 140(n. 12)

Fall, Albert, 33, 36, 113
Farm Advisory Council, plan for, 131
Farm Bloc, 118, 128, 130, 142(n. 34)
Farm marketing cooperatives. *See* agricultural marketing cooperatives
Farm problem. *See* Agriculture, problems of
Farmers Union, 117
Federal Cooperative Marketing Board, 131
Federal Farm Board, 120, 136
Federal Marketing Board, plan for, 120-21
Federal Reserve Bank of New York, 155-56
Federal Reserve Board, 156-57
Federal Trade Commission, 49, 62
Federated American Engineering Societies, 28-29, 48, 59, 84, 88-91
Feiker, Frederick, 51, 53, 70(n. 33)
Firestone, Harvey S., 198-99, 203, 207-09
Firestone Company, 194, 196, 199-200
Fite, Gilbert C., 136
Follett, Mary, 68(n. 11)
Food Administration, 125
Forbes, Charles, 36
Fordney-McCumber Tariff Act, 164, 202
Foreign cartels: campaigns against, 166, 185-210, 214-15; defense of,

202-04; loan policy toward, 162, 190, 193-96, 202; threats from, 216
Foreign combinations. *See* Foreign cartels
Foreign loans, 60, 158, 161, 162, 168-69, 179(n. 70), 181, 190, 193-95
Foreign Trade Financing Corporation, 48, 53, 71(n. 49)
France: and armament limitations, 158; and debt adjustment, 160; and security concerns, 170
Frayne, Hugh, 97
Freeman, Roger A., 244-46
Frelinghuysen Bill, 55, 72(n.57)
Functionalist diplomacy, 148, 150-51, 172(n. 2)

Galambos, Louis, 10
Gary, Elbert, 27-29
Gaskill, Nelson, 62
Gay, Edwin, 51, 70(n. 44)
Geneva Economic Conference, 152
Geological Survey, 56, 72(n. 59)
Germany: and currency depreciation, 158; and foreign loans, 169; and reparations adjustment, 158-59, 167; reintegration of, 170
Glass, Carter, 125
Globalist diplomacy, 148-50, 172 (n. 2), 181
Gold standard, restoration of, 155-57
Gompers, Samuel, 27, 48, 86, 88-91, 97-98
Goodman, Paul, 8
Goodrich Tire Company, 188, 196
Goodyear Tire Company, 188, 196
Gore, Howard M., 129-30
Grain futures, regulation of, 138(n. 3)
Green, William, 98
Grew, Joseph, 205
Gries, John M., 22, 54-55, 59, 71 (n. 54)
Guggenheim, Daniel, 20

Hard, William, 3
Harding, Warren G., 34-36, 91, 157; and cabinet making, 19-21; and Hoover, 33-34, 38; and political scandal, 35; reinterpretation of, 17-18; and tax policy, 32; and twelve-hour day, 23-29, 95; and the Unemployment Conference, 25-27
Harding, Mrs. Warren G., 36

Harding Memorial, 37–38
Harding papers, 9, 17
Harding scandals, 36–37, 41–42
Hardwood Lumber Case, 61
Hardwood Manufacturers Association, 61
Hartz, Louis, 221
Hays, Will, 21, 33, 113
Hearst newspapers, 202
Herter, Christian A., 22
Hicks, Clarence J., 96–97, 99, 101
High-wage doctrine, 48
Hilles, Charles, 20
Hobbes, Thomas, 217, 220–21, 233–34, 249(n. 11)
Hoover, Herbert, 19, 36, 38, 115, 154; achievements of, 92, 181–82; and agribusiness, 145–46; agricultural policies of, 116–18, 120–37, 145–47; and the agricultural public, 128; and Albert Fall, 33; all-around expertise of, 31; on American uniqueness, 234–35; and Andrew Mellon, 32; and antitrust policy, 61–62, 64, 131–32, 143(n. 45), 201, 206, 214, 216; apoliticism of, 40–41, 78–79, 153–55, 164–65, 168; appointed secretary of commerce, 19–21, 48–49; and armaments limitation, 153–54, 157–58; authority of, 155; and aviation, 60; British protests about, 204; on bureaucracy, 233–34; and bureaucratic politics, 41; and the Bureau of Markets, 128–29; and business, 21–23, 140(n. 12), 145, 208–09; and business cycle control, 152; and business planning, 60–61; and cabinet peers, 31–33; and Calvin Coolidge, 37; and central bank cooperation, 155, 157; and Charles Evans Hughes, 32–33; claims credit for economic recovery, 64–65, 76 (n.110); and the coal problem, 24, 33, 55–56, 59, 63, 103; and the Colorado River Commission, 24, 33; and collective bargaining, 85–86; on concentrated power, 231–32; and conservation, 134; consistency of, 216; and corporate statism, 66; criticized for cartel policy, 202–04; and currency stabilization, 155–57; and departmental expansionism, 77–78; as doctor of "sick" indus-

tries, 138(n. 3); and economic growth, 93–94; and economic nationalism, 180–81; economic diplomacy of, 148–71, 179–81, 185; and economic management, 61; and economic stabilization, 43–66; and employee representation, 82–83, 85–87, 95–104; encourages social studies, 103–04; engineering influences on, 254; on engineers as public servants, 88, 107(n. 19), 152; as an enlightened manager, 149–50, 152, 165; envisions new economic system, 82–83, 90, 95, 104; on equality of opportunity, 235, 237, 239–40; and executive reorganization, 140(n. 9); and export promotion, 122; failures of, 168–71, 180; and famine relief, 24; on the farm crisis, 140(n. 12); and farming interests, 22–23; and the farm problem, 56–57, 59, 115–18, 120–24, 126–27, 130–33, 135–36; and foreign cartels, 166, 185–210; and foreign loan controls, 158, 161–62, 169, 181, 190, 193–96, 202; and the French, 168, 170; and George N. Peek, 128–30; goals of, 48–49, 91–92, 112–13; on governmental regulation,152–53, 191, 232, 234; on government in business, 123–24, 150, 153–54; and the Harding Memorial, 37–38; and Harding's Alaskan trip, 34–36; and the Harding scandals, 35–37; and Harry Daugherty, 33; heads Federated American Engineering Societies, 84, 88; and Henry C. Wallace, 32, 118–19, 124–28, 145–46; historical views of, 1–5, 10–13; and hog price supports, 125; and the housing problem, 24, 54–55, 59; on human equality, 229; on human nature, 227–28; ideals of, 77–79; ideology of, 41, 43, 47–48, 185–86, 189–96; on individual liberty, 226–35; influence of, 37; on international relations, 78, 151–53; and James J. Davis, 27, 33; labor policies of, 62–64, 80–81, 92–104, 112–13; on the labor question, 82–84; and laissez-faire, 5, 66; and Latin-American relations, 194–96; and the League of Nations,

154-55; and Louis Brandeis, 216;
and managerial thought, 18, 78,
214-15; and McNary-Haugenism,
120-24, 126, 128, 131, 146-47; and
misuse of factual information, 113-
14, 168; on modern civilization, 154;
and the modern corporation, 102,
145; and national planning, 48, 65,
118; and national self-sufficiency,
139(n. 5), 144(n. 50), 170-71; neo-
traditionalism of, 217-18, 235-36;
and the New Deal, 66, 150, 233; and
the New Freedom, 150; new interest
in, 10; and oil development, 188;
opposition to, 49; and ordered
liberty, 230-31; perceptions of, 1-5,
10-13, 33-34, 119, 202-04; personality of, 31; and personnel management, 96-97; political and social
thought, 217-19, 226-41, 252-
54; political skills of, 31; post-1929
recovery strategy of, 65; and power
development, 60; on preserving
individualism, 240-41; on price
fixing, 121-22, 125, 191-93, 195,
205; on productivity, 82-83, 89-90,
92; progressivism of, 115, 149; and
public relations, 22-23; and public
works planning, 60, 74(n. 81);
Quaker influences on, 254; and
radio, 60; and the railroad problem,
56, 59, 63; and realist diplomacy,
215; and recovery theory, 48; refuses
Department of Agriculture, 135; on
regimentation, 232-33; reinterpretation of, 10-13, 185-86; relevance
of, 243-48; and the reparations
issue, 158-59, 168; reputation of,
29, 31; and rugged individualism,
219, 248-49(n. 2, 3), 254; and rural
development, 146; and Samuel
Gompers, 88-90; and the Second
Industrial Conference, 84-88, 102;
and social contract theory, 226-
35; on socialism, 232-33; and social
organicism, 228-29; and social
pluralism, 229; speaks to AFL
Executive Council, 90-91; and
standardization, 24; and statistical
dissemination, 51-52; study of, 43;
and tax policy, 67(n. 4), 93; teachings of, 219; and trade associations,
24; and trade policy, 52-54, 59-0,

122-23, 127, 132-34, 137, 142(n. 32),
155, 162-66, 169-70, 189-90, 214;
and trade unions, 85-87; and transportation policy, 134; and the
twelve-hour day issue, 27-29, 94-
95; and the unemployment problem,
25-27, 57-59, 94; vision of, 180;
and the war debts issue, 159-61,
167-68; and Warren G. Harding,
33-34; and waste reduction, 50-51,
89; weaknesses of, 41; and William
Jardine, 130-31; and the World
Court, 154; and the world that
might have been, 246-47
Hoover, Theodore Jesse, 100
Hoover Presidential Library, 9
Houghton, Alanson B., 193, 204-05,
207
Housing: problem of, 54; promotion
of, 24
Howard, Sir Esme, 207
Hughes, Charles Evans, 21, 23, 31, 36,
113, 161, 207; and Hoover, 32-33
Humanization of industry, 83
Hunt, Edward Eyre, 50, 57, 64, 89,
91-92
Huston, Claudius, H., 22

Imports, increase in, 163
Individualism, transmission of,
240-41
Individual liberty: Hoover's theory of,
226-35; Mill's theory of, 225-26
Industrial Group, 50
Industrial disputes, plan to settle, 85
Industrial Waste Committee, 50
Intermediate Credit Act, 127, 140
(n. 12)
Interstate Commerce Commission, 56
Isolationism, 149

Jackson, Andrew, 227
Jackson, Henry M., 188
Jardine, William M., 130, 145
Jefferson, Thomas, 227
Johnson, Hiram, 19
Joint Committee on Reorganization,
129
Jones-Winslow Bill, 119
Justice, Department of, and associa-
tional activities, 52, 62, 75(n. 90)

Kellogg, Frank, 193, 195, 201, 204-07

Kellogg-Briand Pact, 153
Kenyon Bill, 60 74(n.81)
King, Mackenzie, 97, 101–02
Klein, Julius, 22–23, 52, 70(n. 44),
    194, 196
Knox, Philander C., 19–20
Koerselman, Gary, 116
Kuhn, Loeb and Co., 188

Labor, Department of, and unem-
    ployment, 27
Labor policy, in the 1920s, 80–81,
    92–93
Labor question, 82, 84
Labor system, in the 1920s, 98–103,
    112–14
Ladd, Edwin F., 142(n. 34)
LaFollette, Robert M., 142(n. 34)
LaGuardia, Fiorello H., 188
Lamb, William, 22, 52
Lamont, Thomas, 160
League of Nations, 154–55
Lee Higginson and Company, 193
Leffler, Melvyn, scholarship of, 148
Legge, Alexander, 97, 102, 145
Leiserson, William, 99, 112
Leitch, John, 68(n. 11)
Lewis, Ernest, 63
Lewis, John L., 103
Lewisohn, Sam, 72(n. 65)
Liberia, rubber interests in, 199–200,
    203, 207, 209
Lincoln, Abraham, 227, 253
Lindsay, Samuel, 72(n. 65)
Liquidity, international problem of,
    162, 166–67
Locke, John, 217, 220–21, 223–24
Lockean liberalism, 221
Lowden, Frank O., 119
Lynd, Helen and Robert, 93

MacElwee, R. L., 70(n. 44)
Machiavelli, Niccolo, 217, 220–23
Macroeconomic management, 45, 66
Malin, James C., 2, 43
Mallery, Otto, 72(n. 65)
Managerialism, 80
Managerial state, 44–46, 66
Marcuse, Herbert, 8
May, Henry, 1
McConnell, Grant, 146

McCormick, Medill, 198
McIlvaine, George, 61
McNary-Haugen bills, 115–16, 119–24,
    126, 128, 130–31, 136, 146–47
Meat packing, regulation of, 138(n. 3)
Mellon, Andrew, 20, 28, 31, 36–37,
    45, 66, 193; and Hoover, 32
Mill, John Stuart, 217, 220, 225–26,
    231, 235, 249(n. 6), 250(n. 19, 20)
Miller, Adolph, 156
Miller, Franklin T., 54–55, 71(n. 52)
Miller, Thomas, 36
Mills, C. Wright, 8
Mitchell, Broadus, 8
Mitchell, Wesley, 51
Modernization theory, and historical
    perceptions, 6–7
"Moderns," in political theory, 217,
    219–26, 253
Morgan, J.P., and Company, 196, 198
Morrison, Frank, 90
Multinational corporations, 188
Murray, John C., 223–24
Murray, Robert, scholarship of, 17–18

National Agricultural Conferences,
    134
National Association of Manufac-
    turers, 51, 117
National Bureau of Economic Re-
    search, 103
National Bureau of Standards, 24
National Civic Federation, 84
National Coal Association, 56
National Coffee Council, 196
National Federation of Construction
    Industries, 55
National government: capabilities of,
    244–46; complexity of, 242; growth
    of, 242, 244, 252–54; power of, 243
National Industrial Conference Board,
    51
National Livestock Producers Associ-
    tion, 117
National Paving Brick Manufacturers,
    51
National planning, 118; and Hoover,
    48, 65, 118
Neo-libertarianism, and historical
    perspectives, 9
Neo-mercantilism, 215–16

Neo-traditionalism: and historical perspectives, 9; and Hoover, 217–18, 235–36
Netherlands, The, and rubber controls, 199
New Economic System, 82, 90, 95–96, 103–04
New Era: contemporary perceptions of, 1–4; historiography of, 1–11, 117; as perceived after 1930, 4–9
New Era diplomacy: flaws in, 168–70, 180–81; importance of, 171; nature of, 150–51, 170–71, 180–81, 214; perceptions of, 115, 148
New Freedom, 118, 145, 150
New Left historiography, 8–9, 112
New Nationalism, 77, 118, 145
Newton Bill, 200
Noggle, Burl, 9
Norris, George, 56, 74(n. 81), 133, 142(n. 34)
Norris-LaGuardia Act, 113

Oil industry, 188–89
Open Door, 154, 157, 204–06, 209, 215
Open price plans, 52, 77–79
Ordered liberty, Hoover's conceptions of, 230–31

Parity principle, 122
Patent Office, 22
Payne, Will, 65
Pearl, Raymond, 61
Peck, Gustav, 104
Peek, George N., 128–30, 133–34, 136, 146
Penrose, Boies, 19–20
Permanent Court for International Justice, 154
Personnel managers, and employee representation, 96–97
Philippines, The, and rubber development, 209
Pinchot, Gifford, 19
Pisar, Charles J., 204
Planning. *See* Business planning; Construction, planning of; National planning; Public works, planning of
Potash cartel, 190, 193
Price fixing: Hoover's views on, 121–22, 125, 191–93, 195, 205; of

rubber, 187, 191; during and after World War I, 125, 141(n. 24)
Production control, in agriculture, 126–27, 130, 135–36
Productivity: and employee representation, 90–91; Hooverian theme of, 82–83, 89–92
Progressive Era, 117–18
Progressive history, 4–5, 7
Progressivism, 145, 209
Public Works: expansion of, 25–26, 58–59; planning of, 60

Radio industry, 60
Railroad industry, 56, 59, 63–64
Railway Labor Act, 63
Railway Labor Board, 56, 59, 63
Raw materials crises, 187–88
Recent Economic Changes, 100, 103
Recent Social Trends, 100, 104
Redfield, William, 68(n. 12)
Reily, E. Mont, 34
Reorganization Committee, 50
Reparations, 158–59, 167–68
Reproductive loan criteria, 161, 164, 168, 181
Republican Party, and labor, 80
Research, promotion of, 24
Rockefeller, John D., Jr., 68(n. 11), 101–02
Roosevelt, Franklin D., 59, 117, 227, 239, 243, 246
Roosevelt, Theodore, 118, 209, 227, 253
Rossiter, William S., 70(n. 35)
Rothbard, Murray, 10
Rousseau, Jean Jacques, 217, 220–21, 224, 250(n. 17)
Rubber: alternate sources of, 194, 198–99, 202, 208–09; conservation of, 202; as contraband, 192; negotiations over, 199, 201, 204–07; price of, 200–01, 208; price fixing in, 187, 191, 197–98, 206–08; reclamation of, 201
Rubber Association of America, 198–200, 205–07
Rubber manufacturing industry, 196, 199, 206; buying pool in, 189–90, 199–202; organization of, 188; profiteering in, 188, 203

Rubber plantation industry, 196
Rubber question, editorial comment
   on, 202-04
Rugged individualism, Hoover on,
   248(n. 2), 254
Russian famine, relief of, 24, 133

Sawyer, Charles E., 36
Scientific management, 84, 88
Scientific tariff making, 164, 170
Seager, Henry, 72(n. 65)
Second Industrial Conference, 84-88,
   106(n. 12)
Shaw, Arch, 69-70(n. 33)
Sherman Act, 206
Shop councils, 80, 85-87, 90-91,
   96-99, 101-02, 110(n. 47)
Silk, Leonard, 188
Simplified practice conferences, 51
Simplification programs, 51, 59, 73
   (n. 70)
Slosson, Preston W., 2
Smith, Alfred E., 130
Smith, Jesse, 35
Social contract theory, 223-27
Soule, George, 136
Special Conference Committee, 102
Stabilization. See Currency stabiliza-
   tion; Economic stabilization
Standardization, 24, 51
Stanford Food Research Institute, 122
Starrett, Henry P., 202
State, Department of, and foreign
   lending, 161-62
Statistical programs, 55, 59, 61-62,
   127, 152
Steel industry, 27-29, 95
Stevenson, Sir James, 199, 201
Stevenson Act, 197
Stevenson Plan, 197-99, 202-08, 215
Straus, Oscar S., 21
Strauss, Leo, 220
Strikes, 63-64, 82, 98, 100, 103
Strong, Benjamin, 155-57
Superpower, 60
Survey of Current Business, 51-52

Tariff Commission, 164
Tariff policy, 53, 127, 131-32, 137,
   142(n. 32, 34), 163-64, 166, 169-70,
   202
Taussig, Frank, 52

Taylor, Alonzo E., 122
Taylor, Frederick W., 84
Tilson, John Q., 194
Trade: balance of, 163; invisible items
   in, 163, 166-67, 178(n. 66); tri-
   angular nature of, 163, 166
Trade policy, 52-54, 59-60, 155,
   180-81, 209. See also Tariff policy
Trade association manual, 62
Trade associations, 43, 47, 53, 61-62,
   75(n. 90); for farmers, 119
Trade unionism, 85-86, 97-99, 102-03
Trade war, 192, 201
Treasury, Department of the: and
   currency stabilization, 156-57; and
   foreign lending, 162; and war debt
   adjustment, 167
Turner, Frederick Jackson, 3
Twelve-hour day issue, 27-29, 94-95
Twelve-hour Day Study, 28-29
Tyron, Frederick, 59

Unemployment, 25-27; relief and
   prevention of, 57-59, 74(n. 82), 94
Unemployment Conference, 25-27, 39
   (n. 15), 57-60, 72(n. 65), 76(n. 110),
   94, 103
United Mine Workers, 63
United States Coal Commission, 64,
   103
United States Employment Service, 58
United States Grain Corporation, 122,
   125
United States Railroad Labor Board,
   92
United States Rubber Company, 188,
   196, 198
Utopian Socialists, 238

Valentine, Robert, 88
Vanderlip, Frank, 20
Veterans Bureau, 36

War debts, adjustment of, 160, 167-68
War Finance Corporation, 56
War Industries Board, 99
War Labor Board, 83
Washington Conference, 154, 157
Washington treaties, 153, 157
Waste in Industry, 89
Waste reduction programs, 50-51, 55,
   62

Waste Survey, 48, 50–51, 89
Walling, William English, 97
Wallace, Henry A., 124–25, 128
Wallace, Henry C., 22, 31, 115–16,
  118–21, 124–28, 133–35, 140
  (n. 9, 10), 142(n. 32), 145; and
  Hoover, 32
Wallace, L. W., 89
Webb-Pomerene Act, 52, 198, 200
Weberian rationalization, 180, 254
Weeks, John, 20, 33
Welfare capitalism, 83, 97–99, 101
Welfare state, 241, 244–46
White, Charles, 75(n. 90)
Whitley Committee, 106(n. 11)
Wilbur, Ray Lyman, 36
Wilkerson injunction, 33, 63, 113
Williams, William Appleman, 8, 10,
  79
Wilson, Joan Hoff, scholarship of,
  115

Wilson, Woodrow, 84, 118, 192, 209,
  227
Wing, David L., 62
Winston, Garrard, 167
Wolf, Robert, 48, 88, 91
Woll, Matthew, 97
Wolman, Leo, 72(n. 65), 93, 99–100,
  104, 112
Woods, Arthur, 26, 58
Working conditions, in the 1920s, 103
World Court. *See* Permanent Court
  for International Justice
World War I, influence of, 45–46
World War Foreign Debt Commission,
  160, 164, 167, 169

Young, Allyn, 51
Young, Owen D., 60, 165
Young Plan, 168

Zieger, Robert, scholarship of, 80